Additional praise for *Schools as Imagined Communities: The Creation of Identity, Meaning, and Conflict in U.S. History*

From the nineteenth-century common school movement to contemporary struggles over redistricting neighborhood attendance zones, Americans have sought to build communities around local schools—and sometimes to restrict access to outsiders. This anthology of historical case studies brings together rich narratives on this dynamic and the surrounding contexts of race, class, gender, sexuality, and disability. In particular, the editors' excellent introduction draws meaningful insights from various scholarly fields and taught me how to think about "communities" with fresh eyes.
—*Jack Dougherty*, Trinity College

Individually and collectively, the essays in this volume ask readers to think deeply, more critically, more thoughtfully, about the unspoken assumptions and the political implications of our common tendency to conceptualize schools as "communities." Issues of nostalgia, of inclusion and exclusion, of racial and social and sexual differentiation, are all deftly handled, highlighting new contributions in the history of American education. Well done.
—*Michael Fultz*, University of Wisconsin-Madison

Schools as Imagined Communities

The Creation of Identity, Meaning, and Conflict in U.S. History

Edited by

Deirdre Cobb-Roberts

Sherman Dorn

Barbara J. Shircliffe

SCHOOLS AS IMAGINED COMMUNITIES
© Deirdre Cobb-Roberts, Sherman Dorn, and Barbara J. Shircliffe, 2006.

All rights reserved. No part of this book may be used or reproduced in any manner whatsoever without written permission except in the case of brief quotations embodied in critical articles or reviews.

First published in 2006 by
PALGRAVE MACMILLAN™
175 Fifth Avenue, New York, N.Y. 10010 and
Houndmills, Basingstoke, Hampshire, England RG21 6XS
Companies and representatives throughout the world.

PALGRAVE MACMILLAN is the global academic imprint of the Palgrave Macmillan division of St. Martin's Press, LLC and of Palgrave Macmillan Ltd. Macmillan® is a registered trademark in the United States, United Kingdom and other countries. Palgrave is a registered trademark in the European Union and other countries.

ISBN 1–4039–6471–8 (hard)
ISBN 1–4039–6472–6 (pbk.)

Library of Congress Cataloging-in-Publication Data

    Schools as imagined communities : the creation of identity, meaning, and conflict in U.S. history / edited by Sherman Dorn, Deirdre Cobb-Roberts, Barbara J. Shircliffe.
      p. cm.
    Includes bibliographical references and index.
    ISBN 1–4039–6471–8 (hard)—ISBN 1–4039–6472–6 (pbk.)
    1. Community and school—United States—History. 2. Education—Social aspects—United States—History. I. Dorn, Sherman. II. Cobb-Roberts, Deirdre. III. Shircliffe, Barbara J.

LC221.S37 2006
371.19′0973—dc22   2005050211

A catalogue record for this book is available from the British Library.

Design by Newgen Imaging Systems (P) Ltd., Chennai, India.

First edition: January 2006
10 9 8 7 6 5 4 3 2 1

Printed in the United States of America.

To students of the history of education in the United States

Contents

Notes on Contributors   ix

Acknowledgments   xi

Introduction   Schools as Imagined Communities   1
Barbara J. Shircliffe, Sherman Dorn, and Deirdre Cobb-Roberts

Chapter 1
Education in an Imagined Community: Lessons from
Brook Farm   33
Vicki L. Eaklor

Chapter 2
Crafting Community: Hartford Public High School in the
Nineteenth Century   51
Melissa Ladd Teed

Chapter 3
Student-Community Voices: Memories of Access versus
Treatment at University of Illinois   79
Deirdre Cobb-Roberts

Chapter 4
From Isolation to Imagined Communities of LGBT
School Workers: Activism in the 1970s   109
Jackie M. Blount

Chapter 5
School and Community Loss, Yet Still Imagined in
the Oral History of School Segregation in
Tampa, Florida   125
Barbara J. Shircliffe

Chapter 6
Imagined Communities and Special Education   143
Sherman Dorn

Chapter 7
The Glover School Historic Site: Rekindling
the Spirit of an African American School Community   181
Elgin Klugh

Index   211

Notes on Contributors

Jackie M. Blount is a professor in historical, philosophical, and comparative education at Iowa State University. Her research focuses on the history of sexuality and gender in school employment. She has written *Fit to Teach: Same-Sex Desire, Gender, and School Work in the Twentieth Century* (2005) and currently is writing a biography of Ella Flagg Young.

Vicki L. Eaklor is a professor of history at Alfred University, where she teaches courses in American history and culture. She is the author of numerous publications concerning American cultural and intellectual history, including *American Antislavery Songs: A Collection and Analysis* (1988); "Striking Chords and Touching Nerves: Myth and Gender in *Gone With the Wind*," *Images: A Journal of Film and Popular Culture* (www.imagesjournal.com); and "The Gendered Origins of the American Musician," *The Quarterly Journal of Music Teaching and Learning* (Winter 1993/Spring 1994). Her current research is in GLBT history and theory.

Deirdre Cobb-Roberts is an associate professor of social foundations at the University of South Florida. She is the author or co-author of many articles and book chapters on the history of higher education and multicultural education. She is currently working on a book documenting the academic and social experiences of African American students at two land grant universities in the post–World War II era.

Sherman Dorn is an associate professor of social foundations at the University of South Florida. He is the author of *Creating the Dropout: An Institutional and Social History of School Failure* (1996) as well as the author or coauthor of articles and book chapters on the history of special education, graduation, and high-stakes accountability policies.

NOTES ON CONTRIBUTORS

Elgin Klugh is an assistant professor of anthropology at Montclair State University. He attended Morehouse College and earned a Ph.D. in Applied Anthropology from the University of South Florida. His dissertation, "African American Schoolhouses: Community, History, and Reclamation," explores the educational histories and ongoing school preservation efforts of communities in Bealsville, FL and Silver Spring, MD. Dr. Klugh's future research interests include issues of heritage and memory in African and the Diaspora, Cultural Resource Management, race, and ethnohistory.

Barbara J. Shircliffe is associate professor of social foundations at the University of South Florida. She received her doctorate from the State University of New York at Buffalo in 1997. Dr. Shircliffe's research has focused on the desegregation of historically black high schools in Florida. She has published articles related to this research in *Oral History Review* and *Urban Review* as well as in her book, *Best of that World: Historically Black High School and the Crisis of Desegregation in a Southern Metropolis* (2005).

Melissa Ladd Teed is an associate professor of history at Saginaw Valley State University whose current research focuses on nineteenth-century women's education and public activism. Research for this chapter was supported by a National Academy of Education / Spencer Foundation Post Doctoral Fellowship. She has most recently published articles in the *New England Quarterly* and *Gender and History*.

Acknowledgments

An edited book can only exist with the discipline of its contributors and the help and forbearance of dozens connected to them. We cannot say enough about the contributors who have worked with us through the book's publication. Our current and past colleagues at the University of South Florida have provided the opportunity to work on collaborations such as this as well as invaluable confidence in our judgment as professionals. Through their actions and support over the past several years, Erwin V. Johanningmeier, Larry Johnson, Harold Keller, Sister Jerome Leavy, Deanna Michael, Terry Richardson, and Tomás Rodriguez have made this volume possible. Amanda Johnson has been encouraging and patient as our editor at Palgrave Macmillan.

The History of Education Society and American Educational Studies Association are small scholarly organizations whose annual meetings welcome new scholars in the history of education. The work of Bealsville, Inc., is described in chapter 7. Royalties from this volume will go to these organizations.

Finally, our families have seen both our own research and the editing of this book swallow time over the past few years. To Darrell James Roberts, Darrell Tashan Roberts, Devaun James Roberts, Daiton Cobb Roberts, Elizabeth Griffith, Kathryn Dorn, Vincent Griffith, and Clint Perigard, we can definitely say that our debt to you is not imagined in the least.

Introduction

Schools as Imagined Communities

Barbara J. Shircliffe, Sherman Dorn, and Deirdre Cobb-Roberts

We often envision schools as communities. Some of us picture a little red schoolhouse where all the children in the neighborhood came to learn and play together. Others have memories of a school down the road they could not attend because they were shipped off to other neighborhoods far away. And, finally, there are those who remember a school that denied them access and made no other educational provisions. This last type of memory makes imagining schools as communities problematic. At first glance we would like to see a school as a place where children, teachers, and parents gather with a shared sense of purpose. The image of everyone working together has been an ideal. In an 1899 lecture, John Dewey said, "What the best and wisest parent wants for his own child, that must the *community* want for all of its children. Any other ideal for our schools is narrow and unlovely; acted upon, it destroys our democracy" (emphasis added). In the midst of industrialization and the growth of bureaucracies within schools, Dewey was trying to justify humanitarian treatment of children by reference to supposedly bygone communal values.[1]

But do schools always work as the communities we often imagine and hope they can be? Many of the controversies over education policy in the past half-century have revolved around conflicts over the proper community of a school. The most obvious historical example is desegregation: should the demographic composition of students be a primary mechanism for improving schools? Those who continue to argue for desegregation as a priority of education policy, such as Gary Orfield, claim that children of color, who are disproportionately from poor communities, cannot command the resources and expectations necessary to educational success when in racially isolated schools. In contrast, historian Vanessa Siddle-Walker has argued that the segregated schools of the early twentieth century were able to support academic achievement where a community pooled its resources together. Other questions of education policy likewise address the question of what makes up a school community, either the definition of an individual school, pieces within a school, or what schools try to teach. Jennifer Hochschild and Nathan Scovronick argue that fights over bilingual education, multicultural curriculum, tracking, vouchers, and charter schools are about whom we include and exclude from "our" schools and different definitions of the American dream. Whether one thinks that education policy is targeted at "our" children or at "other people's" children makes a difference in how one views or supports that policy.[2]

As we look beyond the superficial nature of what we believe schools to be and delve into the many purposes schooling has served and the many practices that schools have used, a different portrait emerges. We *imagine* schools to be more like communities than they often are. We take the title of this book from anthropologist Benedict Anderson's controversial argument that the newly independent nations of the twentieth century were imagined communities of nationalism.[3] In the United States, we talk about schools as communities for many reasons, and some important social science and education writers have used their ideas about communities as central to what they want schools to do.[4] For example, sociologist James Coleman wrote about the *social capital* a community has, or the social networks that serve to supplement the individual and family resources available to support children's well-being and intellectual development. In a different way, for 35 years psychologist James Comer has argued that schools must become *community schools*, using the resources of the children's families and neighborhoods.[5] These writers are thoughtful, and schools that effectively marshal community resources *can* make significant differences in the lives of their students. We think, though, that the discussions of social capital and communities glide over the definition of a school community. In many ways, their blind spot is similar to that of John Dewey, who assumed that the "best and wisest" parents would all agree on a single direction for schools. In other ways, they assume that a consensus would be productive: What if the binding glue focuses on athletics to the exclusion of academics?[6] Those types of blind spots comprise the subject of this book. We think of schools as communities, but with the knowledge that communities can push out as well as pull in people, divide as well as unite. This anthology of historical case studies investigates the problems with imagining schools as communities. The contributors to this book address some historical and contemporary questions regarding schooling and community and how these "imagined communities" often have excluded significant groups of children, teachers, and parents.[7]

This dual nature of community is illustrated by the 1990s debate over the construction of a new elementary school in Tampa, Florida. When the school board authorized the establishment of a new school in the predominately white and middle-class suburb of Tampa Palms, a local parents group organized a protest. The school administration had proposed establishing a second elementary school to serve Tampa Palms children who lived on one side of a busy highway that cut through the residential area. On the east side of the highway, Tampa Palms Elementary School had been serving the entire suburb. The new school, which would be located on the west side of the highway, would alleviate the overcrowding at Tampa Palms Elementary School.

Calling themselves One Community, One School, one parents' group felt that the establishment of a new elementary school would split their community.[8] Instead, One Community, One School advocated that the new school split grades with the existing school, forming one school with two campuses (as opposed to two K-5 elementary schools). With two campuses, one serving K to second grades and the other third to fifth grades, they argued that the one school would eliminate competition over resources and establish a unified school community. One parent felt as though a new school would "split the community . . . Everyone needs to come out of the same school if we're going to have a successful community."[9]

Beneath this rhetoric, several observers point out that the underlying issue was social status. Parents were fighting to maintain Tampa Palms as one exclusive community, and some believed that the section of Tampa Palms served by the new school would lose that identity. A school administrator recalled the conflict and offered insight into this dimension:

> The parents who lived on the east side of [highway], in what was the original Tampa Palms, where Tampa Palms Elementary sits, were comfortable staying at Tampa Palms (Elementary School). The boundary was going to be [the highway] and some of the homes that are not as expensive or exclusive on the west side of [highway] where [the new] elementary school was going to be built. So mainly the parents from the west side of [the highway] started the petition to keep one school on two campuses . . . so you would not split that community. In actuality, they did not want the homes on the west side to be divided from the east side . . . it is not uncommon. It just happened up in [another suburb] too. So what you are seeing is the very exclusive versus the exclusive homes. And there is a lot of concern that "my house is only

350,000 [dollars] but those houses are 6(00,000), so if you build a new school (my status will go down)."[10]

According to this official, current conflicts are often between "the haves" and the "have mores" as much as the "haves" and "have nots." Still, this scenario illustrates how people associate schools with the status of the community, and key institutions for maintaining social status.

Several Tampa Palms parents defined a successful community as children attending the same school, having access to the same resources, and then having the ability to live in the same community that produced them. These parents thus saw their school as necessary for maintaining the social cohesion and mobility of their community. But if this notion is extended a little more, we should be wary of endorsing a role of schools that reinforces the boundaries of a community. If schools serve only this role, which some parents in this debate appeared to sanction, then schools truly are agents of social reproduction. If this dynamic is true for one well-off community, then the argument can be extended to communities that are not as rich in resources and opportunities. Here, social reproduction refers to the role schools can play in maintaining the class structure of society. The lack of educational opportunities and poorly equipped schools promotes low academic achievement among poor children residing in impoverished communities and promotes social *im*mobility. So here is the danger we see in the debate over an elementary school in exclusive suburbs: the notion of schools as communities can reflect a hierarchal societal structure. Do our notions of community schools—and, by extension, nationalism, democracy, and freedom for all—only work if you live in the "right" neighborhood?

Tampa Palms parents were fighting vigorously to keep one school in the community for a variety of reasons. First, families moved into this area because of the school; second, there is a strong PTA that has raised funds to support the school and its endeavors; third, these children have grown together over the years; and, finally, maintaining one school would keep outsiders out (by redrawing the boundaries of school attendance zones). It is the last explanation that concerns us. Who has been designated as an outsider, and what makes this person an outsider? The outsider is "a person not part of a particular group," to choose one definition.[11] In the Tampa Palms community, outsider/insider status designations were class constructions, whose racial dimensions became more evident when several parents opposed an attendance zone for the new school that included low-income children from a predominately African American community.

When the school board rejected the two-campus plan and established boundaries for the new K-5 elementary school, several Tampa Palms parents protested the attendance zone established for the new school because it included a predominately Black-low-income neighborhood. Most rational individuals do not like to cite changes in racial balance at a school as a reason for opposing redistricting; however, some Tampa Palms parents felt quite adamant that the proposed change was unfair because it would increase the ratio of minority to white students at "their" school while the race ratio would remain the same in other schools in the area. Tampa Palm's parents argued that these students would need "more resources like volunteers, tutoring programs, and donated uniforms and supplies." In other words, they felt an increase in minority enrollment would bring the larger burdens of poverty into their school. Assuming all minority students were poor and lived outside their area, parents who opposed the new attendance zone asserted that their community did not have the resources for children who "come to school hungry" and have special learning problems. Ironically, more than half of the "minority" children assigned to the new school lived in Tampa Palm's neighborhoods and not the area targeted for busing. One parent commenting on this irony stated to a local reporter, "The scariest thing is that most of the African American children whose attendance they would like to limit live in their neighborhood."[12]

In this community, parents felt their housing investment provided certain advantages to protect through the school attendance zones. Those privileges were the rights to live in a "good" community, have their children attend a "good" school, receive a "good" education and live a "good" life. In this view, school is a place that will provide the type of education that prepares them for a life that is deemed successful by the community. So in essence the school becomes an extension of the neighborhood community and its values. This particular example affirms the idea of school as community. These parents only wanted the best for their children and thus advocated this "one community, one school" ideology.

But this image of a school as a community restricts access based on race-ethnicity and religion, not just residential boundaries. People can be excluded from communities and schools within their community based on race, ethnicity, and social class. In recent decades, wealthy communities have controlled the social-class membership of neighborhoods by limiting mixed-income housing developments, keeping housing costs out of reach of other socioeconomic groups. As we saw in our own area, wealthy communities can also protest attendance zones that include children from lower-income residential areas.

Furthermore, people who gained access to the community through personal wealth (through houses) can be targets of exclusion due to race or ethnicity (and possibly religion and sexual orientation).

This small vignette from our city illustrates some of the complexities in talking about schools as communities. An historical perspective is important for two reasons. First, there is a nostalgic myth about some idyllic relationship between schools and communities that some are sure existed in the past, as one manual for "how to deal" with parents asserts:

> Gone are the "good old days" when educators were revered and respected for their wisdom and position by parents. Now, we have to earn our respect the old-fashioned way: Work for it. As one beleaguered administrator told me, "Twenty years ago, all I had to do was keep the teachers and the parents happy. Now, I need to get results."[13]

This nostalgia may be consistent with the experience of individual parents or educators, but it does not reflect our national history with its crosscutting arguments about communities and schools. As the authors in this book discuss schools as communities in our country's history, they look carefully at the historical definitions of outsiders, whether based on geographical boundaries, role within a school, race, class, religion, or sexual orientation. They also examine the broader definition of community and who has been responsible for identifying members and defining the terms of membership. An alert observer must ask whether viewing schools as communities has been inherently problematic or whether it has reflected the type of community that schools have propagated? What have we meant by terms such as "school as community"? And, finally, why have we imagined schools as communities?

These questions focus on our flexible use of *schools* and *communities* as language.[14] We would like to believe that we live in a rational world in which everyone agrees that all are created equal and that equality should extend itself to schools. The battle over the new elementary school, however, is one example that speaks to issues of how social divisions based on social status and role can propagate inequitable educational opportunities. The rest of this introduction briefly explores historical changes and continuities in defining school communities, describes the substantive chapters that follow, and explores different theoretical perspectives on schools as imagined communities, the problems involved with such visions. This anthology explores how schools have served as imagined communities, documenting the importance of educational change in American history.

School Communities in History

If there is any clear pattern in the history of *school community* in the past two centuries—whether one is speaking of rhetoric, policy, or practice—it has been a subtle shift in the focus from battles over what constitutes a *school within a community* in the nineteenth century to battles over what constitutes *a school community* in the twentieth. In the early nineteenth century, when local control still flexed considerable muscle, considerable experimentation in the forms of schools led to debates over what was a good school and who properly controlled it. By the end of World War I, by contrast, increasing state control made schools much more standardized in form, commonly part of bureaucratic systems that were either fully centralized or consolidating a centralized form. This standardization created a common understanding of a "real school" and shifted debates over who controls the school community into fights over access, inclusion, and exclusion from desirable communities.[15] This shift was not universal nor did it preclude debates over communities in the nineteenth century—in the heyday of American communes, there certainly were arguments, and parents and teachers could fight bitterly—but debates over school forms and control were more frequent and widespread. And while there have been debates in the last hundred years about the proper form of schools, the larger political battles in the past century have been about inclusion and exclusion—or a path from *Outside In*, as the title of Paula Fass's book suggests.[16]

This shift had its origins in the disorganized origins of formal schooling in colonial British North America in the seventeenth and eighteenth centuries. In the northern British colonies, there were a variety of school types from village shacks that hosted short school sessions, "dame schools" in the houses of town women, and other private schoolmasters, to grammar schools, academies, and colleges. In southern colonies, settlements and towns were less likely to have the same school infrastructure as in the north, and private tutors were more common for wealthy families, but schools still existed. When the American Revolution started (and finished), there were schools, but not school systems.[17]

Several overlapping developments dominated the history of schools—and the definition of school communities, more narrowly—over the next 80 years. In several ways, schools became tightly associated with urbanization and settlement. Although there had been attempts to link towns and schools as early as the 1640s, there are several signs that town building and school building became linked efforts in the early 1800s. First, the 1785 land ordinance passed by the

Continental Congress established a clear legal link between the creation of towns and the support of schools through the reservation of land within a settlement for the support of schools. In addition, several New England states began crafting laws requiring towns of a certain size to support high schools. But the linkage extended beyond laws. In the Ohio River and Mississippi River valleys, town boosters often started religious-supported colleges in an attempt to make the settlement more visible. These uses of schools were frequently poorly conceived and fictional—the laws were poorly enforced, and the startup colleges often switched denominations or failed quickly—but they suggest some common understanding that school building and town building were ideally linked. This linkage came before the common association of primary schooling with citizenship, even while the definition of "public schooling" was in flux.[18]

That experimentation with the form of public schools and nascent school systems dominated the first two thirds of the nineteenth century. Schools operating in the 1830s included one-room shacks and schools of several hundred students taught by one adult, single schools managed by local town elders and large school systems managed by the equivalent of nonprofit corporations, high schools using public funds and academies relying on private donations—a breadth of experimental forms that was the focus of pitched political battles between common-school reformers and their adversaries over the next several decades. In that debate, there was little discussion about inclusion and exclusion in communities. In fact, the largest change in access to primary schooling in our nation's history—the coeducation of America's elementary schools—happened without any substantive, deliberate debate.[19] Similarly, elementary schools slowly excluded the youngest children, again without much debate. That silence on both matters suggests the extent to which inclusion and exclusion were not at the heart of debates, even at a time when most children attended schools that truly were in their own neighborhoods.[20]

There were two greatest exceptions to this broad antebellum silence over inclusion and exclusion. One was based in race, whether racial segregation in northern antebellum schools or the growing restrictions on the education of African American Southerners, free or slave. The other battle was over religion, focused on the relationships between Catholic communities and the public schools. As a result of hostility and political battles over religious education and the distribution of public funds, Catholic bishops in the United States built a network of schools separate from and parallel to public schools.[21] These battles over the demarcation of school communities grew dramatically in the 80 years after the Civil War. Again, the most obvious area was in race and ethnicity. The conflicts over the inclusion and exclusion of children based on race included not only the segregation of African American students but also situations as disparate as Chinese American communities surviving in the Mississippi Delta and conflicting ethnic identities among Latinos in Colorado.[22] But the growing consciousness of boundaries was much broader.

Between the Civil War and the post–World War II civil rights movement, schools became much more like each other in form and content. By the end of World War I, schools that most Americans attended had become part of larger systems, and those school systems themselves were under several forces pushing consolidation in the twentieth century. Three broad trends were at work in this partial standardization of educational experiences: bureaucratization, migration, and increasing attendance. First, schools became increasingly bureaucratized in the closing decades of the nineteenth century. Burgeoning cities developed school systems with larger numbers of administrators and rules that attempted to circumscribe the behavior of individual schools and teachers. State governments also pushed for centralization in the twentieth-century effort to consolidate small rural schools into much larger systems. But school experiences also became more common as children became much more likely to live in major metropolitan areas. This shift came both because the late nineteenth- and early twentieth-century wave of immigration concentrated immigrants in cities and also because internal migration shifted the greatest pace of urbanization from small cities and towns to larger cities. Between 1860 and 1920, the proportion of Americans living in urban areas expanded from just under 20 percent to over 50 percent. Finally, children spent a higher proportion of their childhood in schools by the mid-twentieth century than they had a century earlier. Much of the increased attendance came from a shift in where teenagers spent their time, from full-time labor to full-time school attendance. But younger children were also somewhat more likely to attend schools by the end of the Great Depression, as truancy laws and child-labor laws were enforced more vigorously.[23]

One consequence of these changes was the disappearance of experimental school forms. For example, the academy largely vanished as a high school competitor by the late nineteenth century. And, when competitors did appear, school systems often moved quickly to reacquire their position as the primary legitimate educational institution. In the early twentieth century, high schools duplicated the business clerical skills that proprietary vocational schools used to draw students. Later, mainstream educational administrators attacked federal youth programs that had educational components, primarily the National

Youth Administration and the Civilian Conservation Corps. By and large, however, experimentation in form was on the margins of North American education. By 1950, the majority of young adults in the United States had experienced an education that was far more uniform than any prior generation in the nation's history.[24]

By 1950, "local control" was disappearing from the reality of school systems in many ways. What remained in the control of local schools was not the broad range of early-nineteenth-century experimentation but a more limited menu of options in the post–World War II era. In some ways, school reform had become an "add-on" to existing structures rather than a replacement of those structures, leading to a curriculum and school form that was later termed the "shopping-mall high school." Some choice remained in curriculum matters that were politicized and controversial.[25] One such set of controversies was the direction and scope of history, with vigorous arguments about the presentation of the American Civil War and the contributions of different minority groups. Jonathan Zimmerman has argued that the end result has not been a variety of perspectives or a lively debate but a set of pablum-filled texts that allows any group to insert its set of heroes, as long as the overarching narrative is about the triumphal American nation. The other area of significant local control was defining boundaries of the school community. In one area—race—segregation laws in the South eliminated local control through the early twentieth century. Schools outside the South often did segregate by race and ethnicity, even without the mandates of state law. And, after *Brown v. Board of Education*, local school boards had at least the nominal ability to craft their own path to desegregation. (Most chose to delay and circumscribe desegregation for years.) But in most areas, including sex and disability, local school systems had great leeway to provide or restrict access to education between the Civil War and the modern civil rights movement.[26]

The consequence of educational standardization was not necessarily a greater rift between schools and surrounding communities. As William Cutler notes, there were two significant forces that pushed schools and parents closer during the growth of school bureaucracies. While bureaucracies can alienate and craft artificial distinctions, school bureaucracies also took the sting out of the very local politics of education pitting teachers against parents in the early and mid-nineteenth century. What was lost in intimacy may have been gained in some mutual interest acquiring resources and respect for schools. The other force pulling teachers and some mothers together was the growing feminization of elementary teaching in the United States. By the mid-twentieth century, elementary-school teachers and middle-class mothers often shared perspectives that grew from both gender and social class similarities.[27]

Despite those similarities, the responsibilities and role of teachers represent one significant exception to the historical shift in debates over school and community. From the earliest days of colonization in North America, those who oversee schools in various ways have been concerned with the qualifications of teachers. Through the late nineteenth century, moral probity was far more important than academic or pedagogic skills. With the growth of normal schools, teacher training institutes, teachers colleges, and schools and colleges of education on university campuses, school boards and state departments of education could afford the luxury of being concerned with academic qualifications of teachers in the twentieth century. And, surrounding all of these issues of qualification came the broader issue of how teachers fit into a broader community. Among others, William Cutler has documented the frequently vivid hostility between teachers and parents in the nineteenth century. That complicated role of teachers has continued. As Jack Dougherty has pointed out, the battles over desegregation involved the role and position of teachers as well as students. In New York City, teachers were both civil rights activists and also the symbol of resistance to decentralization efforts; their role was intimately tied up with the definition of school communities in a 1968 teachers strike pitting the predominantly white teachers union against activist African American parents in the Ocean Hill–Brownsville area of the city.[28]

Why Does Anyone See Schools as Communities?

People often identify schools with communities and see schools as types of communities. Because the concept of a school community is so deeply embedded in educational politics, some explanation is necessary before the topical chapters that follow. We start with the assumption that the notion of community is not universal. Rather than asking why anyone sees schools as communities, one's first instinct may be to ask the opposite question: "Why would anyone *not* see a school as a community?" When we are so close to a situation, looking at it in an unusual way is often revealing. Substitute "discount store" for "school," for example, and one can easily see a crucial difference between the two. Many adults will frequent a discount store, drive or walk by the store, and otherwise live nearby without ever thinking of it as a unique part of a community. Who, for example, buys a house to be within a mile of a specific Wal-Mart?[29] No one, certainly, names a chain store after famous people; there is no "Thomas Jefferson Target." The attempts by some developers to suggest that large shopping centers are, instead, community gathering sites is generally unsuccessful; in our metropolitan area, residents rarely refer to the "Citrus Park Town Center," using the common noun "mall" instead. Schools are different. People buy houses to live near particular schools, and residents often vigorously fight for their favored school names. Something, therefore, must be special about schools that make us think of them as closely tied to communities. *We imagine schools as communities regardless of whether the description fits well in the individual circumstances.*

Below, we describe four general categorical explanations of what makes schools qualify as imagined communities and important examples of those explanations. We do not agree with all of them, but we list all the plausible reasons social scientists would provide for thinking of schools as communities so the reader can make an informed judgment about which theories may fit specific situations. Roughly speaking, these theories fall into what we refer to as functionalist, materialist, opportunistic, and institutional-identity explanations of schools as imagined communities.[30] One can categorize these theories by the questions they can answer:

- *Functionalist*: What role does a school as imagined community serve in a society we assume is rationally organized?
- *Materialist*: Who benefits in a concrete way from the identification of schools as imagined communities?
- *Opportunistic*: What opportunities do schools provide through the creation of imagined communities?
- *Institutional-identity*: How does the institution of schooling shape the roles and identities individuals assume in other aspects of their lives and how they imagine their communities?

These categories as stated earlier are ahistorical, for the related questions do not openly recognize change over time. A section later in the introduction raises historical questions about the way people have imagined schools as communities (not just how they do so now). For the moment, this simple set of categories can help explain why schools might serve as imagined communities.

Functionalist Explanations of Schools as Imagined Communities

One can examine schools with the sociological "trick" of assuming that schools serve as a rational role in a society and identifying what roles schools would serve if society were like some clockwork mechanism.[31] In this view of education, schools can help raise children to be functional members of society in various senses. Thus, education can increase the human capital of a society, socialize children into adult roles, and help manage the ambition of the population.[32] The identification of schools either *as* a community in itself or as *part* of a broader community is different from these examples, however, for it concerns how schools and communities of adults interact (rather than focusing on the rearing of children). One functionalist explanation for identifying schools as communities, especially with the vast majority of people in the United States in metropolitan areas, is that schools can help replace the social control of small communities with a more artificial, but still functional, mechanism for maintaining social order. In this view, the imagining of communities in metropolitan areas is a substitute for the more intimate social order of small, rural communities. Schools can serve to facilitate this social control, in theory, by providing an institution to focus adult socialization and observation of children.[33] Imagining schools as communities might help adults (both parents and others) believe that they are rearing children with the support of like-minded individuals. Children who see the adults in their lives as part of a close network might be more likely to obey adults and less likely to believe that their behavior will go unnoticed or unmentioned.

A second functionalist explanation for imagining schools as communities might be as a practical way for adults to work on matters of mutual interest. Parents who otherwise disagree about various matters (such as political affiliation or the desirability of new taxes) are often willing to work in concert when their children attend school together, use the same texts available in that school, and have the same (good or bad) teachers. Schools can thus serve as the focus for interest-group politics, as parents fight for resources, better teaching, and the like. In the broader theory of pluralist politics, interest groups serve as a way for individuals to aggregate in policymaking, avoiding more confrontational ways of seeking political goals.

Materialist Explanations of Schools as Imagined Communities

A second way of looking at schools is to assume that, in contrast to a functionalist approach where *society* is a single unit, schools are the arenas for conflict over the distribution of resources (both tangible and intangible) in society.[34] In this view, different groups might use school resources for their own ends. One way of using a conflict-oriented perspective on schools is to identify specific material advantages individual groups seek to gain through schooling—or, as the converse, attempts to withhold those resources from other groups. Again, as with a functionalist view, one can identify the uses of schools in connection to childrearing and also tied to purely adult purposes. Thus, one materialist explanation of imagining schools as communities might be that groups of parents (and others with emotional ties to a group of children) see schools as a way to advance the interests of those children. Here, the interests of the children are central. Many parents organize to fight for the best education of their children. This behavior is certainly common enough in individual families, who may bargain with school officials for various resources (for example, in individualized education planning meetings for children using special education services). The limits of such resources guarantee that parents and guardians face a conflict between the fact that opportunities in public schools should in theory be available to all and the natural desire to hoard that opportunity for one's children or the children of one's friends.[35] One parent may find out about a specialized science program for her children, and she may pass along the news of the program (including the key person to contact) to a few friends. If all children in the system applied, her children's chances to enter would be minimal. Passing along information on how to access the program to a limited few may be viewed as an act of generosity. Yet, if information about programs is only transmitted through such informal channels it becomes, in effect, selective access and, in effect, opportunity hoarding.

Such opportunity hoarding becomes a matter of imagining communities in two ways: First, people make opportunities available only to those they identify as being part of the same community. Few parents would stop a stranger on the street, for example, and describe how to apply successfully to a magnet program. This passing of information (and thus opportunities) occurs privately, between friends and acquaintances. It is a form of sponsorship. Almost by definition, the social networking that can perpetuate opportunity hoarding is an informal way of defining and making material advantage of a community. The second aspect of hoarding opportunities through imagined communities is when parents and other allies organize to fight for the interests of *groups* of children. A school district transfers a beloved teacher to another school, and parents may call the school board members demanding that the action be reversed. A school decides to distribute computers from a single classroom throughout the school instead, and parents of the children who used the computers before may demand the status quo ante. In metropolitan areas across the South in the late twentieth century, issues over rezoning involved explicit discussions of who should have the opportunity to attend schools that suburban parents identified as *their* (own) schools. Later, we discuss the problems with identifying communities as schools based on how definitions of communities determine who is *not* eligible for access to various educational resources. For now, we note that in this view, parents would not generally recognize a distinction between opportunity hoarding through social networking and organizing. All this behavior is, after all, in the interests of their children.

Yet some uses of schools as communities do focus explicitly on the interests of adults. The reputations of schools, for example, affect property values. Thus, homeowners who have no direct connection with local schools have an interest in the schools that, if the reputation is good, they would want to characterize as *their* schools. This associated "property value" of a school is important not only for those selling to parents but also to all homeowners, who do not know who might eventually purchase property from them. A recent paper by David Figlio and Maurice Lucas has documented that the value of each grade increment in the Florida system of assigning single-letter grades to schools (implemented in 1999 by Governor Jeb Bush) was worth approximately $9,000 for the value of a home in Alachua County. Thus, school reputation plays into the speculative aspect of real estate.[36]

Opportunistic Explanations of Schools as Imagined Communities

A third category of explanations for why many imagine and use schools as communities is that schools serve as a practical occasion to build community.[37] Children and adults meet at schools for a variety of purposes (not always for academics), and thus schools can serve as gathering sites for adults as well as children. Two sociologists argued that in the 1920s in Muncie, Indiana, high school served in part as a way to cement adult ties to the community through common attendance at basketball games. In a very different way, the Lexington School for the Deaf in Manhattan is a focal point of the Deaf community in the New York City area as adults come to the school for meetings in a welcoming environment.[38] Parent–Teacher Association meetings, fish fries, and carnivals at schools all serve, like interscholastic athletics, the dual purposes of helping the school's more direct mission of rearing children and also being chances for adults to meet and share a symbolic affiliation.

The terms *social capital* and *cultural capital* represent the utilitarian and symbolic connections built up by the definition of schools as communities in this way. *Social capital* is the development of skills and knowledge shared among people who know each other. When a volunteer tutor forms a lasting friendship with a student, that tutor then becomes part of the social network of the student and the student's social capital. The tutor can share knowledge about educational opportunities, professional requirements, and other knowledge that other individuals in the student's social network (including the student's immediate family) may not have. *Cultural capital* is the knowledge of common cultural resources that allow people to share cultural values, referents for discussion, or even a common group affinity. Pierre Bourdieu cynically described cultural capital as one of the ways families and schools help reproduce inequality; knowing which paintings of Claude Monet are in the Art Institute of Chicago may not be relevant to doing a job competently but may convince a potential employer that you're the type of person he or she wants as a worker and colleague.[39] E. D. Hirsch turned this argument on its head and said that, if cultural capital exists, then schools must provide those touchstones of commonality to its students.[40]

Schools are not the only places where adults can consciously build community. As Benedict Anderson argued in the book that inspired the title for this volume, that nations becoming independent in the twentieth century were "imagined communities" built through the earlier rotation of colonial civil servants, whose journeys defined colonial territories as more than lines on a map. Those journeys propagated the idea that everyone living in that territory had a shared interest. The role of the colonial civil service was crucial, according to Benedict, because they were key agents in the propagation of an idea that made the most sense to *them*, a group whose lives were dominated by travel in a territory (but never service in the colonial capital). Sexual minorities in the twentieth century also used the chances afforded them to build social networks and a consciously created community. According to John D'Emilio's history of gay communities the years after World War II provided a variety of means for homosexuals to meet, realize common interests, and begin to organize for the rights of gays, lesbians, and bisexuals. In both these stories, occasions to build social networks can turn a fragile sense of common interest into a stronger, consciously articulated community.[41]

Institutional-Identity Explanations of Schools as Imagined Communities

The last category of explanations we describe sees the institutional characteristics of schools as tied to their identity as communities because they might be unbearable to contemplate otherwise. We now live in an institutional world, with large organizations whose primary purpose is to serve the needs of individuals "from cradle to grave," in the words of utopian writer Edward Bellamy.[42] Whether these organizations are private or public, nonprofit or moneymaking, is largely irrelevant to the individual who faces a large bureaucracy as an obstacle or facilitator. Those working within these organizations try to imagine them as better than a bureaucracy and often use language to create different images, of a "team" or "family." These metaphors are not just for public relations, as they also are means for resolving the psychological gap in scale between the individual lives we lead and the huge organizations that shape our world.

Seeing schools as communities is one example of this use of language to struggle with imagining a huge organization (and one's relationship to it). In the nineteenth century, many cities in the United States had schools far larger than typical factories.[43] As more urban areas developed, educators and their critics searched for metaphors—often borrowed from military and business organizations—to help them describe what they wanted.[44] The depiction of schools as communities or as families suggests a far more intimate relationship than the description of a school as a set of bureaucratic cogs. No one wants to send one's child to or work in a set of bureaucratic cogs. Thus, identifying with or creating one's community within the school is a way of blunting the institutional characteristics of a school.

Problems with Imagining Schools as Communities

We have considered why we imagined schools as communities from differing theoretical perspectives. Now we examine the very real problems with imagining schools as communities. First, although we often discuss schools as communities through the rhetoric of inclusion, imagined communities are necessarily exclusive. Ira Katznelson and Margaret Weir note that despite the democratic notion of "schooling for all," public schools have historically been sites of ethnic and territorial conflict and exclusive practices that denied some groups access to educational resources.[45] The exclusive nature of bounded communities brings us to consider a second problem with imagining schools as communities. We imagine schools as bounded communities of shared interests. Yet seldom do such communities exist. As Albert Hunter and Gerald Suttles state, sociological models of the local community neglect the role of external forces and internal divisions and create "representations which are faulty, limited, unreal, or artificial."[46]

Examples of these faulty representations in academic discourse are bountiful such as "the African American community values discipline" or "the Jewish community resisted vocational education." Finally, a third problem is we often imagine schools as communities through nostalgia, raising questions about the reliability of our memories of the past. Through nostalgia one can express a yearning for something lost that is no longer recoverable except through one's imagination. Through nostalgia we invoke romanticized memories of past schools as communities in an effort to cope with and critique the problems of contemporary institutional life. The following discussion explores these three problematic areas.

Rhetoric of Inclusion, Reality of Exclusion

Though we can imagine communities as all-inclusive as in the "global village," in reality any notion of a school as a community is exclusive, whether based on residential area or group identity. As stated earlier, exclusive aspects of schools often function to maintain a status quo within society despite the ideal of the American meritocracy, the notion that individuals can climb the social ladder on their merit. Rather than merit alone, individual success in school and the workplace are often results of family background, social networking, and elite cultural traits, as well as individual effort. The policy of Ivy League institutions to grant admissions to the sons of school alumni regardless of academic qualifications is one obvious example of how educational resources can be inherited rather than earned through individual effort. Even public schools, which are purportedly open to all children, have particular constituencies often differentiated by location, social class, or ethnic, cultural, and other characteristics attributed to its members. As bounded communities, schools have designated insiders and outsiders so we can distinguish between "our" school and "theirs." Indeed, most extracurricular activities, particularly sports, band, and academic competitions, are predicated on rivalries between school communities. Though competition may bolster school spirit and community pride, they also reinforce the exclusive nature of school as communities.

Social Networks, Social Capital, and the Community of Limited Liability

But exclusion is not restricted to the boundaries of a school's attendance area. Imagined communities can also mask internal divisions. As Gerald Suttles described, an imagined community may be cemented by common interests—the community of limited liability—but those common interests do not end the internal differentiation, external influences, and the fragmented involvement of people in community life in the United States.[47] Suttles pointed out that communities are not self-contained entities whose members share identities and activities as well as interests. Despite our references to "the" community, even close-knit and seemingly enclosed communities are composed of individuals with differing interests and statuses, multiple roles, and varying degrees of involvement.

Consider the following excerpt from an interview with Carlton Williams as he discusses growing up and going to school in the segregated Black community of Tampa. Williams describes his "subset" of Tampa as a "small town," where everyone knew everyone through shared membership in schools and churches. Williams explains that "no matter where or what part of Black Tampa you lived in somebody in the family or the neighborhood knew who you were." This close knit community was not without internal divisions, as Williams recalls:

> You can live side by side, but you can also maintain separate interaction, separate transactional sets. You can be a neighbor, but not go to tea with your neighbor ... I do now remember that there were, perhaps, certain restrictions on who was welcome as a playmate of mine. Since I knew them all and my parents knew them all, and they (playmates) would either be Cadillac'd or Buick'd in from wherever they lived to play with me, and I would be Buick'd out to them to play with them, rather than [I] join the neighborhood, sand-lot baseball team.[48]

Williams's description of life in Black Tampa captures Morris Janowitz's concept of "community of limited liability." As Suttles contends, not all members need to identify or be identified with a community for it to maintain cohesion. William's parents may not have welcomed the children on the "sand-lot" baseball team as their son's playmates, but they were nevertheless part of the Black community.

When we think about looser coalitions based on interest—an expanding community of limited liability, according to Suttles—we can understand fragmented "communities" as territorial and socially constructed entities, and we can also understand why internal and external actors and institutions can maintain community identity despite its changing boundaries, internal divisions, and external pressures. Within a given school community further differentiation can occur such as the "nerds," "Goths," and "druggies" of the local high school. In this sense, imagined communities are not monolithic, and the underlying tensions among its members and nonmembers suggest a complexity underneath the simple term "school community."

All too often, this tension is hidden in rhetoric about the need to support communities or build social capital around children. Of course children deserve to belong to supportive social groups. But talk about community cannot paper over the divisions that prevent many children from accessing that support—division between schools and parents, among parents of children attending a school, and within the residential neighborhoods of children, such as violence based in the drug economy. Because the talk about school communities emphasizes local ties, the importance of resource differences is marginalized. For parents with enough resources, long-distance social networks and resources can compensate for divisions in a neighborhood. If you can drive your child to a private school, to a tutor, or to a playgroup, you do not need close ties with your neighbors. And if you do not have those resources, talking about reliance on one's community may be unrealistic.

Nostalgia: Remembering Schools as Communities

We cannot consider schools as communities without noting that school and school experiences can be significantly romanticized. People commonly idealize school community relations in their memories of the past. Strikingly, oral histories of students who attended poor, segregated schools reveal testimonies about the family-like atmosphere of these schools where "everybody knew everybody and cared about everybody."[49] The nostalgia for past schools of one's childhood often provides a social commentary on the present as much as fragmented and selective memories of the past. We tend to be nostalgic for relationships and experiences we see absent today. One fundamental problem with nostalgia is its potential to distort the historical record by advancing a superficial understanding of the past and contemporary problems. Commenting on the nostalgia for historically Black schools, Gary Orfield and Susan Eaton argue that critics of desegregation erroneously assume the failure of desegregation to expand opportunities because some inequalities and problems still persist.[50] Stephanie Coontz also contends that nostalgia for the past can fabricate history.[51] Romanticizing the "traditional" family, Coontz argues, creates a "nostalgia trap" that prevents people from developing viable solutions to the contemporary family crisis.

The existence of nostalgia challenges historians to find value in the frail memories of the past. To be sure, we must scrutinize romanticized memories of schools as communities. Nevertheless, what meanings people attached to nostalgic reflections also deserve examination.

Key to the themes of this book is how and why people imagine schools as communities, and in the case of nostalgia, how they remember schools as communities. By studying nostalgia for school communities, we examine how individuals invest past experiences with new meanings informed by present circumstances. Whether the memory is of segregated schooling, spankings received as a child, or other events, recollections are both memories and also judgments about the present. Nostalgia is a way we invest past events and experiences with significance largely informed by present concerns. Therefore, the nostalgia for "neighborhood schools" in public discourse can be read as reflective of an increasing angst about current social and demographic changes.

Imagining Schools as Communities: Historical Case Studies

With this theoretical discussion behind us, we now move to the case studies that form the bulk of the book. The broader story sketched earlier in the chapter—the shifting focus from defining the proper school to defining the proper school community against the more constant debates about population minorities and the role of teachers—is the backdrop for this book. Each chapter in this anthology discusses how schools have been imagined as communities among diverse communities throughout the United States. Each author provides a unique framework from which to consider ways and potential problems with imagining schools as communities. Each of these frameworks illustrates the complexity of school–community relations in the United States, in many cases intertwined with the struggle for educational equity.

We have arranged the chapters thematically. The first two chapters focus on the creation of imagined school communities among educators in nineteenth-century America. The first chapter by Vicki Eaklor, "Education in an Imagined Community: Lessons from Brook Farm," explores the construction of school as an imagined community during a period when the utopian and egalitarian goals for public schools were first being articulated. Eaklor's chapter focuses on the activities and role of the school at Brook Farm Institute for Agriculture and Education (1841–1847), one of the most famous utopian communal experiments in U.S. history. Eaklor examines Brook Farm in the contexts of the local "school community" on the one hand and the larger "community"—the (northern) United States—of which the Farm was but a small part on the other. Paradoxically, it was the brainchild of New England Transcendentalists whose reputation in their time and since has revolved around the antithesis of community, individualism. In seeking to balance the principle of individual freedom with a communal ideal, the founders and residents of the Brook Farm can be viewed as a microcosm of America itself, where these elements have been in perpetual tension.

The Brook Farm School gained notoriety for its rigorous curriculum and "success" as an educational institution at precisely the time that a more general educational reform, in the call for public education for all children, was gaining popularity in America. The roots of this success seem to lie in the relation between the School and the Farm, with the latter taking over the role of community building with which public schools in the United States have been burdened. Thus the Brook Farm School, though short-lived, provides a fascinating window into both a moment in U.S. history when educational ideals and the role of schools were hotly debated and a more general consideration of the relationship, real and imagined, between schools and community.

The second chapter by Melissa Ladd Teed, "Crafting Community: Hartfold Public High School in the Nineteenth Century," also explores the creation of an educational community. After months of intense public debate in 1847, the residents of Hartford, Connecticut, agreed to construct a coeducational public high school. Over the next several years, the city witnessed the creation of a new kind of educational community in which young teachers from other parts of Connecticut and New England imported fresh ideas and attitudes about the meaning of education. By using a single institution as the starting point, Melissa Ladd Teed analyzes the impact of this educational community on the lives of the first generation of women teachers at Hartford Public High School (HPHS). Although many were newcomers to Hartford, this group of women teachers did not remain isolated from city life. To limit the disruption that the new institution might bring to the city, the new teachers were immediately "adopted" by the city's elite in an attempt to socialize them to the community's norms. Olivia Day and Sophia Stevens, for example, two early teachers at HPHS, quickly became friends and joined a circle of young women from the most respectable Hartford families, thereby creating a mutually sustaining web of social relations. Yet this socialization process was not unidirectional.

Melissa Ladd Teed demonstrates that the educational community that was created at HPHS acted as a catalyst for some to question the city's traditional gender boundaries. Despite the aspirations of the town fathers who encouraged the creation of the HPHS, the meaning and outcome of the experience of teaching could not be controlled.

As women such as Day and Stevens negotiated the inevitable period of adjustment to the new school and community, they also reconsidered the possibilities for their own lives. Teaching in Hartford presented opportunities for women not simply to socialize with Hartford's elite, but also to develop their skills in the classroom and to create informal mechanisms to exercise authority over the educational process itself. Their friendships with city residents, their solidarity as teachers, their commitment to the educational experiment, and their drive to excel together created the foundation for women to move beyond the classroom and play a role in building a viable institution. As the site for the negotiation of these issues, HPHS provides an opportunity to explore the reciprocal relationships between school, city, and teachers, and in the process, to assess the nature of the community that was formed.

Though the idea of education for all children became increasing popular, not all groups of Americans had access to educational institutions. The next two chapters examines community building as it relates to politics of racial identity, sexuality, and equality of access and treatment in schools. In her chapter "Student-Community Voices: Memories of Access versus Treatment at University of Illinois," Deirdre Cobb-Roberts analyzes the academic and social experiences of African American students at the University of Illinois at Urbana-Champaign, during the post–World War II era. Using oral history and traditional archival research, this chapter examines the complexity of access versus treatment. Prior to 1945 few African American students attended the University of Illinois. After World War II, more African Americans were able to enroll due to the GI Bill. Once these students began to enter the University in "larger" numbers, the university was faced with issues of treatment. The voices of students and community members in addition to various manuscript collections specifically outlined the life of African American students on the campus during the post–World War II and pre–Civil Rights movement era. There exists a significant amount of research on the higher education of African American students, but precious little on their experiences at majority white college campuses outside the South. In conclusion, this chapter provides a critical analysis of race and higher education at the University in the context of memory versus historical documents.

Like students at University of Illinois, teachers also built communities to challenge discrimination, and in the case of the next chapter, fought against heterosexist oppression. In this chapter, "From Isolation to Imagined Communities of LGBT School Workers: Activism in the 1970s," Jackie Blount describes the formation of early Lesbian Gay Bisexual Teacher (LBGT) organizations. During the cold war, teachers who centered their lives on persons of the same sex learned either to hide this part of their identities—or to leave the profession. Witch-hunts, inspired by Senator McCarthy's successful government purges of homosexuals, became commonplace in states such as Florida, California, and Idaho as well as in communities around the country. Consequently, teachers who identified as homosexual quickly learned that to keep from raising suspicion, they needed to isolate their social lives from work. They especially needed to exercise extreme caution when interacting with teachers like themselves. A common tactic of the time was for investigators to identify one allegedly homosexual teacher and then to press him or her for as many names as possible, producing a snowballing roster in the process.

After the Stonewall riot in 1969, however, LGBT teachers, energized by the fledgling gay rights movement, began to fight for their rights. In the mid-1970s, lesbian and gay teachers organized professional groups that would press larger education associations for support, inclusion, and fully equal rights. Meanwhile, though, conservatives eager to beat back early victories of the larger gay rights movement soon focused their assaults on LGBT teachers. Critics such as Anita Bryant successfully evoked the specter of organized homosexual teachers preying on the young. They exaggerated the extent to which LGBT teachers could comfortably connect with each other, much less organize and form community. Examining this history, Blount compares the sense of community engendered among these groups with the imagined threat they posed according to conservative critics.

As these case histories shed insight on the community building and the struggle against discrimination, the next three chapters deal with historical memory and imagined communities of the past during the era of school segregation. Barbara Shircliffe's chapter, "School and Community Lost, yet Still Imagined in the Oral History of School Segregation in Tampa, Florida" explores the nostalgia for historically Black schools closed during desegregation. In their testimonials, former students of Blake and Middleton High Schools, two historically Black high schools in Tampa closed as a result of a 1971 desegregation plan, construct an idealized school-community of the past. Shircliffe argues nostalgia functions as a critique of a desegregation process circumvented by white interests. The construction of school-community in narratives about Blake and Middleton High Schools reflect current tensions in Tampa's Black community over the need to fight resegregation and the desire to have schools that they can call "ours." This discussion broadens our understanding of how notions of past school-communities are informed by the contemporary social and economic context.

Though most discussion of school as communities has focused on ethnic/racial/gender identification, the final two chapters of this anthology explore social movements and organizations as imagined and problematic communities of interests. Sherman Dorn's chapter, "Imagined Communities and Special Education" examines how the history of special education in Nashville, Tennessee, represents both attempts to craft a community of common interests and also the fractious nature of those imagined and real networks. One illustrative thread follows: Individuals from a broad variety of backgrounds—researchers, teachers, and parents—formed and maintained an organization for children with mental retardation from the 1950s onward, and that organization combined with others to push for advances in state programs for students with disabilities. The culmination of those efforts was a state civil rights law in the early 1970s guaranteeing education for students with disabilities. Yet the same law threatened those imagined common interests in several ways, in part by threatening to change the prep-school nature of the state's school for the blind by reserving space for children with multiple disabilities at the state school.

Elgin Klugh's chapter, "The Glover School Historic Site: Rekindling the Spirit of an African American School Community" explores the present situation, and historical context of efforts to preserve segregation era African American schoolhouses. Many of these former community institutions were established shortly after slavery, and later strengthened under the guiding paradigm of the Rosenwald Fund. Now, after years of decay and noneducational use, community groups seeking a revival of educational spirit, facilities to offer supplemental educational programming (such as tutoring and educational museums), and/or space for other community activities have, independently, started to return their gazes upon the actual structures that once served as educational centers. Using the theoretical backdrop of cultural capital, and research methodology based in anthropological fieldwork, Klugh explores the work of one community group—Bealsville Inc. in rural Hillsborough County, Florida—and its efforts to preserve, rehabilitate, and reclaim segregation era schoolhouses.

These case studies point to the powerful role schools play in U.S. history and how community life and struggles often center around the schoolhouse. Schools not only serve as one source of community identity, but they also symbolized the path toward social mobility and community uplift. When schooling or educational resources are denied, communities of people often organize and demand change. This mobilization comes from the concrete interests that groups find in activism but also from the historical association of schools with communities in the United States.

Notes

1. John Dewey, *The School and Society* (1899), reprinted in *The School and Society* and *The Child and the Curriculum* (Chicago, IL: University of Chicago Press, 1990): 7; Carol Merz and Gail Furman, *Community and Schools: Promise and Paradox* (New York: Teachers College Press, 1997), 19; William W. Cutler, III, *Parents and Schools: The 150-Year Struggle for Control in American Education* (Chicago, IL: University of Chicago Press, 2000), 26–29. Jonathan Zimmerman argues that Dewey's principles did not extend the notion of the school as a community to popular input into school operations; Zimmerman, *Distilling Democracy: Alcohol Education in America's Public Schools, 1880–1925* (Lawrence: University Press of Kansas, 1999), 144–145.
2. Gary Orfield, Susan E. Eaton, and Elaine R. Jones, *Dismantling Desegregation: The Quiet Reversal of Brown v. Board of Education* (New York: New Press, 1996); Vanessa Siddle Walker, *"Their Highest Potential:" An African-American Community in the Segregated South* (Chapel Hill, NC: University of North Carolina Press, 1996); Jennifer Hochschild and Nathan Scovronick, *The American Dream and the Public Schools* (New York: Oxford University Press, 2003); Lisa Delpit, *Other People's Children: Cultural Conflict in the Classroom* (New York: New Press, 1995).
3. Benedict Anderson, *Imagined Communities: Reflections on the Origin and Spread of Nationalism* (London: Verso Editions, 1983).
4. The modern "classic" on the topic is Thomas J. Sergiovanni, *Building Community in Schools* (San Francisco: Jossey-Bass, 1994). As Gail Furman points out, "community" has been written about both as school–community relations (as if the two are separate) and as a community *within* schools; "Introduction," Furman, ed., *School as Community: From Promise to Practice* (Albany, NY: State University of New York Press, 2002), 8–10. Furman's writings are grounded in the German sociological notions of *Gemeinschaft* and *Gesellschaft*; see Furman, "Introduction," and Merz and Furman, *Community and Schools*. Frank Lutz and Carol Merz focus on political theories—Wirt and Kirst's observations of low participation in education elections contrasted with dissatisfaction theory; Frank W. Lutz and Carol Merz, *The Politics of School/Community Relations* (New York: Teachers College Press, 1992). Some writings call for an idyllic synergy of school and community; Anne Wescott Dodd and Jean L. Konzal, *How Communities Build Stronger Schools: Stories, Strategies, and Promising Practices for Educating Every Child* (New York: Palgrave Macmillan, 2002). Other more instrumental writings about school and community still derive from the early-twentieth century notion of manipulating parents and surrounding communities through public relationships; e.g., see Donald R. Gallagher, Don Bagin, and Leslie W. Kindred, *The School and Community Relations*, 6th ed. (Boston: Allyn and Bacon, 1997); Elaine K. McEwan, *How To Deal with Parents Who Are Angry,*

Troubled, Afraid, or Just Plain Crazy, 2nd ed. (Thousand Oaks, CA: 2005); as well as the historical description in William Cutler, *Parents and Schools: The 150-Year Struggle for Control in American Education* (Chicago: University of Chicago Press, 2000), esp. 42–69, 177.

5. For example, see James S. Coleman, "Social Capital in the Creation of Human Capital," *American Journal of Sociology* 94 (1998 Supplement): S95-S120; James S. Coleman, *Foundations of Social Theory* (Cambridge, MA: Belknap Press, 1990); James P. Comer, *School Power: Implications of an Intervention Project* (London: Free Press, 1980).

6. Robert S. Lynd and Helen M. Lynd, *Middletown: A Study in Modern American Culture* (New York: Harcourt Brace Jovanovich, 1929), describe how the winter life Muncie, Indiana, revolved around the high school basketball team. In *Beer and Circus: How Big-Time College Sports Is Crippling Undergraduate Education* (New York: Owl Books, 2001), Murray Sperber argued that college athletics has corrupted undergraduate education in the United States.

7. For others who have written about exclusivity and tensions in the notion of school community, see Furman, "Introduction," 3; Ulrich G. Reitzug and Mary John O'Hair, "Tensions and Struggles in Moving Toward a Democratic School Community," Furman, ed., *School as Community*, 119–141.

8. "Two schools or one?" *St. Petersburg Times*, May 28, 2000.

9. "Two schools or one?" *St. Petersburg Times*, May 28, 2000.

10. Person, William, interview with Barbara Shircliffe (February 6, 2002).

11. Random House, Webster's Dictionary.

12. Michelle Sager, "Tampa Palms parents debate minority ratios," *The Tampa Tribune*, December 8, 2000.

13. McEwen, *How To Deal with Parents Who Are Angry, Troubled, Afraid, or Just Plain Crazy*, 3.

14. For a discussion of the fluid imagery of "community" today, see Lynn G. Beck, "The Complexity and Coherence of Educational Communities: An Analysis of the Images that Reflect and Influence Scholarship and Practice," Furman, ed., *School as Community*, 23–49.

15. Mary Heywood Metz, "Real School: A Universal Drama amid Disparate Experience," D. Mitchell and M. E. Goertz, eds., *Education Politics for the New Century: The Twentieth Anniversary Yearbook of the Politics of Education Association* (Philadelphia: The Farmer Press, 1990), 75–91.

16. Paula S. Fass, *Outside In: Minorities and the Transformation of American Education* (New York: Oxford University Press, 1989).

17. Among others, see Carl F. Kaestle, *Evolution of an Urban School System* (Cambridge, MA: Harvard University Press, 1973); Theodore R. Sizer, *The Age of the Academies* (New York: Teachers College Press, 1964); Nancy Beadie and Kim Tolley, eds., *Chartered Schools: Two Hundred Years of Independent Academies in the United States, 1727–1925* (New York: RoutledgeFalmer, 2002).

18. Land Ordinance of 1785, *Journals of the Continental Congress*, May 20, 1785; Maris Vinovskis, *The Origins of Public High Schools* (Madison: University of Wisconsin Press, 1985), 60–68; see Daniel Boorstin, *The Americans: The National Experience* (New York: Random House, 1965), *passim*, on town boosterism; Ira Katznelson and Margaret Weir, *Schooling for Al: Race and the Decline of the Democratic Ideal* (New York: Basic Books, 1985), on the growing ties between education and citizenship in the nineteenth century.
19. Tyack and Hansot, *Schooling Together*.
20. Michael B. Katz, *Reconstructing American Education* (Cambridge, MA: Harvard University Press, 1987), 24–57; David Tyack and Elisabeth Hansot, *Schooling Together: A History of Coeducation in American Public Schools* (New Haven: Yale University Press, 1990); Carl F. Kaestle and Maris A. Vinovskis, "From Apron Strings to ABC's: Parents, Children and Schooling in Nineteenth-Century Massachusetts," John Demos and Sarane Boocock, eds., *Turning Points: Historical and Sociological Essays on the Family* (Chicago: American Journal of Sociology supplement 84, 1978–1979).
21. Leon Litwack, *North of Slavery: The Negro in the Free States, 1790–1860* (Chicago, IL: University of Chicago Press, 1961); Lawrence A. Cremin, *American Education: The National Experience, 1783–1876* (New York: Harper and Row, 1980), 103–147; Diane Ravitch, *The Great School Wars: New York City, 1805–1973* (New York: Basic Books, 1974), 20–76; James W. Sanders, *The Education of an Urban Minority: Catholics in Chicago, 1833–1965* (New York: Oxford University Press, 1977).
22. Sieglinde Lim de Sánchez, "Crafting a Delta Chinese Community: Education and Acculturation in Twentieth-Century Southern Baptist Mission Schools," *History of Education Quarterly* 43 (2003): 74–90; Ruben Donato, "Hispano Education and the Implications of Autonomy: Four School Systems in Southern Colorado, 1920–1964," *Harvard Educational Review* 69 (1999): 117–149.
23. David Tyack, *The One Best System* (Cambridge, MA: Harvard University Press, 1974); David Tyack and Elisabeth Hansot, *Managers of Virtue* (New York: Basic Books, 1982); "Population: 1790–1990," *1990 Census of Population and Housing*, "1990 Population and Housing Unit Counts: United States," (CPH-2), Table 4, retrieved February 28, 2005, from <http://www.census.gov/population/censusdata/table-4.pdf>; Paul Osterman, *Getting Started* (Cambridge: MIT Press, 1980); Sherman Dorn, "High-Stakes Testing and the History of Graduation," *Education Policy Analysis Archives* 11, 1 (2003), available at <http://epaa.asu.edu/epaa/v11n1/>; Miriam Cohen, *Workshop to Office* (Ithaca: Cornell University Press, 1993), 156–160.
24. William J. Reese, *The Origins of the American High School* (New Haven: Yale University Press, 1995), 256–261; Harvey A. Kantor, *Learning To Earn* (Madison: University of Wisconsin Press, 1988);

Edward A. Krug, *The Shaping of the American High School, Vol. 2: 1920–1941* (Madison: University of Wisconsin Press, 1972), 319–327.
25. For key discussion of curriculum debates, see Herbert M. Kliebard, *The Struggle for the American Curriculum, 1893–1958* (Boston: Routledge & Kegan Paul, 1986); Lawrence A. Cremin, *The Transformation of the School: Progressivism in American Education, 1876–1957* (New York: Alfred A. Knopf, 1961); Diane Ravitch, *Left Back: A Century of Battles over School Reform* (New York: Simon & Schuster, 2000).
26. Arthur G. Powell, Eleanor Farrar, David K. Cohen, *The Shopping-Mall High School* (Boston: Houghton Mifflin, 1985); Jonathan Zimmerman, *Whose America?* (Cambridge, MA: Harvard University Press, 2002); Joseph Moreau, *Schoolbook Nation* (Ann Arbor: University of Michigan Press, 2003); Diane Ravitch, *The Language Police* (New York: Knopf, 2003); Ruben Donato, *The Other Struggle for Equal Schools* (Albany, NY: State University of New York Press, 1997); Guadalupe San Miguel, *Brown, Not White* (College Station, TX: Texas A&M University Press, 2001); Seymour Sarason and John Doris, *Educational Handicap, Public Policy, and Social History: A Broadened Perspective on Mental Retardation* (New York: Free Press, 1979). For another controversial curriculum issue (sex education), see Jeffrey P. Moran, *Teaching Sex: The Shaping of Adolescence in the 20th Century* (Cambridge, MA: Harvard University Press, 2000).
27. Cutler, *Parents and Schools*, 3–4, 5, 17. Also see Merz and Furman, *Community and Schools*, 8–10, 55, 59–60, 63–64, 66, 82–83, 87, 92, for a discussion of how efforts to craft new school–community relationships often entail the growth of bureaucratic layers.
28. Willard S. Elsbree, *The American Teacher: Evolution of a Profession in a Democracy* (New York: American Book Company, 1939); Paul H. Mattingly, *The Classless Profession* (New York: New York University Press, 1975); William Cutler, *Parents and Schools*, 20–23; Jack Dougherty, *More Than One Struggle: The Evolution of Black School Reform in Milwaukee* (Chapel Hill, NC: University of North Carolina Press, 2004); Daniel H. Perlstein, *Justice, Justice: School Politics and the Eclipse of Liberalism* (New York: Peter Lang, 2004). Also see Willard Waller, *Sociology of Teaching* (New York: Russell and Russell, 1961), 49–50, for a discussion of teachers' relationships to communities. Melissa Teed's chapter is an important counterpoint to Waller's deterministic view.
29. Modern songwriters have used the expansion of Walmart stores in small towns as material for their work; see Dave Carter, "Ordinary Town," in Dave Carter and Tracy Grammar's *drum hat Buddha* (Signature Sounds, 2001 [sound recording]).
30. We skip in the text an extended discussion of the differences among structural–functionalist, conflict-oriented, and institutional theories in sociology and historical sociology. The classics in each area, respectively,

include Talcott Parsons, *The Social System* (New York: Free Press, 1951); Karl Marx, "The Eighteenth Brumaire of Louis Napoleon," trans. Daniel De Leon (Project Gutenberg: 1998), available on-line at <ftp://ftp.ibiblio.org/pub/docs/books/gutenberg/etext98/mar1810.txt>; Alexis de Tocqueville, *The Old Regime and the French Revolution*, trans. Stuart Gilbert (Garden City, NY: Doubleday, 1955).

31. Howard Becker, *Tricks of the Trade: How To Think about Your Research While You're Doing It* (Chicago, IL: University of Chicago Press, 1998).

32. Gary Becker, *Human Capital: A Theoretical and Empirical Analysis, with Special Reference to Education*, 3rd ed. (Chicago, IL: University of Chicago Press, 1993); Robert Dreeben, *On What Is Learned in School* (Reading, MA: Addison-Wesley Pub. Co., 1968); Samuel Bowles and Herbert Gintis, *Schooling in Capitalist America* (New York: Basic Books, 1976). The phrase "managing ambition" comes from the nonfunctionalist book by Steven Brint and Jerome Karabel, *The Diverted Dream: Community Colleges and the Promise of Educational Opportunity in America, 1900–1985* (New York: Oxford University Press, 1989). Many will quibble with our description of Bowles and Gintis's book as functionalist. They certainly did not agree with the system they described, but they write demonstrably about how schools maintain both inequality and the appearance of meritocracy (and thus the political legitimacy of the "system").

33. We are extrapolating here from Gerald Suttles' argument in *The Social Construction of Communities* (Chicago, IL: University of Chicago Press, 1972).

34. For a broader discussion of functionalist and conflict theories of education, see Martin Carnoy and Henry M. Levin, *Schooling and Work in the Democratic State* (Stanford, CA: Stanford University Press, 1985); Ira Katznelson and Margaret Weir, *Schooling for All: Class, Race, and the Decline of the Democratic Ideal* (New York: Basic Books, 1985).

35. See Charles Tilly, *Durable Inequalities* (Berkeley: University of California Press, 1998).

36. David N. Figlio and Maurice E. Lucas, "What's in a Grade? School Report Cards and the Housing Market," *American Economic Review* 94 (2004): 591–604.

37. We use the word "opportunistic" here even though there may be confusion with the term "opportunity hoarding" described earlier.

38. Robert S. Lynd and Helen Merrell Lynd, *Middletown: A Study in American Culture* (New York: Harcourt, Brace, and Company, 1929); Leah Hager Cohen, *Train Go Sorry: Inside a Deaf World* (Boston: Houghton Mifflin, 1994).

39. Pierre Bourdieu, "The Forms of Capital," John Richardson, ed., *Handbook of Theory and Research for the Sociology of Education* (New York: Greenwood Press, 1986), 241–258. Also see John Guillory,

Cultural Capital: The Problem of Literary Canon Formation (Chicago, IL: University of Chicago Press, 1993), for an application of cultural capital to controversies in the curriculum.
40. E. D. Hirsch, *Cultural Literacy: What Every American Needs To Know* (New York: Vintage Books, 1988).
41. Anderson, *Imagined Communities*; John D'Emilio, *Sexual Politics, Sexual Communities: The Making of a Homosexual Minority in the United States, 1940–1970* (Chicago, IL: University of Chicago Press, 1983).
42. Edward Bellamy, *Looking Backward, 2000–1887* (Mineola, NY: Dover Publications, 1996).
43. A number of cities had Lancaster or monitorial schools with enrollments in the hundreds, while many factories even in cities like Philadelphia had ten or fewer workers. See Carl F. Kaestle, *Joseph Lancaster and the Monitorial School Movement: A Documentary History* (New York: Teachers College Press, 1973); Bruce Laurie, *Working People of Philadelphia, 1800–1850* (Philadelphia: Temple University Press, 1980).
44. Sherman Dorn and Erwin V. Johanningmeier, "Dropping Out and the Military Metaphor," *History of Education Quarterly* 39 (1999): 193–198.
45. Katznelson and Weir, *Schooling for All*.
46. Suttles, *The Social Construction of Communities*, 45.
47. Morris Janowitz advanced the concept of the community of limited liability as a framework for understanding and describing the differentiated, partial, and voluntary roles groups play in forming, preserving, and defending community identity. See Suttles, 47; Morris Janowitz, *The Community Press in an Urban Setting: The Social Elements of Urbanism*, 2nd ed. (Chicago, IL: The University of Chicago Press, 1952).
48. Williams, Carlton, interview with the author, (February 24, 2000).
49. Otis Anthony, "Remember" (Poem, Collection of Author). Also see Siddle Walker, *passim*.
50. Gary Orfield and Susan E. Eaton, *Dismantling Desegregation: The Quiet Reversal of Brown v. Board of Education* (New York: The New Press, 1996), 82.
51. Stephanie Coontz, *The Way We Never Were: American Families and the Nostalgia Trap* (New York: Basic Books, 1992).

Chapter 1

Education in an Imagined Community: Lessons from Brook Farm

Vicki L. Eaklor

Brook Farm (1841–1847) is one of the most famous utopian communal experiments in U.S. history. Paradoxically, it was the brainchild of some New England "Transcendentalists" whose reputation in their time and since has revolved around the antithesis of community, individualism. In seeking to balance the principle of individual freedom with a communal ideal, the founders and residents of the Brook Farm Institute for Agriculture and Education can be viewed as a microcosm of America itself, where the individual and the community have been in perpetual tension. If Brook Farm is notable despite its short existence, the schools established there have been considered among the most viable in educational history, and remembered as perhaps the only genuine success of the community itself. "The three schools were a success from the start," wrote Edith Curtis, for example, "and for three years they stabilized the finances and enhanced the reputation of Brook Farm; and the interest which accrued in spiritual dividends for posterity is still accruing."[1] To understand more fully why and how this happened, the activities and role of the Brook Farm School (as the three schools are usually called) must be examined in the overlapping contexts that merged to create this unique institution: the climate of antebellum (northern) America, in which reform generally became ever more prominent, and the specific causes of educational reformers, Transcendentalists, and utopian socialists.

The Ambivalent Impulses of Reform

The United States, the ultimate imagined community within which the smaller ones have emerged, has been shaped by a curious conglomerate of democratic, capitalist, and Protestant Christian ideals, at times remarkably in sync—when supporting "conservative" values such as obedience to authority, sobriety, and the like, for example. Each system, however, has within it both conservative and liberal impulses, and when one or another of these has seemed to prevail, the potential conflicts have been clearer: How does a "good" American reconcile capitalist competition with Christian brotherhood (and sisterhood)? When is democratic freedom of thought more threatening than supportive of all three institutions? Such are the questions that have animated American thought and action; in no time since the antebellum era have they been asked more pointedly, perhaps, and in no other institution than the school have they been so confused and combined without being answered.

The history of formal education in the United States, like that within any other country, is particularly revealing of the concerns, goals, and developing self-image of the nation. Unlike many other nations, however, the United States developed its educational ideas and systems in a dialectic with two rapidly evolving systems: a democratic republic and an industrial capitalist economy. As if this were not enough, the tensions within and between these processes were ignored as often as they were acknowledged, as were those added by the insistence that America's destiny has been to fulfill (a Protestant) God's mission.

Educational reform was but one of many causes that seemed to burst suddenly on the scene, in the North and especially in New England, in the three decades preceding the Civil War. In that period enough distance was gained since the American revolution to render those events and recently passed heroes already more mythical than historical. Especially in the North, Americans were struggling to define themselves and their place in the world amid the rapid changes brought by industrial capitalism, immigration from Europe and emigration to the West, and an increasingly volatile political climate. Probably as a response to these upheavals, the United States experienced its first wave of social reform that would recur every 30 years or so: born in a climate of both hope and anxiety and nurtured by evangelical Protestantism, such causes as temperance, antislavery, women's rights, and improving conditions in factories and correctional institutions, as well as public education and communal living, found numerous supporters.

Fears for the survival of the republic generated as much activity as did a more Romantic faith in the United States as the "world's last best hope" for liberty, equality, or any other ideal. That survival, in turn, depended in many thinkers' minds on a virtuous citizenry—those both apprised of their duties and willing to perform them—and a concern for training those citizens fostered a conservative element even in the most progressive-looking efforts. In general, reformers placed great emphasis upon preserving their notions of morality and social order through the established institutions of family, church, and government.When they created new institutions, as in the case of public schools and communal experiments, those institutions remained basically new means to old ends, and thus both backward- and forward-looking in character.

Seen in this context, the educational reform of the era, particularly the movement for common schooling, was another means to the greater end, and reflected a more general duality of anxiety and confidence in its structure and implementation. Free public education, for example, could be seen as part of the democratizing process *and* as an antidote for its possible evils. Ideally, it might assure equal opportunity for material success regardless of the disparate socioeconomic backgrounds of the students, while the common knowledge and morals instilled in the children (hence the term "common" school) were to prepare them to be literate and responsible citizens (or mothers of citizens) and thus offset the potential for "mobocracy" always lurking under the surface. The common school was but one solution, though, and by no means brand new. (Puritan laws, whether enforced or not, had mandated education and a limited form of community schools since the 1640s in language revealing concerns strikingly similar to those of common school reformers.) As antebellum educational reformers pondered these social tensions, their ideas and activities ran the gamut from reforming the existing hodgepodge of urban and rural schools to introducing new private as well as public institutions, the former usually in conjunction with additional reformist goals.

Similarly, urbanization and industrialization contributed to the advent of educational reform, with the school again acting as both agent of change and conservative sanctuary in which rural values could be preserved. Many reformers perceived cities and factories, and especially the immigrants who came to live and work in them, as harbingers of poverty, ignorance, crime, and immorality; the question of which were cause and which effect was less important than finding a cure for all, and the proposed remedy was public education.[2]

Finally, a process of secularization, to some a contributing factor to social instability, became an additional stimulus to educational reform. By this time Enlightenment principles of humans' natural goodness had contributed to some shift away from the severe Calvinistic view of children as innately wicked, and influenced both social and educational theory. As Europeans "discovered" childhood as a separate stage of human development, Jean Jacques Rousseau and Johann Heinrich Pestalozzi applied natural law philosophy and theories of social responsibility to the principles and practices of education. Rousseau's view, in *Emile* (1762), was of a "natural" education that would correspond to Emile's phases of growth, while in Pestalozzi's works (*Leonard and Gertrude*, 1781; *How Gertrude Teaches Her Children*, 1801) the school became a means of improving society through moral and social as well as intellectual and physical education. What was in Europe a general, idealistic interest in society's regeneration became in the United States a particular concern for the survival of America as a refuge of freedom and democracy. Advocates saw the common school as a means to insure this vision of the future, but again by preserving such values as order, industry, respect for property rights, obedience to laws, sobriety, and charity, all espoused as republican as well as Christian virtues, and all dependent more on conformity than on the agency or "freedom" of individuals.[3]

A Transcendental Utopia

Among those concerned for America's future and proposing a variety of changes to ensure it, the Transcendentalists may be among the least understood. Transcendentalism, often presented in the context of literature or philosophy, was most essentially the religious expression of a handful of New England malcontents during the second quarter of the nineteenth century. Objecting to the more austere and authoritarian aspects of American Protestantism in general and Unitarianism in particular, these advocates of "Newness" began to voice their concerns to each other in a series of meetings in 1836. This "club" continued to convene, with varying "membership," until 1840, and by 1845, the fundamental tenets of the faith had been outlined and published by such figures as Ralph Waldo Emerson and Charles Mayo Ellis.[4]

At the basis of their beliefs was their conviction that humans are inherently good and (therefore, to them) capable of perfection. These were not new ideas, but rather revived by the Transcendentalists in the context of a more general "ferment of reform" in the United States at the time and then taken in unique directions. Out of these convictions came probably the most famous tenet they shared, the "spark of divinity" they felt was in us all. This was also the most controversial, and that which engendered the most ridiculed at the time (besides Emerson's notorious comment, "I become a transparent eyeball," that is[5]). Essentially, their interpretation of the Christian message was that Jesus, himself divine, exhorted us all to emulate him. In Ellis's words, "it is absurd to call on us to imitate one of a different nature."[6] The difference between Jesus and the rest of us was not in any gap between human and divine, but instead the *degree* to which he had experienced and expressed his divinity in practice. Having been infused with this spark (as were all living things), any person could attain perfect spirituality, and the more people that did, the greater the societal improvement.

Despite agreement on this key principle, it would be a mistake to conceive of Transcendentalism as a "movement"—much less a literary or aesthetic one in its origins—with designated "leaders"; indeed, this would be to violate its basic premises. It is true that Emerson, A. Bronson Alcott, Henry David Thoreau, Margaret Fuller, and others came to be regarded as preeminent in expressing the general ideas of the group, but it would be difficult to select a "typical" Transcendentalist due to the nature of those very ideas.

Ironically, the element that provided much of the identity of the group was agreement on the principle of individualism; as the saying goes, they agreed to disagree. This stemmed from a rejection of the Lockean view of all knowledge being gained through the senses and reason in favor of a Romantic (and neoplatonic) conception of ideas existing in the mind of God, to which humans have access by way of introspection. Denying neither the senses nor the reasoning capacity as means of verification, the Transcendentalists saw the most important knowledge—Truth, Virtue, and Beauty—as that which could be obtained only from a direct communication with the Divine. Each soul, however, ultimately gained the same knowledge from the same source and subsequently recognized its oneness not only with God but with humanity as well. Thus individualism provided the means rather than the end of the Transcendental vision.

The variety of thought and action represented by the group, then, was a result of energies flowing in several different directions in an attempt to work out that problematic relationship between the one and the many, a relationship with which many Americans—whether from a religious, political or social perspective—had grappled since colonization. While Thoreau promoted a type of arch-individualism, for example, Emerson supported various causes without actually joining any of them. Yet others, such as Alcott, Margaret Fuller, Theodore Parker, and Elizabeth Peabody, participated in various movements and experiments of the day, from women's rights, temperance, and especially antislavery, to educational reform and communal living. Again, however, their differences in approach often stemmed more from short- versus long-term views of change than from disputes over fundamental aims.

Despite their differences over means to a greater end, an important area of relative agreement among them was a general dedication to "education" in all its forms. As privileged New Englanders, they valued knowledge generally, and as heirs of Calvinism (even if they departed drastically from its tenets) Transcendentalists especially sought spiritual and self-knowledge as well as more concrete information. Typically, their programs varied from writing and speaking on principles to applying them practically: Hiram Fuller, Elizabeth Peabody, the Thoreau brothers, and A. Bronson Alcott were among their notable teachers.

Alcott's Temple School (1834–1838), in fact, was an important experiment that exposed the limits within which educational and Transcendental reformers operated, separately and together. In the School, Alcott taught 30–40 girls and boys less than ten years of age, using principles and practices derived from his Transcendental faith. He considered the "Contemplation of the Spirit" the "first principle of Human Culture and the foundation of Self-Education" and his curriculum was divided into subjects and activities for the Spiritual, Imaginative, and Rational Faculties.[7] Among his pedagogical models were Socrates and Jesus, and in teaching such common subjects as English, geography, and Latin, he used discussion and journal-keeping as means of leading the children to a realization of their divinity. This latter goal, coupled with his admission of an African American girls to the School, led to its demise. When his *Conversations with Children on the Gospels* were published in 1836 and revealed the radical nature of his Christianity, parents began removing their offspring.[8]

If the Temple School revealed the limits of the Transcendentalists' principles in practice, so did Brook Farm, one of their few forays into communal living (in addition to Alcott's and Charles Lane's Fruitlands). Given their devotion to separate paths to Truth, the Transcendentalists might be the last people one might expect to try to form a community. As with all their causes, though, they came to throw the ideas and activities of their time, and the contradictions of American life, into sharp relief.

If the United States itself was founded as an imagined community, or utopia, it is almost predictable that critics would emerge from a variety of perspectives and with a variety of programs to demonstrate where the nation had gone astray. A number of communities were based in religion, for example, whether imported (Shakers, Rappites) or home-grown (Hopedale, Mormons). Others, such as Nashoba, Icaria, and Oneida, were somewhat more secular, at least in their impetus and governing philosophy. The Transcendental Brook Farmers combined religious and secular impulses (as did most Americans then) and joined the ranks of those addressing the relation between the individual and society.⁹

Brook Farm and Its School

A community based upon Transcendental principles, while paradoxical, was far from inconsistent with the main concerns of the group. Only a society that recognized the basic unity of creation, they believed, would be secure enough to allow and even foster true freedom of expression; that very freedom, in turn, would serve to strengthen, not erode, a sense of harmony. In an attempt to prove these ideas in the present, some of their number, led by George and Sophia Ripley, founded the Brook Farm Institute for Agriculture and Education in 1841.

Unlike some communal experiments, Brook Farm was less a retreat from the world than it was an effort to change the world by offering a model of attitudes and relationships to be copied. "We propose a radical and universal reform rather than to redress any particular wrong," stated a later constitution of the community, and even at the outset, according to George Willis Cooke, it was only after "a careful and serious study of the needs of humanity," that Ripley "calmly reasoned out a method for saving society."¹⁰ Part of this method involved uniting two previously separate areas of action—agriculture and education—into a new world view by partially expanding the definition of both. In Ripley's famous letter soliciting Emerson's support, he explained that the aims of the future Brook Farmers were

> to insure a more natural union between intellectual and manual labor than now exists; to combine the thinker and the worker, as far as possible, in the same individual; to guarantee the highest mental freedom, by providing all with labor, adapted to their tastes and talents, and securing to them the fruits of their industry; to do away the necessity of menial services, by opening the benefits of education and the profits of labor for all; and thus to prepare a society of liberal, intelligent, and cultivated persons, whose relations with each other would permit a more simple and wholesome life, than can be led amidst the pressure of our competitive institutions. To accomplish these objects, we propose to take a small tract of land, which, under skillful husbandry, uniting the garden and the farm, will be adequate to the subsistence of the families, and to connect with this a school or college, in which the most complete instruction shall be given, from the first rudiments to the highest culture.¹¹

Despite his implicit critique of capitalism, or of at least some of its results, Ripley never really strayed very far from the economic practices and assumptions of the larger society. From the beginning, Brook Farm was considered a business as well as a social reform enterprise, with a return promised to any investor who subscribed to the joint stock company. Once underway, the main sources of revenue, besides visitors and boarders, outside investors, and new members bringing property, were to be farming and the schools.[12] If the reformers were realistic enough to recognize the need for income, however, in actual practice their successes were reaped more often in the social and intellectual than in the economic sphere. The community operated at a loss until the third year, in fact, and even when it turned a profit the financial structure was too frail, it seems, to bear the weight of numerous other complications.

In its relatively short history, Brook Farm experienced significant changes and problems. In 1843 the farm began to move away from its relatively informal origins toward a more rigidly planned and structured community. By March 1845 the farmers had adopted a new constitution and a new name, the Brook Farm Phalanx, which reflected the trustees' conversion, via Albert Brisbane and Horace Greeley, to the principles of French social theorist Charles Fourier. Work was now divided and subdivided into series and groups within series, with a complicated system of elected chiefs ultimately directing the Phalanx. In this last, Fourierist phase, financial problems were compounded by an outbreak of smallpox, a fire that destroyed the Phalanstery, internal dissensions, and an increasingly negative public image deriving from even the partial adaptation of Fourierism. At its peak, Brook Farm had only about 100 members (considerably less than the 1620–1800 people recommended for a Phalanx), and in August 1847 the "brightest and happiest of American utopias" was disbanded.[13]

Through it all, though, the original objective of cultivating both crops and minds furnished some material stability, and provided some continuity amid changes in personnel, organization, and ideological focus. In fact, education eventually came to overshadow agriculture in application as well as in the community's reputation, and one fed upon the other to the point that the schools of the community at times provided its only income. Indeed, to John S. Dwight, "From the first the educational object was made more prominent at Brook Farm than agriculture itself,"[14] and an observer recorded in 1843, that

> This is almost exclusively an Educational establishment, relying mainly upon the income of its excellent school, which, from the peculiar nature of its organization and management is, in our opinion, the best in the country, and depends but slightly upon its industrial income.[15]

By 1846 James Kay, Jr., had written to Dwight, "The education must be your chief source of income; and all other pursuits must be contingent and subsidiary," advice now more descriptive of their situation than prophetic.[16]

The organization of formal education at Brook Farm was not unlike that of the evolving public system. There were two schools for younger children—a primary school for students ages 6–10 and an infant school for those less than six—and a set of college preparatory courses projected to last six years. George, Sophia, and George's sister, Marianne Ripley, acted as supervisors as well as teachers, and were assisted by apparently able instructors throughout the farm's career. Besides George and Sophia Ripley, George P. Bradford, Charles A. Dana, and John S. Dwight taught in the preparatory school, whereas Georgiana Bruce, Frances Dwight, Marianne Dwight, Abby Morton, Hannah Ripley (George's niece), and Marianne Ripley were among those who lent their abilities mainly to the younger students. In addition, there was a three-year program in agriculture and horticulture, taught by John S. Brown, reflecting again one of the primary objectives of the experiment. The sexual division that paraleled the age of the students and hence subject matter—women teaching younger children and men teaching older ones—eventually became entrenched in the U.S. public school system, where it was based on accepted notions about both women's "natural" affinity for small children and the role of the primary school. Apparently Brook Farmers did not dispute all of their culture's assumptions, with Sophia Ripley a notable exception.

Nor did the Brook Farmers' curriculum depart significantly from contemporary practice. The curriculum of the young men planning to attend college, usually Harvard, was similar to that of other (private) preparatory schools: philosophy, history, mathematics, literature, music, Greek, Latin, and modern languages. For the younger children, as in the new common schools, there was instruction in music and drawing as well as the "three R's.[17]

At the same time, those involved perceived some key differences between education at Brook Farm and that available in the public sphere, and it is these rather than the similarities that offer the most insight into the nature of both the larger (the U.S.) and smaller communities. Beneath most of these differences, it seems, is a fundamental discrepancy in the very definition of "education" and hence in its proposed role within and relation to the group in question. Dwight summed up the distinction while reiterating the School's financial role:

> The great point aimed at was to realize practical equality and mutual culture, and a common-sense education for the children in a larger

sense than prevails in ordinary society. The educational phase consisted partly in our education of one another and partly in the school, which was also one of the means of support of the community.[18]

In addition to the usual subject matter, for example, students of all ages, boarders from outside and children from member families, were expected to spend an hour or two a day doing some sort of manual labor. This was intended not just "to combine the thinker and the worker . . . in the same individual," but in turn to create a sense of the dignity of *all* labor. To the more egalitarian Transcendentalist this ultimately might erode the class attitudes that were seen to promote division and conflict in society and encourage the unity they envisioned. At the same time, others made finer distinctions within the concept of equality that are reminiscent of perennial constitutional debates; as "Charlie" wrote to his sister from the Farm in 1845, "The Brook Farmers have never preached social *equality*, but social *rights*."[19] Also labor, particularly that done outdoors, was thought to promote health, morality, and a certain self-sufficiency within a broader context of interdependency.

The idea that labor, especially that associated with farming, helped to create virtuous, independent yet community-minded citizens was not itself unusual, of course, and was to some degree a throwback of Thomas Jefferson's nation of yeoman farmers. In other social reform institutions—prisons, asylums, and hospitals—work was a common part of the routine, driven by the assumption that work was healing for the spirit as well as productive to the institution. The contemporary Romantic religion of nature added an even greater emphasis. Abandoning the view of their Puritan ancestors that uncultivated nature was suspect or downright evil, the Transcendentalists instead saw in the wilderness a primary source of divine Truth and hence an ideal place for contemplation or simple relaxation. In this way, nature became part of both the formal and the more general educational plan at Brook Farm, with students embarking on frequent excursions into the woods in search of spiritual as well as scientific knowledge.[20]

If manual labor and nature walks served to distinguish the Farmers' school slightly from those then being formed in New England, the application of their most fundamental educational concepts gives it the appearance of a different institution altogether. The word most frequently used in reminiscences of former students, it seems, is "freedom"—freedom to study when and where one pleased, freedom of interaction between students and teachers (and even males and females), and especially intellectual freedom. As Edith Curtis put it, "In that happy summer of high hope, 1841, educational policy at

Brook Farm was based on perfect freedom of thought between students and teachers."[21] This was manifested in a number of ways and based on the principle that in the ongoing search for Truth—the ultimate aim of Transcendental education—the roles of students and teachers could be interchangeable. Consequently the learning process, though structured and somewhat traditional, appears to have been far less dogmatic and authoritarian than that in the emerging public system. If common school education was created to encourage conformity to republican ideals, that at Brook Farm was characterized more by "informality and spontaneity."[22]

Preparatory school student James Burrill Curtis, for example, mentioned the greater opportunity he perceived for "free growth."[23] Similarly, a former pupil of Sophia Ripley's recalled many years later that, "One peculiarity was the entire freedom of speech between pupil and teacher" while George Willis Cooke wrote, "In the mingling of old and young in the process of education the association was unique in its methods, few restraints being put upon the young, while the old were constantly invited to keep fully alive their intellectual interest."[24] Even Charles Lane, who in 1843 described Brook Farm as a place where "there are eighty or ninety people playing away their youth and daytime in a miserable, joyous, frivolous manner," wrote highly of the school a year later:

> In education, Brook Farm appears to present greater mental freedom than most other institutions. The tuition being more heart-rendered, is in its effects more heart-stirring. The younger pupils as well as the more advanced students are held, mostly if not wholly, by the power of love. In this particular, Brook Farm is a much improved model for the oft-praised schools of New England. It is time that the imitative and book-learned systems of the latter should be superseded or liberalized by some plan, better calculated to excite originality of thought, and the native energies of the mind. The deeper, kindly sympathies of the heart, too, should not be forgotten; but the germination of these must be despaired of under a rigid hireling system. Hence, Brook Farm, with its spontaneous teachers, presents the unusual and cheering condition of a really "free school."[25]

In similar fashion, Margaret Fuller's father testified to the spirit of inquiry that distinguished education at Brook Farm:

> A lady asked me not long since where she should send her daughter to school. I said at once, to the *Community*, for there she would learn for the first time, perhaps, that all these matters of creed and morals are not quite so well settled as to make thinking nowadays a piece of supererogation,

and would learn to distinguish between truth and the "sense sublime," and the dead dogmas of the past. This is the great benefit I believe you confer upon the young.[26]

Such freedom appears not to have harmed the substance of the education offered at the schools: Both memoirs and later scholarly evaluations consistently have attested to its quality. Of the preparatory school, Frederick Pratt recalled (though somewhat ungrammatically), "we had one of the best Schools there, with some of the finest teachers I was ever with."[27] Apparently officials at Harvard agreed, for they recommended the school to students aspiring to their ranks, to the effect that it came to attract pupils not just from the region, but occasionally from areas as remote as Florida, Cuba, and the Philippines.[28] Memories of the primary education are equally positive and those of both younger and older students repeatedly support John Codman's assertion that he "never knew a pupil that was not pleased and delighted with the school."[29]

This is not to say that the schools and the communitarians did not invite criticism. It must be remembered that as a group the Transcendentalists were a tiny minority of New England, much less of American society, and the faction of them that formed Brook Farm even more so. Holding unorthodox religious, social, and economic views, to many of a more conservative bent they were suspect, even dangerous. At any rate, sometimes-unacceptable views of former pupils were attributed, probably correctly, to training at Brook Farm. One "practical soul" who questioned George William Curtis's stand on the equality of women explained it away in the statement, "there must be a screw loose somewhere in a man who graduated from the lunatic school at Brook Farm."[30] After the partial adoption of Fourierism in 1845 the community, and hence the school, came under attack that eventually contributed to its demise. As Fourier's unconventional principles regarding sexual and family relations were circulated in the press, anxious Victorian parents withdrew their support and their children, regardless of the fact that those ideas, as with most of Fourierism, were never really put into practice.[31] Despite its partial application, though, Fourierism did alter the original spirit and actions of Brook Farmers. In Mark Holloway's words,

> ... now the school itself was neglected for interminable discussions concerning Groups and Series; and although the injection of so much Fourierist claptrap first acted as a stimulant, raising the membership and causing a whirlwind of unnatural activity, the reaction from it rapidly followed. *The Harbinger*, which became the most important Fourierist

journal, brought the germs of officialdom to the Phalanx, and they infected not only lectures and meetings, but also amusement, which no longer grew organically from the peaceful activities of a group of people united by a gentle culture, but was organized into whist drives and other deadening pastimes. Theatrical entertainments, readings from the classics, costume parties, and picnics gradually ceased; Emerson, Thoreau, and other literary figures no longer paid visits to the Farm. The unique atmosphere which had infused every activity of the Farmers with spontaneity and enjoyment had gone.[32]

A Successful Failure

> Perhaps the reason [for the lack of a history of Brook Farm] is that it never had any result, except upon the individual lives of those who dwelt there . . . It was a beautiful idyllic life which we led, with plenty of work and play and Transcendentalism; and it gave place to the Roxbury poorhouse.[33]
>
> (Arthur Sumner, 1894)

Despite the final unfortunate chapter in the history of Brook Farm and its schools, the latter have continued to receive nearly unqualified praise for both the content and methodology of their educational programs, often with an implication of the superiority of those programs to those in the public sphere.[34] Transcendentalism itself, with its faith in humanity and emphasis upon the individual religious experience, certainly provided a basis for an alternative approach to education, as did the founding of a utopian community, Transcendental or otherwise.[35] It is the combination of the two, though, that offered the greatest opportunity to depart from the assumptions and regimen of the public schools.

Although similar in many respects, there was a fundamental difference in the proposed role of each school within its given community. A new and not yet accepted institution in the United States, the antebellum public school, as noted previously, was rooted in the idea of a common education for all. Implied in this idea is a certain sameness that can be interpreted in various ways. On the one hand it entails the laudable democratic goal of offering equal opportunity to those previously denied it, but on the other is an emphasis on conformity that seems an inevitable by-product of such an effort. In a nation that was still striving to define itself and its values, a concern with uniformity is understandable and rendered the school essentially a device for creating, or at least crystallizing, a very large community—a nation—from diverse elements.

This national role for the school is in direct contrast to that of the Brook Farm School, where questions of community solidarity, if not settled, were automatically addressed in the experimental setting. Brook Farm seems to have achieved, if only for a short time, the difficult balance inherent in a community of individuals; common ideals, revolving around educating the mind, body, and spirit inside and outside the classroom, united them. To place a school *within* that setting (that is, Brook Farm was a community inside a community) was to offer it an unusual chance to serve the needs of individuals. Of the reformers of their day, the Transcendentalists required perhaps the least outward manifestations of the unity they believed to exist among them, and this was especially true once they formed an actual community. In making education their main focus (even farming was a type of education to them), they provided a unique laboratory in which to test a system in which "freedom of thought" was a *practice* rather than a common cultural principle to be memorized. Thus the roots of the school's success, however temporary, seem to lie in the relation between the school and the farm, with the latter taking over the role of community building, in the very act of living communally as well as in shared goals, with which public schools in the United States have been burdened. If they failed in achieving a perfect balance between the needs of the group versus those of its members, it was due more to the task than the effort; George Ripley could have been describing any society, but especially the United States in its ongoing quest to reconcile liberty and equality, when he wrote, "The great problem is to guarantee individualism against the masses, on the one hand, and the masses against the individual, on the other."[36] The Brook Farm School, though short-lived, provides a fascinating window into both a moment in U. S. history when educational ideals and the role of schools were hotly debated and, more important, a more general consideration of the relationship, real and imagined, between schools and community.

Notes

1. Edith Roelker Curtis, *A Season in Utopia: The Story of Brook Farm* (New York: Thomas Nelson and Sons, 1961), 73.
2. See Lawrence A. Cremin, *The American Common School: An Historic Conception* (New York: Columbia University Press 1951), 44–45; Carl F. Kaestle, *The Evolution of an Urban School System: New York City, 1750–1850* (Cambridge: Harvard University Press, 1973), 138.
3. Useful primary sources are Samuel R. Hall, *Lectures on School-Keeping* (Boston: Richardson, Lord and Holbrook, 1829, reprinted as *Hall's Lectures on School-Keeping*, ed. Arthur D. Wright and George E. Gardner (Hanover, NH: Dartmouth Press, 1929); and Horace Mann *Life and Works of Horace Mann* (Boston: Lee and Shepard, 1891),

vols. II–IV (see especially the Ninth, Tenth, and Twelfth Annual Reports of the Massachusetts Board of Education, and "The Necessity of Education in a Republican Government," vol. II, pp. 143–188). Among the works that support the view of early public education as essentially a tool of nationalism are Lawrence A. Cremin, *Common School*; Carl F. Kaestle, *Pillars of the Republic: Common Schools and American Society, 1780–1860* (New York: Hill and Wang, 1983); Michael B. Katz, *The Irony of Early School Reform* (Cambridge: Harvard University Press, 1968); and Stanley K. Schultz, *The Culture Factory: Boston Public Schools, 1789–1860* (New York: Oxford University Press, 1973).
4. See, e.g., Ralph Waldo Emerson, "Divinity School Address" and "The Transcendentalist" Edward Waldo Emerson ed., *The Complete Works of Ralph Waldo Emerson*, (Boston, 1903–1921); [Charles Mayo Ellis], *An Essay on Transcendentalism* (1842; Gainesville, FL: Scholars' Facsimiles and Reprints, 1954).
5. Emerson, "Nature," ch. I, The Complete Works.
6. [Ellis], *Essay*, 82.
7. [Elizabeth Peabody], *Record of a School: Exemplifying the General Principles of Spiritual Culture*. 2nd. ed. (Boston: Russell, Shattuck and Co., 1836; New York, 1969), iii. The curriculum and schedule can be found on the inside front cover, and on page 176.
8. A. Bronson Alcott, *Conversations with Children on the Gospels; Conducted and Edited by A. Bronson Alcott* (Boston: James Munroe Company, 1836). Also see the Appendix to Peabody's *Record* for extracts from students' journals.
9. A good brief overview is Mark Holloway, *Heavens on Earth: Utopian Communities in America, 1680–1880*. 2nd ed. (New York: Dover Publications, Inc., 1966). An entertaining account of Fruitlands is Louisa May Alcott's *Transcendental Wild Oats and Excerpts from the Fruitlands Diary* (Harvard: Harvard Common Press, 1981).
10. Preliminary statement of the 1844 Constitution, quoted in John Thomas Codman, *Brook Farm: Historical and Personal Memoirs* (Boston: Arena Publishing Company, 1894), 42; Cooke, *Dwight*, 18.
11. Boston, November 9, 1840, quoted in Sams, *Autobiography*, 6. Emerson's letter to Ripley of December 15, 1840 (quoted in Sams, 11–12), replies in part, " 'In regard to the plan as far as it represents the formation of a School or College, I have more hesitation, . . . a concentration of scholars in one place seems to me to have certain great advantages. Perhaps as the school emerges to more distinct consideration out of the Farm, I shall yet find it attractive. And yet I am very apt to relapse into the same skepticism as to the modes & arrangements, the same magnifying of the men—the men alone. According to your ability and mine, you and I do now keep school for all comers, & the energy of your thought & will measures our influence.' "
12. Sams, *Autobiography*, 7; also see Codman, *Memoirs*, 211.

13. Quote from Alice Felt Tyler, *Freedom's Ferment: Phases of American Social History from the Colonial Period to the Outbreak of the Civil War* (New York: Harper and Row, 1962), 184. For Fourierism see Holloway, *Heavens*, 134–159.
14. John S. Dwight, quoted in George Willis Cooke, *John Sullivan Dwight: Brook-Farmer, Editor, and Critic of Music* (Hartford, CT: Transcendental Books, 1973), 19. John S. Dwight taught music and Latin in the preparatory school and went on to become the nation's foremost arbiter of musical taste.
15. "The Roxbury Community," *Phalanx or Journal of Social Science* I (October 5, 1843), 15–16; quoted in Henry W. Sams, ed., *Autobiography of Brook Farm* (Englewood Cliffs, NJ: Prentice-Hall, 1958), 84.
16. Letter of March 2, 1846, quoted in Sams, *Autobiography*, 165.
17. Music and drawing, especially the former, were seen as useful adjuncts to a well-rounded moral education, and thus were introduced into many of the common schools as early as the 1830s. See Vicki L. Eaklor, "Roots of an Ambivalent Culture: Music, Education, and 'Music Education' in Antebellum America," *Journal of Research in Music Education*, 33 (Summer, 1985), 87–99.
18. Cooke, *Dwight*, 20.
19. Letter of September 9, 1845; quoted in Codman, *Memoirs*, 268.
20. For Transcendental ideas about nature, one might begin with Emerson's "Nature," found in any edition of his collected works, and any of Thoreau's writings.
21. Curtis, *Season*, 71.
22. Tyler, *Ferment*, 181.
23. Curtis letter of July 23, 1842, in Joel Myerson, "James Burrill Curtis and Brook Farm," *New England Quarterly* 51 (September, 1978), 408.
24. Mrs. Nora Schelter Blair, "Some School Memories of Brook Farm [1892]" Joel Myerson ed., "Two Unpublished Reminiscences of Brook Farm," *New England Quarterly* 48 (June, 1975), 259; Cooke, *Dwight*, 19.
25. Letter to the *New Age*, July 30, 1843, quoted in Sams, *Autobiography*, 83; "Brook Farm," *Dial* 4 (January, 1844), 352–353.
26. Richard F. Fuller, quoted in Codman, *Memoirs*, 22.
27. Quoted in Myerson, "Reminiscences," 255.
28. See, Curtis, *Season*, 70; and e.g., Sams, *Autobiography*, 248.
29. Codman, *Memoirs*, 214.
30. Quoted in Lindsay Swift, *Brook Farm: Its Members, Scholars, and Visitors* (New York: Macmillan, 1908), 87.
31. Curtis, *Season*, 210–215, and Codman, *Memoirs*, 213–214, are among those who discuss the effect of Fourierism on Brook Farm's reputation. Codman noted also on page 204, "The principle ground of attack was that the 'Fourierites' were 'disorganizers,' that they were unsettling the foundations of society and that they wished to make

their Associations entering wedges to disrupt the marriage relation and produce promiscuity and general anarchy."
32. Holloway, *Heavens*, 153.
33. Arthur Sumner, "A Boy's Recollections of Brook Farm," *New England Magazine* 10 (May, 1894): 313.
34. Later evaluations praising the Brook Farm schools include those of Cooke, *Dwight*; Curtis, *Season*; and Myerson, in "Reminiscences."
35. Arthur Bestor, i.e., noted the "close affinity" between the goals of utopian and educational reformers in his classic *Backwoods Utopias* (Philadelphia: University of Pennsylvania Press, 1950), 134–135.
36. Draft of letter, ca. 1845–1846, in Codman, *Memoirs*, 148.

Chapter 2

Crafting Community: Hartford Public High School in the Nineteenth Century

Melissa Ladd Teed

When Abby Dodge joined the faculty of the Hartford Public High School (HPHS) in 1854, she reported that the school was housed in "a fine three-story brick building, classical department on the first floor, general assembly room on the second, gymnasium on the third, laboratory, dressing-room, etc., in the basement. Everything is entirely different from any private school I was ever in. . . . There seems to be much more machinery." Dodge had worked for two private female seminaries and the economic support for the coeducational public high school clearly stood out. Noting the quality of the building and the classroom, Dodge correctly determined that Hartford residents were interested in the school and "spent their money freely."[1] Committed to boosting Hartford's standing in New England and providing a thorough education for all students, several influential citizens had contributed sizable amounts to found the school. In addition to money, the supporters of the school also took a keen interest in selecting teachers and in establishing the qualifications for admission to HPHS. After the school opened in 1847, a school visiting committee made up of city residents was charged with monitoring the progress of both scholars and teachers alike.[2]

Many examinations of nineteenth-century public high schools start with this formal governing body, the all-male school board, and then explore how these boards implemented their vision. The work of historians David Tyack, Elisabeth Hansot, and William Reese has examined the foundation and operation of coeducational high schools from this key perspective. Building on their work, historians such as Kathleen Weiler, Victoria-Maria MacDonald, and Geraldine Clifford have attempted to recover the voices of women teachers in educational institutions. As Clifford has argued, "the challenge lies in recovering the experiences and perceptions of the clients and agents of education, rather than of the presumed spokesmen and indisputable savants of traditional histories of educational thought and institutional development." Teachers, predominantly women, played an active and vital role in determining the meaning of the educational experience for the scholars who attended the schools, and their contributions need to be examined.[3]

To recover these experiences, this chapter relies heavily on manuscript sources to examine the educational community that emerged at HPHS in the mid-nineteenth century. It places the faculty at the center of this community and investigates how they interacted with city residents, board members, and students. HPHS provides an opportunity to explore the reciprocal relationships between school, city, and teachers, and in the process, to assess the nature of the community that emerged. Groups of residents, teachers, and students—sometimes in competition, sometimes in cooperation—claimed the authority to determine what was best for the school. Grounded in a set of relationships between teachers and between teachers and students, an imagined educational community emerged at HPHS in the mid-nineteenth century. It conceptualized the school as a place in which women educators were valuable contributors to a noble experiment in democratic schooling and whose knowledge and experience were crucial in defining their institution's identity and future. Because of the high turnover in the faculty, this imagined community was unstable, sometimes fleeting. It nevertheless took on sharp focus and meaning in moments of conflict with forces in Hartford society that sought to define the school's function differently.

In the first section, I explore how and why city residents integrated new teachers into the wider Hartford society. Not only was inclusion into the city's social life a mechanism to attract and retain qualified applicants, but educational reformers also hoped to impart their vision for the school to the teachers. These city residents claimed responsibility for identifying who would work at the school and what their function would be. Yet this model of community formation assumes that the teachers would simply carry out the board's wishes. The experience of teaching in the school, however, acted as a powerful countervailing force. In the second section, the focus shifts from their world outside of school to the school itself. As a group, the teachers believed they represented a new kind of educational community that was charged with realizing the school's potential. The relationships established between teachers fostered the perception that they shared a common identity. Described in the first paragraph of this chapter, Abby Dodge was one of 21 women and 20 men who worked at HPHS between 1847 and 1861. Collectively, they became a dynamic group who shared similar aspirations for the future of the institution and who effectively worked and socialized together. The community of teachers not only constituted an alternate power structure at HPHS, but it also imagined the school's function and identity in ways that did not always coincide with the school board's vision. In the final section, I explore how the community and its distinctive understanding of HPHS functioned at a moment of crisis in the life of the institution. Teachers and students self-consciously banded together to implement changes in the school that conformed with their aspirations for the educational experience, even when that meant opposing the board and the principal. In the process, they did their best to preserve the community of teachers who would make HPHS "a bright & shining light."[4]

Integrating Teachers into Hartford Society

Those who founded HPHS sought to create an institution that would be consistent with the city's commitment to Congregational Protestantism, political conservatism and elite governance. Unlike many antebellum northeastern cities, Hartford had retained a remarkable degree of homogeneity and the city's core elite retained power, even in the face of significant social and demographic change. As the city's economic base diversified from its colonial roots in the West Indies trade, Hartford developed a small manufacturing sector and also became a center for insurance and publishing. The population of Hartford grew substantially, from 6,900 in 1820 to 29,150 in 1860, but it nevertheless remained small by nineteenth-century standards. Like most nineteenth-century institutions in Hartford, the school board was made up of prominent men from business, politics and religion. Horace Bushnell, who helped found HPHS, was the well-known theologian and minister of Hartford's North Congregational church. Members of Bushnell's church and other Congregational churches in the city dominated the board, although other religious denominations such as the Episcopal church also had representatives. Antebellum Hartford retained elements of its religious, political, and social homogeneity well into the nineteenth century, in contrast to large urban centers such as Boston that were marked by a higher degree of diversity and social fragmentation. Educational reformers wanted the new institution to enhance and not disturb the existing social relationships.[5]

After opening its doors in December 1847, HPHS attracted teachers from all over New England to staff its ranks. Of the ten female teachers and five male administrators who worked for HPHS between its opening and 1851, none were native to Hartford and only three had direct ties to the city. Hired in the fall of 1851, Erskine Hawes, son of the longtime minister of Hartford's First Congregational Church, was the first resident to teach at the high school. The need to look outside the city was further reduced in 1858, when the school's own graduates were hired. Whether newcomers or residents, however, the faculty of the HPHS turned over with a high frequency. Of the first ten women teachers, only three worked at the school for more than one year and the high turnover rate included administrators as well. Helen Wheaton, for example, taught mathematics at HPHS from 1847 to 1851 under four different principals. Because of the rapid change in the composition of the school's faculty, school administrators were constantly on the lookout for qualified teachers. In many instances, the school's wealthy supporters became active recruiters of teachers, and then they worked hard to integrate these newcomers into the city's social fabric.[6]

Promoters of the high school often drew on their personal connections to select teachers. James Bunce, for example, who contributed $1,000 to establish the high school and then served on the committee to oversee its operation, encouraged his niece to teach in Hartford. Faculty positions were, in fact, initially reserved for the relatives of prominent residents or the recommendations of trusted friends. Highlighting the selectivity of the process, one teacher remarked that the school committee was "anxious to keep *caste* & engage only *ladies*." Once hired, new teachers were offered accommodations with some of the city's best families and given access to a social world of polite teas and parties. As one newcomer noted, "All the teachers board in some of the first families & consequently [are] in the first circles of society." The new teachers, therefore, were immediately "adopted" by the city's elite in an attempt to integrate them into the highest circles of Hartford's social life. For some the fit was natural. While she taught in Hartford, Olivia Day, the daughter of Yale's president, lived with her uncle. Those without family connections, boarded not in rooming houses, but with elite families. John Olmsted, a retired dry goods merchant and one of the wealthiest men in Hartford, opened his home to Mary Brognard, Sophia Stevens, and Malvina Gore. After being offered a teaching post at HPHS, Mary Torrey and Marion Goodrich were encouraged to consider the benefits of boarding with James Bunce, who could offer them the "comforts & luxuries of a wealthy family," and who would "introduce them into society." By offering excellent accommodations and access to elite society, HPHS hoped to attract and retain well-qualified teachers.[7]

For one of these women, Sophia Stevens, the transition from Vermont to Hartford entailed more than a geographical change. Stevens's father, a farmer, postmaster, book collector, and founder of the Vermont Historical Society, provided a solid education for all his children, but needed their paid labor to supplement his income. Sophia Stevens's abilities as a teacher gave her access to a social world wholly unlike the one she experienced at home. "I like the society here very much," she assured her parents. "I am in the very best circle too." Demonstrating the impact of Olmsted's wealth and refinement on a young woman from rural Vermont, Stevens took special care in her letters home to list the elegant furnishings in his rooms, including marble tabletops, imported carpets, an extensive library, and frescoes on the walls. Corroborating Stevens's impressive list, a visitor in the 1840s commented that Olmsted's house was "better in its way than anything I had seen, and, if I mistake not, better than anything then in Hartford."[8]

While living in the Olmsted household, Stevens was treated like a member of the family. She described cold winter evenings when she would sit in a rocking chair and read and talk with John Olmsted or his son. Access to the extensive Olmsted library allowed Stevens to read books such as John Ruskin's *Modern Painters* that would help cultivate her aesthetic interests and contribute to her social refinement. In fact, Stevens read Ruskin aloud with Frederick Law Olmsted and it formed the context of their socializing. Olmsted informed his brother that he "spent the evening reading and discussing Modern Painters with Miss Stevens who is much interested in it.... The Modern Painters improves on acquaintance and Miss Stevens forms an amalgam with it in my heart." After a particularly trying week at school, Sophia Stevens and Olivia Day took an evening ride on the frozen Connecticut River with Frederick Law Olmsted that provided the context for their application of Ruskin's ideas. As Olivia Day wrote to a friend, "[E]verything reminded us of that book, and illustrated its principles."[9]

Those elite families who had worked hard to create the high school attempted to ensure its success by offering an attractive package to potential teachers such as Sophia Stevens that included not just employment at the school but also access to Hartford's social amenities. In addition to putting some of their own money behind the school,

David and Anne Robinson encouraged their daughter to write to prospective teachers and act as an ambassador for the city and the school. In one letter, Sarah Robinson wrote encouragingly of the fine scenery, houses and people that made up Hartford. "In our enlightened land," Robinson proclaimed, "teachers are loved & respected ... as much as any members of society." Believing that the social world was at least as much an incentive as the school, Robinson assured Sophia Stevens that if she accepted the post in Hartford she would be introduced to the city's "best young ladies, the admired of all admirers."[10]

As Robinson predicted, Hartford's high school teachers were indeed offered the opportunity to form friendships with the daughters of prominent families. Sophia Stevens, for example, proudly informed her mother that she saw "a good deal" of Eliza Trumbull, the governor's daughter. Stevens's inclusion in a selective group of young women "who call me 'Sophia' " appealed to her. In addition to Trumbull, her new circle of friends included Emily Perkins, Sarah Robinson, and Elizabeth Hamersley, all of whom were from socially and economically powerful families. These women gathered together on Wednesday evenings for their "Now and Then" meetings, which Stevens called a "small sewing society of select girls." In addition to the sewing society, women teachers were also asked to join their new friends once a week for Bible study. Both activities were common outlets for women in Hartford and suggest that women teachers were encouraged to replicate conventional gender patterns.[11]

The process of incorporating newcomers into accepted social patterns occurred in formal and informal settings. Teachers at HPHS made note of their many opportunities to talk informally with prominent members of the community at public lectures or at one of the city's bookstores. Abby Dodge, for instance, would visit Rev. Beadle and his wife whenever she needed cheering up after a difficult day teaching. Letters indicate that teachers also attended social gatherings regularly, sometimes three or four times a week, and became enmeshed in the active social life that young men and women conducted in Hartford. Abby Dodge informed her parents that her free time was filled with activities that ranged from gatherings where they made molasses candy to parties and teas. One fancy dress party, where all the guests dressed up as historical figures or characters from popular books, captivated attention. "The fame of it has spread abroad & every body is anxious to have the party at their house," one guest noted proudly, but added, "It will not be made very public." While these gatherings might be commonplace for the daughters of wealthy families, the exclusivity of the social relationships was heady stuff for some of the teachers. The importance of these cultural exchanges was not lost on the teachers themselves, and one noted that she was "gratified to find teaching so genteel a business as it is in Hartford." Part of the attraction of the teaching position, therefore, was that it offered refinement and status.[12]

Despite the careful efforts by the city's elite to create an educational community whose values were coterminous with theirs, it would be a mistake to assume that the teachers were indistinguishable from polite society in Hartford. The primary distinction, of course, was that the teachers supported themselves with their wages. Living "respectably" in Hartford society cost money, more money than some teachers had available to them. To attend these gala affairs, fashionable dresses needed to be made or old ones ornamented. Abby Dodge was grateful for the advice she received from one Hartford matron about how to wear her dresses more stylishly. When she attended a lavish party celebrating the graduating class of 1856, Dodge borrowed jewelry and accessories from various Hartford friends to ornament her dress. Hoping she would not have to appear at parties in shabby clothes, Sophia Stevens asked her parents to pay the cost of a new black silk dress for spring. Although she assured her parents that she would not adopt "city notions and extravagances," Stevens had to balance the expectations of her new friends with those of her parents in Vermont. While Sophia acceded to some of her father's wishes, she did not agree to refuse all invitations, adding "I have no desire to make myself conspicuous by my oddities."[13]

Despite links between the daughters of respectable families and women teachers, the two groups, in fact, did not always share the same expectations for their role as women. Although Sarah Robinson acknowledged that "It is an excellent thing for a young lady to teach," she never sought that path herself. Ultimately, the desire of some women to teach or the economic necessity that propelled their vocational choice distanced them from the more comfortable and conventional world of women such as Sarah Robinson. At one point, Robinson even voiced irritation that Stevens's schoolwork interfered with her willingness to attend parties. This palpable cultural distance necessarily influenced how women teachers were perceived by Hartford society.[14]

While the whirl of Hartford's social life initially proved exciting to the teachers at the high school and offered a welcome respite from the periodic drudgery of their work, it did not define the parameters of their lives. Soon the novelty of parties wore off and they instead represented an opportunity for women teachers to voice opinions and even to influence substantive policy decisions about the school.

Studying the "spirit of the community" as carefully as she studied books, Sophia Stevens determined that social gatherings provided an excellent opportunity for a woman to make her views known. "A gentleman over a plate of hot oysters or a cup of coffee will most readily promise his name . . . to a project proposed by a spirited young lady who entertains him with wit & pleasantries," she informed her parents.[15] Two years working with and more importantly socializing with the Hartford elite had taught Stevens how to influence the school board. Despite the parties they attended, teachers such as Stevens formed their strongest relationships at school with their colleagues and students.

Building an Educational Community

Board members expected that the careful selection of teachers and their inclusion into the city's social life would ensure that the school functioned according to their plans. Despite their best efforts, however, the educational community was not simply a microcosm of the wider Hartford society. The views and aspirations of teachers at the school were not so easily contained, in large part because of their self-conscious professional identities. As they became more experienced and confident, HPHS teachers became convinced that they, more than the school board or other city residents, should determine the future of the school. Alternate images of educational institutions were created by and grounded in the diverse experiences of those who were connected to them. The educational community that emerged around key faculty at the high school became the source of this unexpected assertiveness. Through their shared experiences in creating a viable school that would realize its crucial educational functions, they came to identify themselves as part of a group whose understanding of the school should carry significant weight. In moments of crisis at the school, this sense of shared identity encouraged collective action. The self-conscious community of teachers at HPHS became a source of opposition to the school board when it attempted to make substantial alterations to the school. Before examining the impact of the educational community at HPHS, however, the process of its creation needs to be investigated.

To negotiate the inevitable period of adjustment to the new school and community, teachers formed their strongest relationships not with the sons and daughters of the elite but with other teachers. While they happily interacted with Hartford society, the teachers at the high school developed their own community that sustained them during their professional struggles. Bonds between teachers helped newcomers adjust to the environment at HPHS and to resolve any doubts they had about teaching. The teachers who staffed the high school in its early years manifested a common purpose or commitment to creating an important institution. To improve the school, they also worked together to enhance their impact on the students, who also represented an important element of the educational community at HPHS. With the support of the students, teachers not only were able to experiment with new pedagogies and forms of discipline, but they also had advocates in Hartford society, independent of the school board. This examination of the high school community, therefore, will focus on the interaction among the teachers themselves as well as their relationships with their students.

One of the difficulties in studying the educational community at HPHS is that its members changed unpredictably and rapidly and such changes constituted a substantial challenge to the community's ability to sustain its vision of the school over time. In this way, the school board and the city's elite families enjoyed an advantage in imprinting their views of the school's identity. In addition to students who came and went and board members whose term lasted for only one year, the faculty of the high school also changed with alarming frequency. In September 1851, only William Capron, the head of the classical department, had any experience in Hartford—all of the other teachers and the principal were new. A variety of factors contributed to the high turnover rate. Low pay, health issues, and dissatisfaction with teaching were some common causes. In addition, for most of the men and women at HPHS, teaching represented a temporary and not a lifelong avocation. Along with the reshuffling of personnel, another challenge revolves around source material. Many examinations of public high schools use published school reports as an important source. Unfortunately, these sources have little to say about the interaction of faculty and scholars. The private correspondence of teachers and students at the high school is a rich source for the educational community, but nineteenth-century manuscript sources for HPHS are limited. The bulk of the available correspondence centers on the high school under two popular principals, Thomas Beecher (1848–1850) and Thomas Curtis (1851–1861). Coherent, self-conscious communities did emerge around these two dynamic leaders. As they set the tone for the school and defined its mission, Beecher and Curtis inspired loyalty from both teachers and students alike.

When teachers from around New England arrived in Hartford, they faced the isolation of a new job and a new city. In response, many teachers hoped that friends from home would be hired to fill vacant positions. Pleased that both she and her friend were offered jobs in

Hartford, Marion Goodrich remarked, "It has always been a dream of Mary's and mine to teach together but it is seldom that such an opportunity offers." Debating whether to accept a post in Hartford, Nancy Johnson assured her friend, "It would be no small part of the temptation that you would be my 'fellow laborer' and companion."[16] In addition to teaching at a school with a companion from home, new friendships were formed. Olivia Day and Sophia Stevens, for example, quickly became friends and Stevens would often spend the school vacations in New Haven with Day's family. Stevens's early letters to her parents testify to the depth of her admiration for her "sister Teacher." Referring to Olivia Day as a "rare girl" whom she loved "exceedingly," Sophia Stevens described her as a genius who was "most deeply taught in both heart & intellect. . . . Her wit is exceedingly sharp—but delicious. She has deep toned piety." While Stevens had a good opinion of many of her acquaintances, no one else received such effusive or extensive praise. Their shared experiences in Hartford as women teachers in a new school created a powerful bond between the two women.[17]

For Abby Dodge, her friendly relationship with Thomas Curtis, the principal of HPHS, made her teaching experience more enjoyable. Before working at the public high school, Dodge had taught for one term at the Hartford Female Seminary and had little or no contact with the distant principal, Anna Crocker. "To go from Miss Crocker to [Curtis]," she informed her parents, "is like . . . going from one who ignores your existence to one who feels you are worth at least a three-cent piece." Curtis valued Dodge as a teacher and hoped to retain her services for as long as possible. When Dodge considered leaving HPHS in 1856, Curtis informed her parents that he regarded her as a "permanent fixture" at the school and he argued that Dodge was "filling a sphere of useful labor here which no one before her has yet done, and which I sincerely believe we can find no one else to fill." After Caroline Tallant and Mehitable Snow announced they would be leaving at the end of the term, Abby Dodge felt pity for Curtis's "forlorn situation" and reassured him that she would remain for another year.[18]

These relationships went well beyond the formal and professional. In addition to their obvious professional respect for one another, Curtis and Dodge also established a personal friendship that permitted jokes at the other's expense. In one instance, Dodge sent a friend a note in her own hand that stated, "This certifies that Mary Abby Dodge by her diligence, good conduct and orderly habit and sobriety of deportment merits my approbation," and signed it "Simon Simple." As evidence of her irreverence, she claimed that her principal had written the testimonial, and suggested that his "nom de plume," although unusual, fit him perfectly. Curtis was not merely on the receiving end, as he poked fun at Dodge's foibles on numerous occasions. Imagining the benefits of wealth, Dodge proclaimed that if she were rich she would not even comb her own hair. Agreeing with her, Curtis teasingly added, "It is as much as ever you do it, now you are poor."[19]

Beyond fostering friendships, teaching at the high school also created circumstances for romantic relationships as well. Between 1850 and 1861, there were four marriages involving HPHS teachers. Sarah Hooker, who taught for two years at HPHS, married William B. Capron, head of the classical department and together they served as missionaries in Madura, India. Bertha Olmsted, who taught at HPHS from 1858–1861, married her colleague, William W. Niles (1858–1860) and HPHS principal Thomas Curtis married Virginia Hubbard (1860–1861). Residents felt free to comment on whether they thought one individual was good enough for the other, but it was the marriage of Olivia Day that received the most attention. Between her set of friends in New Haven and her uncle's circle in Hartford, Day socialized with many eligible young men. However, the marriage proposal that she accepted came not from her New Haven or Hartford social circle, but from Thomas K. Beecher, the principal of HPHS. Hoping to avoid any hint of impropriety, Beecher and Day carefully concealed their attraction until after Day had resigned her position at the high school. Writing to his sister about his engagement, Beecher exulted, "The day that Livy left the School—it opened the floodgates of my heart—& poured out mightily. . . . And now at last—the valiant Tom—the careless Tom—the foolish Tom—the teacher Tom—is the accepted one—more than this—the loved one of Livy Day." Beecher's letter indicates not only that he had been suppressing his feelings for Day while she was a member of the community of teachers at HPHS, but also his relief that his identity as "the teacher Tom" was no barrier to his marriage into one of Connecticut's first families.[20]

Writing about Day's engagement, John Olmsted did voice some doubts about Beecher's suitability for the favored "Livy." "I hardly know what to think of it," Olmsted wrote. "It is strange and will make a great sensation. . . . I hope he will change very much, & presume he will. As he is now, he decidedly does not deserve Miss Livy."[21] As the accomplished daughter of the president of Yale and the niece of one of Hartford's most prominent families, Olivia Day had been sought after by several young men of Olmsted's elite circle of friends. His chagrin at the Day-Beecher engagement suggests a sense among this group that Beecher did not measure up to their understanding of Day's social worth. Whatever Olmsted and other members of the Hartford community thought of the marriage, however, Day herself had successfully negotiated the boundaries between teachers and elite society. Indeed, two of her most important relationships—her friendship with Sophia Stevens and her marriage to Thomas K. Beecher—grew out of her decision to *teach* in Hartford. This suggests that the educational community at the high school was powerful enough to reshape the expectations and aspirations of its members.

Not only were various social relationships created among those who worked at the high school, but also a reciprocal concern for the institution itself existed among members of this educational community and became a central part of their claim to define its identity. As part of the first generation of teachers at HPHS, Day and Stevens were aware that they were crucial components in the success of an educational experiment and they avidly followed the school's progress. "The High School is knit to my heart," remarked Olivia Day, "and sometimes I have to feel the pain of it." The youth of the institution allowed its early teachers to shape its identity and the principal, Thomas K. Beecher, inspired the teachers to commit themselves to the creation of an exemplary school. As a result of his efforts, the teachers expressed excitement about their work and optimism about its significance. Even after they left the high school, many teachers continued to be concerned with its welfare. By specifically referring to the HPHS as "our beloved institution," Mary Torrey consciously identified herself as part of the group anxious about the school. The work of creating a viable school, in fact, encouraged their identification as a distinct community and they keenly felt the departure of anyone in that group. "I cannot bear to think of what Hartford and the High School must seem without Mr. Beecher, Minnie or Miss Brognard," lamented Mary Torrey after the three had left Hartford. "Its charm would be nearly lost to me I am sure." The school was inseparable in their minds from the community of men and women who worked there.[22]

Despite their pride in their work and the friendships they created, HPHS teachers confronted challenging and dispiriting conditions. Abby Dodge, for example, was periodically overwhelmed by the monotony of teaching and dreamed instead of a literary career. "As for wearing out my life, and soul and brain, and lungs, in teaching and getting just enough to keep body and soul together, I won't do it any longer. . . . I have tried teaching some four years, and I think it is quite time to see whether something else will not be as profitable and less wearisome and wearing." Far from profiting from her hard work,

Dodge spent her meager salary on her room and board, and then had difficulty meeting her other expenses. "Sent my class out at half-past eleven, and had a cry," she wrote her parents at one particularly low point.

> I am not sick, nothing in particular is the matter, but I am so tired, tired of learning lessons, tired of teaching them, tired of going to school at nine o'clock every day, tired of never visiting anybody, tired of going from one thing to another just as fast as I can, tired of being in a whirl all the time, tired of school, tired of everything—almost.

Fighting frustration and burnout, Dodge considered leaving HPHS, but because she was a successful teacher that the school wanted to keep, they did offer better compensation. In 1855, they raised her salary by $100, bringing it to $500 a year, and the next year they raised it to $600. Though Dodge did at times feel discouraged, she was a talented teacher who received the support and admiration of the educational community of which she was an integral part.[23]

The shared experience of teaching, in fact, served as the basis for solidarity among teachers in the face of adversity and it sustained them as they coped with difficult tasks in the classroom. As a group, they confronted their vocational difficulties and supported new teachers who expressed serious doubts about their abilities. Many inexperienced teachers had trouble adjusting to their students, but Olivia Day actually experienced "cold chills" whenever she thought about teaching in Hartford, and wondered if she should continue. Midway through her first year, Day described her appearance as "forlorn, bedraggled, chalky and school-worn," and she often felt real weariness at week's end. After one class had been "torturing" Day with their "cold, almost insulting *manner*," she sought freedom from the trials of her classroom and expressed deeply ambivalent feelings about teaching that highlight both the pain and the satisfaction associated with her job. "If ever at the close of a recitation I can feel as if I had been *teaching*, in the lowest sense of the word," Day wrote a friend, "I am sufficiently happy." She admitted however, that "There are days when I never have this pleasure, when everything drags—mortifies—perplexes—when my whole connection with the school seems an absurd farce—and even my assumed part is hard to play." Despite these sincere concerns, Day was committed to remaining at the high school, or else, she suggested tongue in cheek, she would have to refund her salary and make "a humble apology to the assembled school, for the humbug of which they have been victims." Although the work was often frustrating, the educational community of teachers and students that existed at HPHS remained an appealing package that Day would not easily relinquish or replace.[24]

While teaching caused some women to experience periodic doubts about their vocation, others became progressively more self-confident and assertive, to the point of ignoring dictates of the school board. Abby Dodge's confidence that she was an effective teacher, for instance, helped her to resist requests from the school board that she believed were unnecessary, intrusive, or insulting. The high school required that all new teachers be examined, a practice to which Dodge objected. When her principal came to her boarding house to take her before the "Fathers of the School" to be tested in arithmetic, geography, and other subjects, Dodge refused to go. After Curtis's 30-minute attempt to convince her, she "parried all his shafts with the clear and simple forcible English declaration, 'I won't go.'" Because she would rather leave the school than consent, Abby Dodge was not examined. In fact, the board altered their procedures so that future teachers could instead choose to have their classes observed. "How grateful ought all my successors to be to me!" exclaimed Dodge. The examination of teachers has been presented by historians as one of several bureaucratic measures designed to centralize control of the school in the hands of the board, but the Dodge case cautions us not to see teachers as hapless pawns in their plan. Confident and assertive teachers such as Abby Dodge who occupied important places in their educational communities actively renegotiated the terms of their employment.[25]

In addition to resisting examinations, HPHS teachers expected that their talent and hard work would be rewarded either with raises or with power at the school. Like the New England women schoolteachers examined by historian Jo Anne Preston, Sophia Stevens exhibited a belief in her own worth and a willingness to assert herself. She accepted the school's offer of $300 per year to start, but Stevens expected a $100 raise each year and confidently asserted, "If I am worth anything I am worth this salary as I believe I shall have proved to them this year." As principal, Thomas Beecher expected all his teachers to become "independent & individually strong" and consequently encouraged such conviction. The community of teachers at HPHS did not merely demand adequate compensation for their labor, but they faithfully advanced the school's mission.[26]

Being part of the first generation of teachers at HPHS created in Sophia Stevens a desire for personal excellence linked to the success of the institution. She launched projects, like the creation of a girls' gymnasium, that would both improve the school and help her carve out a leadership role as well. To be an effective educational leader however,

Stevens believed that she needed to continue her own learning. As she realized that she had the opportunity to achieve a considerable amount at HPHS, her reading became directed to a specific program of study. Proclaiming a "mania for study," Stevens energetically attacked Blackstone and Hume as well as works of English constitutional history and Richard Hildreth's *History of the United States*. Insisting that her ambition did not interfere with her school duties, she asserted, "I find the more I study—the better I can teach." Ultimately, however, her ambition extended beyond excellence in the classroom and she wanted to run a school. For Stevens, the first step on achieving this goal meant that she must develop her intellectual capacities to the fullest.[27]

While personal intellectual development was important, the community of teachers at HPHS placed their primary focus on the students. Identifying the centrality of human relationships at the school, William Capron, the head of the classical department, remarked that "It is good to watch the progress of the scholars to whom you have become so much attached, and this certainly is the strongest cord that binds me to my work." These bonds encouraged some teachers to help needy, but gifted students. William Niles, for example, looked for a patron to pay for college for one talented student who was entirely without means. Niles reported that "all the teachers esteem him very highly and some of us feel a special interest." This "special interest" in particular students represented one reason why the school remained a crucial part of teachers' lives even after they left. Marion Goodrich experienced numerous frustrations as a teacher, but after returning to Burlington, Vermont, she remembered her students, especially her "pet class" in Geometry, when it was time for their recitations. "I wish I could see that Geometry class of mine," wrote Goodrich, "for I shall always claim it." Former HPHS teachers had difficulty adjusting to their departure from the educational community. After the death of her mother necessitated her return to New Haven, Olivia Day thought of the "trials and delights" of her former history class and felt "a deep sense of loss, that I knew not well how to bear it."[28]

These relationships between teachers and their students formed an integral part of the day-to-day functioning of the educational community. During her three years at the high school, Sophia Stevens became a compelling model for young female students, who sometimes called themselves her "adopted daughters." Charlotte Braddock offered this testimonial: "I do believe I never knew a teacher, that I loved more. I hope you will always remember me." Stevens achieved a level of popularity with the students that attested to her personal charisma and professional commitment. As one student noted, Stevens was "generally surrounded by a group of scholars" who competed for her attention and approval. Marion Goodrich received reports from her former students that Stevens was the "best teacher in the school." After Stevens left the school to get married, one student reported dramatically, "I dread to go back to the school and find your place filled by a stranger." Her popularity with the students was enhanced by her willingness to play with them outside of school. Dropping her sober "teacher woman" persona after school, Stevens would "dance and frolic with the school girls." This devotion from students, like the support she had among the teaching corps, gave Stevens a level of power within the high school. Her ability to build support among city residents, students, and teachers both encouraged and enabled her to wield influence at an institution that reserved formal leadership positions for men.[29]

While Sophia Stevens received glowing testimonials from many of her female students, she had more trouble with one of her students, J. Pierpont Morgan, who resented her authority in the classroom. When Stevens had occasion to send him out of class for disruptive behavior, her action was met with disdain from the future financier. Playing the part of the persecuted pupil, Morgan demanded to know how she could treat him in such an "inhumane manner" for "laughing a little too loud," an action he assured his teacher he was "perfectly unable to control and which no punishment will cure me of." In an attempt to reverse the hierarchy of teacher and pupil, Morgan threatened to leave Stevens's classes in history and grammar and move to another section if she would not treat him better. Some of Morgan's indignation no doubt stemmed from the fact that Sophia Stevens stood before him as a confident, powerful woman. The negative comments by Morgan stand alongside the almost worshipful attention she received from many of her female students as indications of Stevens's growing power at the high school.[30]

J.P. Morgan presented specific difficulties for Stevens, but women teachers at HPHS as a group had to confront the challenge of instructing classes filled with high-school aged boys. At HPHS, Abby Dodge taught both boys and girls and expressed initial reservations, hardly surprising in light of her training and teaching experience at single-sex institutions. "Did you ever teach boys?" she asked her mentor.

> I cannot tell you how strange it seemed to me at first. Great burly fellows; they poured into the recitation room the first day, coming upon me like a seventy-four-gun ship till I almost gasped for breath. They frightened me out of my senses. I walked about in a dream the

first week. They seemed so like men. Every time one of them rose to answer me, it seemed to me as if he was going to make a speech.

Despite her initial discomfort, Dodge noted that the boys had "diminished perceptibly in size and numbers and taken together, are really a very gentlemanly set, though I find them in their classes more restless than girls." While particular challenges certainly existed, the letters of women teachers at HPHS emphasize the positive and enduring relationships formed with the students.[31]

These relationships with students were crucial to the educational community's ability to imagine the school as something more than bricks and mortar. Indeed, the rapport that Dodge and other teachers quickly established with their students represented a key ingredient in the group cohesion that developed at the high school. Students and their parents were quick to express their appreciation for talented teachers. The mother of two male students, for example, called Abby Dodge "an oracle" and other students regularly offered flowers or other gifts to their beloved teacher. In one especially memorable instance, a group of students borrowed the nine pence she always wore on a chain around her neck and when they returned it, they had replaced the coin with a gold dollar. Not only was Dodge pleased by the gesture, but also, she remarked jokingly, by the increase in her salary. The students helped create a supportive working atmosphere not just with gifts, but also by offering consolation if she was weary or depressed. This attachment, however, was not unidirectional. Reciprocating their concern, Dodge determined that she would not leave the school until the graduation of her "pet class" in 1858.[32]

Like Sophia Stevens before her, Dodge stood before her students as an engaging, learned woman, and many decided to follow her path to teaching. Five of the ten women in the 1858 graduating class went on to teach in the Hartford school system, two at the high school. Katherine Burbank, in particular, made teaching English and History at HPHS her lifelong career.[33] While Dodge had an impact on the choices her students would make, not all possessed her confidence or independence of mind. When Lilly Gillette, an 1858 graduate of HPHS and keen admirer of Dodge, began teaching in January 1860, she opted for a temporary position at one of the primary schools in Hartford. Although she clearly enjoyed many aspects of teaching, she was torn between her desire to teach and the needs of her family and debated whether she should continue. In February, she wrote, "A pleasant, happy day in my dear school. I am getting to love it so that I really feel sometimes as if it would be hard to give it up in Spring." Yet because illness periodically forced her to miss school, she hesitated to commit to teaching permanently. When Lilly Gillette received an offer to teach at HPHS, she was ecstatic, "A letter from Miss Dodge, asking me, in Mr. Curtis' name to come into the High school to teach, my dream!" Despite her clear happiness, she quickly added, "But I cannot this summer. I ought not for my own health and for Mother's sake too, our family is going to be so large."[34]

Gillette wanted to return to HPHS because she continued to cherish her connection to the educational community at the school long after she graduated. The importance of this connection, for example, prompted her to arrange her class reunion, working hard to make the tableaux vivant an impressive sight for Hartford residents. To maintain her link to the school, Gillette also kept in contact with her former teachers and established friendships with new teachers at the high school. Whenever she had a religious question or needed advice, she visited her former principal, Thomas Curtis. After one visit with Curtis, Gillette remarked "I had had one of those days when everything seems to go wrong, and it did me good to see him." When Curtis offered her the opportunity to teach for only a half day instead of a full day, Gillette found it an acceptable balance between the needs of her family and her desire to once again be "settled into the old school way."[35]

The educational community at HPHS, therefore, was made up not simply of teachers who formed lasting bonds with one another, but also of strong ties between teachers and the student body. These relationships encouraged some students to model their lives after particularly influential teachers. As students became attached to teachers, many found the high turnover rate in the faculty distressing. After Olivia Day resigned from the HPHS faculty, Josie Carpenter took comfort in the fact that there were "other teachers who had been with us from my entrance into the school." Soon however, she reported sadly that only Sophia Stevens and William Capron had been at HPHS as long as she had. While these relationships were important to both students and teachers on a daily basis, they formed the basis of an educational community that took on real coherence in times of crisis. As the school faced repeated conflicts over leadership and authority, some HPHS teachers soon learned that their students' loyalty could be used for practical purposes when alternate images of the school's identity came into conflict.[36]

The Educational Community in Action

Comments like Josie Carpenter's are important windows into the ways in which student desires sometimes conflicted with aspects of school governance. Because students did not want to lose their favorite teachers, they sought to exert pressure on the school board whenever possible. When the board was considering whether they would increase the salary of one teacher, for instance, a group of scholars sent petitions to the board in her favor. After hearing good reports from their children, parents often added their support on behalf of a teacher. In addition to revealing the impact of particular teachers on students' lives, therefore, the loyalty that students exhibited served as an important source of power for HPHS teachers. In one notable instance when the school board attempted to intrude on their educational community, students banded together with teachers to exert pressure on the board to take their views into consideration. More than just a group of scholars and teachers that liked one another, the community at the high school possessed a vision of what the school should be and they would act together to defend it.

HPHS teachers envisioned their community as a place where they were valued as important contributors to an innovative educational experiment and where the improvement of the institution and their own self-improvement were reciprocal values. They expected that those who did the essential work of the institution would have an equal say with other powers, like the school board, in determining the methods of instruction, discipline, and daily management of the school. However, their vision ran headlong into the expectations of the school board, which claimed the authority to make all substantial decisions for the school. What the board failed to understand was that a dynamic educational community had already been created with its own aspirations and understandings of how the school should be run. As a result, their attempts at administrative oversight ran into conflict with both teachers and students at the high school.

Seeking to define both the purpose and nature of the school for themselves, the teachers and students at HPHS resented outside interference with their close-knit community. During his tenure as the principal of HPHS, Thomas K. Beecher, had made converts among the teachers and students, but many on the school board were skeptical of his rejection of rote learning and rigid discipline. The 1849 report of the school visitors, for example, stated that "the theory of discipline, and of instruction" at the high school was "peculiar . . . broad and radical." Beecher and his supporters wanted to encourage principles to emerge in the mind of the student rather than be transplanted there by a book or a teacher. This pedagogical approach and Beecher's opposition to corporal punishment appeared too lax for some in Hartford. Fearing that public opposition to Beecher's methods would hurt the school, the board sought to restrain Beecher's authority. When the school board forced out Beecher in 1850, a group of women teachers used their ties to students and Hartford society as mechanisms to lobby for his reinstatement. Students were devoted to Beecher and many believed that he treated them as adults rather than four-year-olds. If they were running or making too much noise in the hallway, he simply asked them to stop and did not turn minor issues into disciplinary incidents. One student remarked that the school was "melancholy" after Beecher's departure and "it has not seemed at all like the High School of 1848 and 1849." While their efforts failed to bring Beecher back, they did succeed in making it impossible for his replacements to remain. The change in personnel created deep rifts among the school board, teachers, students, and city residents as two short-lived replacements failed to exercise effective leadership.[37]

Using her leadership status in the school community and her connections with Hartford's social elite, Sophia Stevens was instrumental in the dismissal of the two principals who succeeded Beecher. As Stevens actively opposed the replacements, she did so not simply out of her loyalty to Thomas Beecher. She hoped that her fiancé Stephen Hitchcock would be hired and worked behind the scenes to bring this about. Additionally, Stevens had ideas about how the school should be run and wished that her gender did not make it impossible for her to be principal. Her private aspirations for herself and her fiancé fueled Stevens's powerful opposition to the two men who did hold the position. With Stevens's encouragement, teachers and the students quickly determined that McLauren Cooke was not good enough for the position and they therefore rejected him. They felt that they were engaged in important work that required able, intelligent leadership. Hoping that Cooke would fail quickly and then be replaced, the teachers did nothing to help him become a more effective principal, preferring instead to call him "rather stupid" and "too small potatoes." On other occasions, the teachers ignored Cooke's presence, assumed control over school governance, and performed his duties for him. Whether because of his incompetence or the hostility of the faculty and scholars, Cooke was dismissed at the end of one term.[38]

The response to the two men who followed Beecher as principal reveals that the educational community at HPHS was an exclusive one. Teachers and students alike demonstrated little sympathy or respect for those individuals who did not meet their standards. Loyalty to Beecher fueled much of the resentment and the HPHS community resisted any attempt by outsiders to change the direction of the school. Cooke was deemed unacceptable because they found him incompetent, but no such charges could be leveled at his replacement, Cephas Leach. Instead, teachers decided that Leach was ill-suited for HPHS because he was "not well enough acquainted with refined people & city customs." Elevating their school and community over Leach, one teacher remarked, "I fear his ideal is too low for our school. He has lived too much with District Schools and their Teachers." ("District school" was the common nineteenth-century term for local village and neighborhood primary schools in the North.) From the outset, many of the HPHS teachers—and therefore their loyal students who followed their lead—doubted Leach's ability to fit into their exclusive group. Believing that their educational community was both special and superior, Sophia Stevens feared that Leach would diminish the quality of the school and "bring in a bevy of country teachers whom I could not sympathize with." Stevens did not explain precisely what she objected to in either Leach or the "country teachers." Her letters indicate, however that she expected the faculty to possess a certain level of cultural sophistication that would allow them to fit into Hartford society. Additionally, Stevens believed that HPHS was superior to other schools and consequently should be staffed by individuals with a rigorous educational background and a progressive pedagogy. She wanted to exclude anyone that did not measure up to these standards.[39]

Status as an insider or outsider was based not on residence or title, but on whether the existing educational community decided to allow a person to join the group. First Cooke and then Leach found that it was impossible to exercise power at the high school without membership in the educational community. Pledging to pull "the strings to make the puppet go," Stevens encouraged students to petition the school committee for Leach's removal and to voice their support for Beecher's return. Because students were fiercely loyal to Stevens, she was able to use them as her "confidential agents" who would publicly voice her criticisms of the current principal. One student reacted to this atmosphere of open criticism by composing and then circulating doggerel that lampooned Leach as an incompetent fool.[40] Showing no deference to the principal of her school, Ellen Fowler wrote:

> And often fears do seize my mind,
> That on some morning we scholars shall find
> Our principal choked by a great big word
> Some monstrous word we never have heard,
> But in *this* surely I must have *erred*;
> For when "aggravated instances of insubordination"
> And such terrible words as "cooperation"

Can be spoken *at all*, through the knit of the brow
We need have no fears, for our darling now.
He'll giggle and grin, and titter and laugh
Till many a scholar has called him a *calf*.[41]

Stevens understood that she needed to keep secret her intrigues with students because if the board became aware of them, she would be the one to lose her job. Reassuring her worried fiancé, Stevens stated, "I will not do anything rash or notorious. I have plenty of kind protecting friends." Perceiving correctly that Stevens was using her popularity with the students and with many Hartford residents to undermine his leadership, Leach worked to have her replaced with a teacher of his own choosing. During the spring 1851, a power struggle occurred between Leach and Stevens as each plotted to remove the other and to cultivate the support of the board. For Leach to succeed at HPHS, he would need his own power base of teachers who were loyal to him and not Thomas Beecher. Stevens would not resign, but two other teachers did, in fact, opt to leave the school and seek employment elsewhere. After returning home to Vermont, Marion Goodrich expressed relief to be out of the strife and even announced, "I'd rather be sick here than to go back to the High School." Realizing that the internal conflict at the high school was having a corrosive effect on scholars, teachers, and the city's perception of the school, the school board voted to dismiss Leach after one term.[42]

The dismissal of Beecher had set off a chain of events that the school board had not anticipated. While they were responding to outside criticism that the school was not being run properly, the board's actions had the unintended consequence of creating a powerful internal dispute that threatened to destroy the community at the high school. From the point of view of the teachers and scholars, the school board did not appreciate how their institution worked in practice. Teachers such as Sophia Stevens were proud of the institution that they had helped create and bitterly resented the intrusions of the school board that in their view had the potential of wrecking their vision of the school. The loyalty that students felt toward the school and toward their teachers induced them to work against both Cooke and Leach. Teachers, who had once felt a part of Hartford society, increasingly felt at odds with city residents. One teacher remarked with resignation, "I do not think the public care very much who heads the school—it is no such matter of life and death as it seems to us." After two failed attempts to hire a viable principal, board members needed to find someone who could act as a stabilizing force and revive the sense of common purpose of the school's early days. Thomas

Curtis, hired for the fall 1851, faced the unenviable challenge of restoring an educational community that had been polarized. As his first order of business, Curtis had to hire all new teachers. While this was certainly a big job, it allowed him to start with teachers who had no institutional memory of either Beecher or his failed replacements. Like Beecher before him, Curtis soon earned the respect and loyalty of both the teachers and scholars. He led the school for ten years and reestablished a stable community at HPHS.[43]

A vibrant, complex community existed at HPHS in the mid-nineteenth century and it functioned in myriad ways. At its best, the educational community gave purpose and meaning to the lives of the teachers, created bonds among students and teachers, and fostered a supportive environment where individuals could construct alternate identities. Individuals such as Sophia Stevens, Abby Dodge, and Lilly Gillette had a powerful impact on creating and sustaining the educational community at HPHS, and their aspirations were in turn reshaped by their experiences as part of this group. Students and teachers shared a common interest in advancing and protecting this community on their own terms. By constructing a collective identity, they assertively responded when they believed their institution was under threat. At its worst, the educational community was highly exclusive and arrogantly confident that the school would benefit from an unpopular principal's spectacular failure. The divisive events that followed Beecher's dismissal demonstrate the desire of teachers and scholars alike to be involved in the decisions that would fundamentally reshape their institution. HPHS was more than a physical space; it was a community that, at least for a short time, brought people together to act in the name of a common purpose.

Notes

1. H. Augusta Dodge, ed., *Gail Hamilton's Life in Letters*, 2 vols. (Boston: Lee and Shepard, 1901), I: 70–71, 74.
2. *Order of Exercises at the Dedication of the Hartford Public High School*, December 1, 1847 (Hartford: Case, Tiffany, & Co., 1847); *Catalogue of the Hartford Public High School, Tercentenary Edition, 1638–1938* (Hartford: Hartford Press, 1941), 15–16; Emit Duncan Grizzell, *Origin and Development of the High School in New England Before 1865* (New York: MacMillan, 1923), 201–211.
3. Geraldine Joncich Clifford, "History as Experience: The Uses of Personal-History Documents in the History of Education," *History of Education* 7 (1978): 186. For a discussion of the formation of public high schools, see William J. Reese, *The Origins of the American High School* (New Haven: Yale University Press, 1995); David Tyack and

Elisabeth Hansot, *Learning Together: A History of Coeducation in American Schools* (New Haven: Yale University Press, 1992); David Tyack, *The One Best System: A History of American Urban Education* (Cambridge, MA: Harvard University Press, 1974). For analysis of school teaching see Myra H. Strober and David Tyack, "Why Do Women Teach and Men Manage? A Report on Research on Schools," *Signs* 5 (Spring 1980): 494–503; Joel Perlmann & Robert A. Margo, *Women's Work? American Schoolteachers, 1650–1920* (Chicago: University of Chicago Press, 2001); John L. Rury, *Education and Women's Work: Female Schooling and the Division of Labor in Urban America, 1870–1930* (Albany: State University of New York Press, 1991); Kate Rousmaniere, *City Teachers: Teaching and School Reform in Historical Perspective* (New York: Teachers College Press, 1997); Kathleen Weiler, *Country Schoolwomen: Teaching in Rural California, 1850–1950* (Stanford: Stanford University Press, 1998); Victoria-Maria MacDonald, "The Paradox of Bureaucratization: New Views on Progressive Era Teachers and the Development of a Woman's Profession," *History of Education Quarterly* 39 (Winter 1999): 427–453. For rates of school teaching among women, see Maris Vinovkis and Richard Bernard, "The Female School Teacher in Ante-Bellum Massachusetts," *Journal of Social History* 10 (March 1977): 332–345.

4. Olivia Day to Sophia Stevens [SS], January 20, 1851, Doc. 346, Stevens Family Papers, Vermont Historical Society [VtHS]; *Report of the Board of School Visitors to the First School Society of Hartford* (Hartford: Case, Tiffany & Co., 1849); *Report of the Board of School Visitors to the First School Society of Hartford* (Hartford: Case, Tiffany & Co., 1851); *Triennial Catalogue of the Hartford Public High School* (Hartford: Case, Lockwood & Brainard, 1891); *Catalogue of the Hartford Public High School* (1941). SS to Candace Stevens, December 25, 1850; Josie Carpenter to Olivia Day, April 21 [1850], Doc. 346, Stevens Family Papers, VtHS.

5. For information about Hartford in the nineteenth century, see J. Hammond Trumbull, *A Memorial History of Hartford County, 1633–1884*, 2 vols. (Boston: Edward L. Osgood, 1886); Glenn Weaver, *Hartford: An Illustrated History of Connecticut's Capital* (Woodland Hills, CA, 1982), 60–73; Ellsworth Strong Grant and Marion Hepburn Grant, *The City of Hartford, 1784–1984* (Hartford: Connecticut Historical Society, 1986).

6. Biographical data on HPHS teachers is found in *Catalogue of the Hartford Public High School* (1941), 108–111.

7. Grizzell, *Origin and Development of the High School in New England Before 1865*, 204; SS to Candace Stevens, November 26 [1848], Doc. 30, Stevens Family Papers, VtHS; SS to Stephen Hitchcock, January 2, 20, 1850, William Page Papers, Archives of American Art, Smithsonian Institution, Washington, D.C. [AAA]. Boarding teachers in the homes of residents was not unusual and it was a well-established practice for private seminaries. What is unique about the HPHS case is that the

residents who boarded teachers had no economic motive to do so. A comparison of the families who boarded the early HPHS teachers with the families who boarded the women teachers at the Hartford Female Seminary reveals a significant difference in their economic position.

8. SS to Henry Stevens, December 2, 1848; SS to Candace Stevens, December 31, 1848, February 17, 1849, November 26, 1849, Doc. 30, Stevens Family Papers, VtHS. Frederick Kingsbury to Frederick Law Olmsted [FLO], January 31, 1873, FLO Papers, Library of Congress [LC].
9. FLO to John Hull Olmsted, February 10, 1849, FLO Papers, LC; Olivia Day to Elizabeth Baldwin, April 14, 1849, Box 28, Folder 323, Baldwin Family Papers, Yale University Library.
10. Sarah A. Robinson to SS, September 12, 1848; October 31, 1848, Stevens Family Papers, Doc. 30, VtHS.
11. SS to Candace Stevens, February 17, 1849, March 13, 1849, Doc. 30, Stevens Family Correspondence, VtHS; Olivia Day to Elizabeth Baldwin, April 14, 1849, Box 28, Folder 323, Emily Perkins to Elizabeth Baldwin, May 14, 1849, Box 28, Folder 324, Baldwin Family Papers, Yale University Library, New Haven, CT; Libby Hamersley to Sophia Stevens Hitchcock, October 18, 1851, William Page Papers, AAA.
12. SS to Candace Stevens, November 19, 1848, November 26 [1848], June 10, 1849, Doc. 30; SS to Candace Stevens, February 24, 1850, Doc. 346, Stevens Family Correspondence, VtHS; SS to Stephen Hitchcock, November 20, 1849, William Page Papers, AAA.
13. *Gail Hamilton's Life in Letters*, I: 63, 126; SS to Candace Stevens, November 26 [1848]; SS to Henry Stevens, December 10, 1848, Doc. 30, Stevens Family Papers, VtHS.
14. Olivia Day to Elizabeth Baldwin, April 14, 1849, Box 28, Folder 323; Emily Perkins to Elizabeth Baldwin, May 14, 1849, Box 28, Folder 324, Baldwin Family Papers, Yale University Library; Sarah Robinson to SS, n.d. Folder 3, Doc. 346, Stevens Family Papers, VtHS.
15. SS to Henry and Candace Stevens, December 1, 1850, Doc. 346, Stevens Family Papers, VtHS.
16. Marion M. Goodrich to SS, January 7, 1850, Nancy Johnson to SS, January 12, 1850, Doc. 346, Stevens Family Papers, VtHS.
17. SS to Candace Stevens, December 24, 1848, December 31, 1848, February 17, 1849, Doc. 30, Stevens Family Papers, VtHS; SS to Stephen Hitchcock, December 15, 1850, William Page Papers, AAA.
18. *Gail Hamilton's Life in Letters*, I: 71, 128–129, 141.
19. *Gail Hamilton's Life in Letters*, I: 85; Abby Dodge to Mrs. Eunice Cowles, November 16, 1854, Archives and Special Collections, Mount Holyoke College.
20. Thomas K. Beecher to Isabella Beecher Hooker, January 27 or 28 [1850], Acquisitions, Harriet Beecher Stowe Center Library, Hartford, CT. Day's acceptance of Beecher can be contrasted with her

earlier refusal of Frederick Kingsbury, who was an accepted member of her New Haven / Hartford social set. See Emily Baldwin to Roger Baldwin, May 29, 1850, Box 29, Folder 336, Baldwin Family Papers, Yale University Library.
21. John H. Olmsted to Frederick J. Kingsbury, January 9, 1850, FLO papers, LC.
22. Olivia Day to SS, March 15 [1850]; MC Torrey to SS, August 21, 1850, January 8, 1851, Doc. 346, Stevens Family Papers, VtHS.
23. *Gail Hamilton's Life in Letters*, I: 79–80, 112.
24. Olivia Day to Thomas K. Beecher, November 1, 1848, Box 12, Folder 202, Day Family Papers; Olivia Day to Elizabeth Baldwin, April 14, 1849, Box 28, Folder 323, Baldwin Family Papers, Yale University Library.
25. *Gail Hamilton's Life in Letters*, I: 74–75. For further examination of the bureaucratic changes in school organization, see Victoria-Maria MacDonald, "The Paradox of Bureaucratization," 427–453.
26. SS to Candace Stevens, September 24, 1849, Doc. 30; T.K. Beecher to SS, n.d. folder 3, Doc. 346, Stevens Family Papers, VtHS. Jo Anne Preston, "Domestic Ideology, School Reformers and Female Teachers: School-Teaching Becomes Women's Work in Nineteenth-Century New England," *The New England Quarterly* 66 (December 1993): 544–545.
27. Sophia Stevens to Candace Stevens, February 3, March 10, April 7, September 8, October 2, 1850, February 1, June 9, 1851, Doc. 346, Stevens Family Correspondence, VtHS. For information on women's reading in antebellum America, see Mary Kelley, "Reading Women / Women Reading: The Making of Learned Women in Antebellum America," *Journal of American History* 83 (September 1996): 401–424.
28. William B. Capron to Sophia Stevens Hitchcock, January 2 [1852], William Page Papers, AAA; William W. Niles to William Hamersley, April 29, 1859, Hamersley Papers, Connecticut Historical Society; Marion M. Goodrich to SS, January 10, 1851, January 22, 1851; Olivia Day to SS, March 15 [1850], Doc. 346, Stevens Family Papers, VtHS.
29. Marion Goodrich to SS, February 9, 1851, Doc. 346, Stevens Family Papers, VtHS; SS to Stephen Hitchcock, March 17, 1850, William Page Papers, AAA. Lottie Braddock to SS, July 18, 1851, Josie Carpenter to Olivia Day, April 21 [1850], Doc. 346, Stevens Family Papers, VtHS. After Stevens left the high school, several former pupils wrote her letters offering testimonials of her influence on their lives. See e.g., L. Allyn to Sophia Stevens Hitchcock, September 27, 1851, M. Smith to SSH, October 18 [1851], William Page Papers, AAA.
30. J. Pierpont Morgan to Miss Stevens [1850], Mabel Satterlee Ingalls Papers, Pierpont Morgan Library, New York, NY.
31. *Gail Hamilton's Life in Letters*, I: 73–74.
32. *Gail Hamilton's Life in Letters*, I: 81, 112, 121, 127.

33. *Catalogue of the Hartford Public High School* (Hartford: Case, Lockwood & Co., 1858); *Hartford City Directory* (Hartford, 1861); *Catalogue of the Hartford Public High School* (1941).
34. Diary of Lilly Gillette, February 14, May 9, 12,1860, Diaries Misc., Harriet Beecher Stowe Center Library, Hartford, CT.
35. Diary of Lilly Gillette, January 19, 24, February 10, May 16, July 4, 11-13, 1860, Diaries Misc., Harriet Beecher Stowe Center Library.
36. Josie Carpenter to Olivia Day, April 21 [1850], Doc. 346, Stevens Family Papers, VtHS.
37. *Report of the Board of School Visitors, to the First School Society of Hartford* (1849), 8; Josie Carpenter to Olivia Day, April 21 [1850]; Ellen Fowler, "Mr. Beecher," January 24, 1851, Doc. 346, Stevens Family Papers, VtHS.
38. SS to Candace Stevens, October 18, November 1, 1850, Doc. 346, Stevens Family Papers, VtHs; SS to Stephen Hitchcock, September 29, October 13, 1850, William Page Papers, AAA.
39. SS to Candace Stevens, December 25, 1850, January 5, January 19, June 19, 1851, Doc. 346, Stevens Family Papers, VtHs; SS to Stephen Hitchcock, December 15, December 22, 1850, William Page Papers, AAA.
40. SS to Candace Stevens, December 25, 1850, January 5, January 19, June 9, June 19, 1851; Ellen Fowler, "Mr. Beecher," January 24, 1851, Doc. 346, Stevens Family Papers, VtHS; SS to Stephen Hitchcock, September 29, October 13, December 22, 1850, April 28, May 4, 1851, William Page Papers, AAA.
41. Ellen Fowler, "Mr. Beecher," January 24, 1851, Doc. 346, Stevens Family Papers, VtHS.
42. SS to Stephen Hitchcock, February 26, 1851, March 10, 1851, William Page Papers, AAA; Marion M. Goodrich to SS, January 22, 1851, February 2, 1851, Doc. 346, Stevens Family Papers, VtHS.
43. Olivia Day to SS, January 20, 1851, Doc. 346, Stevens Family Papers, VtHS; William B. Capron to Sophia Stevens Hitchcock, January 2 [1852], William Page Papers, AAA.

Chapter 3

Student-Community Voices: Memories of Access versus Treatment at University of Illinois

Deirdre Cobb-Roberts

The main focus of this chapter is on the social and academic experiences and demographic characteristics of African American students at the University of Illinois at Urbana-Champaign (hereafter UIUC) from 1945–1955 and their notion of what a community represented to them. The post–World War II era witnessed many significant changes in American higher education, including sharp increases in the number and proportion of male students as a consequence of the GI Bill. Important changes in race relations occurred as institutions of higher education were forced to reconcile their own traditions with the national and international struggles against Nazism, anti-Semitism, and racism. Various policies and traditions at the University of Illinois, as in other predominately white northern universities, ranged against positive academic and social experiences for African American students.

African American students were constant victims of discrimination from the start of their enrollment at the University of Illinois. The determination of these students, with the assistance of Albert R. Lee, the unofficial dean of African American students, the encouragement of African American elected officials, community individuals, the Student Community Interracial Committee, Student Human Relations Council, and individuals in the nearby cities such as Chicago and St. Louis, enabled them to fight discrimination emanating from varying levels, thus providing a coping mechanism that was essential in the survival and matriculation of African American students. Understanding the history of the founding of the University of Illinois is crucial to understanding the prevailing climate for African American students, outside the mainstream university "community."

This chapter examines the experiences of African American students in the context of post–World War II higher education in America at the University of Illinois. Although each institution has it own traditions and distinctive character, UIUC's history demonstrates the common dynamics that appeared nationwide in majority-white institutions that developed in America by mid-century, particularly of the large public land grant universities. Secondary sources on the history of African American students at similar predominately white universities reveal similar experiences from one campus to another. Many of these campuses were attempting to desegregate their residence halls and eating facilities on and off campus and were dealing with the influx of new students as a result of the GI Bill. Thus UIUC's social context during the 1945–1955 period provides more or less a representative setting for studying the social and academic experiences of African American students in a large, public, predominately white university. The impact of the GI Bill on American higher education, changes in race and gender relations, and changes in student life and culture will form the context for analyzing the behavior and beliefs of African American students during this period as they formed a community within a community.

Currently, there is a paucity of scholarship on the history of black students at predominantly white universities during the postwar era. For example, very few historians have had access to student transcripts and this has precluded any analysis of academic characteristics along race and gender lines. Further, even among existing scholarship on higher education of African American students, researchers have not had access to the kinds of records that form the evidential base for this chapter. Ultimately, this chapter aims to build on and add to the historical scholarship in the areas of African American experiences in predominantly white universities, comparisons of the higher education of men and women, and the history of student life and culture.

This chapter describes the campus and city racial climate for African American students during the postwar era and to focus on issues of struggle, discrimination, commitment, community, and perseverance. The account of African American students presented here depicts how students learned to survive and advance on a racially hostile campus and describes how the university attempted to reconcile its principles of fairness, equality, and nondiscrimination with its practice of institutionalized segregation and racism. Indeed, there is very little that is written about any aspect of African American higher education during this era. Many important questions such as the impact of the GI Bill on African American higher education attainment have not been treated.

African Americans and Higher Education

Much of the material used for this chapter comes from a 1968 project sponsored by the UIUC Archives. The focus of the "Black Alumni and Ex-Student Project" was to identify all African American students who had attended the University of Illinois from 1887 to 1968. Although this project fell short of its target, it was successful in identifying thousands of African Americans who were students at the University of Illinois between 1887 and 1968. Building on this project by using reference files such as University applications for part-time employment (these forms asked students to report their religion, racial descent, and color), yearbooks, transcripts, student directories, card files (these often contained pictures), lists of Black students in fraternities, sororities, and independent houses, and the papers of university presidents, clerks, and deans, a list of approximately 1,400 African American students who attended the university from 1945 to 1955 was compiled.

The pursuit of higher education for African Americans in America has been a difficult one. Traditionally African American students have been denied equal access to predominately white universities and constantly portrayed as intellectually inferior. White women had experiences that were somewhat similar to African Americans because they too were considered to be inferior to White men. Even given these similarities, we have to acknowledge the differences between the experiences of these two groups. African Americans in the South were legally barred from education and often threatened with death if they attempted to pursue it.[1] On the other hand, White women did not have to fear their lives if they so chose the path of education.

Traditionally White men were in charge of educational decision making. They decided whether or not slaves should be educated and similarly if their wives and daughters should be educated. As a result of this white patriarchal system, African Americans were not educated and White women were only educated as it suited the purposes of the larger society. White men saw the education of African Americans as unnecessary because they believed it would undoubtedly lead to problems (i.e., slave uprisings, notions of superiority).

African Americans who were given an opportunity to become educated had different experiences than their white counterparts in the educational realm. For example, Linda Perkins in her article entitled "The Impact of the 'Cult of True Womanhood' on the Education of Black Women" describes how the experiences of Black women were different from their White counterparts experiences. Perkins stated,

> This "true womanhood" model was designed for the upper and middle class white woman, although poorer white women could aspire to this

status. However since most blacks had been enslaved prior to the Civil War and the debate as to whether they were human beings was a popular topic, black women were not perceived as women in the same sense as women of the larger (i.e., white) society. The emphasis upon women's purity, submissiveness and natural fragility was the antithesis of the reality of most black women's lives during slavery and for many years thereafter.[2]

This passage shows how African American women's degraded womanhood is often compared with the elevation of White womanhood.[3] African American women were viewed as less than women because they did not fit the "womanhood" mold as defined by White society. This finding was consistent with the way in which African American women were treated, typically as second-class citizens. Black women had to constantly dispel the myths of their racial and social inferiority, and immorality and perceived lack of dignity, all of which affected their fight for education.[4] This struggle existed for African American men as well.

Education for African Americans had been difficult. Although the Emancipation Proclamation provided freedom, African Americans had to prove their worth as human beings. They had to overcome the fact that they were stolen, beaten, witnessed children sold away, disenfranchised, stripped of personhood and often denigrated to the lowest position. Their struggle to become educated is still one marred by racism. History cannot deny the contributions made by African Americans. History reveals that these forms of oppression have not stifled the desire to learn and become educated. In fact, their desire to pursue an education has been enhanced by it.

The Founding of University of Illinois and African American Students

The University of Illinois was incorporated on February 28, 1867, as the Illinois Industrial University and opened its doors to students on March 2, 1868. At the university's opening, it was clear the institution was intended for White men, despite its public land grant status. The wording of the U.S. Statutes at Large is as follows:

> the leading object shall be, without excluding other scientific and classical studies, and including military tactics, to teach such branches of learning as are related to agriculture and the mechanic arts, in such manner as the legislatures of the states may respectively prescribe, in order to promote liberal and practical education of the industrial classes in the several pursuits and professions in life.[5]

There was nothing in its charter to encourage discrimination against students because of race, sex or class. Indeed, the U of I was chartered for all the children of the "industrial classes" of Illinois. In the original draft of the bill, however, the school was to be for any white resident of the state of Illinois. Although this draft did not specifically exclude women, it was clear that the university was not established with women in mind. Nonetheless, the university opened with 50 White males and a faculty of three, establishing at the outset a critical distinction between democratic rhetoric and the practice of racism and sexism, a distinction that would plague the institution well into the twentieth century.

Changing Student Demographics

The university maintained an all White male population until 1870 when it admitted its first female student, a White woman, marking a significant shift in its student population. This decision to admit a female student was prompted by the fact that the UIUC was a state school and taxpayers demanded that their daughters as well as sons be educated. The Morrill Act of 1862, signed by President Lincoln established the land grant colleges especially for the sons and daughters of the common people. However, even after the university admitted its first female student in 1870, it would be quite some time before White women matriculated at Illinois in any significant numbers. In 1887, two years after the General Assembly changed the name to University of Illinois, the university admitted its first African American student, nearly two decades after the founding of the university.[6] The population of African American students at the university remained at a minimum during the first half of the twentieth century, but there were relatively significant increases during the 1930s, 1940s and 1950s. From 1945–1955 approximately 1,400 African American students matriculated at Illinois.

The first African American to be admitted to the university was Jonathan Rogan, from Decatur, Illinois. He attended the university from 1887–1888. After his short stay the next African American student was not admitted until 1894. George W. Riley, a student in Art & Design, from Champaign, attended the university until 1897. In 1900, William Walter Smith was the first African American student to graduate from UIUC. Walter T. Bailey was the second to graduate with a degree in architecture in 1904 and the only student at that time to finish with a professional degree of Master of Architecture.[7] The first African American woman, Maudelle Tanner Brown, graduated in 1906 with an A.B. in mathematics, which she completed in three years. The first African American to graduate in Law was Amos Porter Scruggs, who completed his education in 1907.[8] There were few African American graduates during the late nineteenth and early twentieth centuries. Enrollment trends for African American students at UIUC were very low until a modest increase occurred during the post–World War II years. This pattern of scarce African American presence at Illinois would follow for years to come.

Albert R. Lee: The Unofficial Dean of Black Students

Albert R. Lee, born on a farm near Champaign on June 26, 1874, attended Champaign Central High School and graduated in 1893. Two years after graduation Lee went to work for the University of Illinois in 1895 as a messenger boy in the office of the President, Andrew Sloan Draper. He spent a period of 53 years working for the University of Illinois in the office of the president in a variety of positions, from messenger boy to the unofficial Dean of African American students. According to his papers, Lee was employed and utilized as messenger "boy," clerk, waiter, doorman at Presidents Draper's and James's houses and unofficial dean of African American students. In his paper, "University of Illinois Presidents I Have Known," Lee describes his duties from the beginning of his time spent working at Illinois. Despite the various positions held, he was never paid for his duties performed in the capacity of unofficial dean of African American students. This was a position that Lee adopted for himself and it became convenient for the university as they recognized him in this position.[9] Despite the lack of pay for his self-proclaimed title, it was obvious from his correspondence that he was dedicated to African American students. Lee worked very diligently for the university with the exception of one year, 1897–1898, when he was enrolled as a student.[10] His dedication and knowledge of the university and its community permitted him the opportunity to successfully assist African American students.

Albert R. Lee went to great lengths to help African American students in whatever capacity he could. He was considered to be the unofficial Dean of African American students.[11] In addition to his other responsibilities in the president's office he was responsible for compiling data on African American students. Lee was very involved in the affairs of African Americans on and off campus. He was a respected leader in the Champaign African American community. His official capacity was that of an office clerk in the office of the president who was responsible for keeping records, accounts, and performing routine assignment. However, he did much more. He was often called upon to address issues related to African American students. Not only did students look to him for guidance and counsel; university officials counted on him as well. It was not always clear why the university relied on him; however, one may surmise that it was the confidence that university officials had in his administrative ability and his commitment to helping African American students. Furthermore, university officials probably assumed he could relate to and understand the students based on their shared ethnic background. The fact that he was the highest-ranking African American in the university illustrates the minor role that African Americans played in the university administration and faculty during this era. Yet, Lee played a major role in the lives of African American students. He served as their mediator, comforter and friend. According to one account,

> He was very well respected in the community and the University, which was a separate community, it still is but not as much as it used to be. He worked his way up from office boy but he was the one who, didn't complain, he wanted people to respect him so he respected other people and he got their respect or he wouldn't have gotten where he was without any education because he was not an educated man. The education he got was from, his experiences working, working with people on the campus and he was very good or he wouldn't have been there as long as he was.[12]

Lee committed the better part of his life to the UIUC and African American students. As evidenced in letters from the families of incoming students, Lee was responsible for almost all aspects of African American student life.[13] His files contain a vast amount of information on African American students and their experiences. When African American parents contacted the university, various deans and administrators on campus would forward those letters to Lee. For example, Lee would frequently receive letters from families requesting information about the university. He felt obliged to provide the requested information.[14] In a letter dated August 17, 1928, Mr. Edward Jacobs called on Lee to assist him in securing housing for an incoming female African American student. In that letter, Mr. Jacobs thanks Lee and reminds him of the assistance he has given him over the last ten years. Lee responded to this letter informing the student of the housing conditions at the University of Illinois.[15] He also took it upon himself to document the number of African American students at the university and regularly submitted the information to W.E.B. DuBois, editor of the *Crisis* the official journal of the NAACP. Lee was definitely a man committed to seeing African Americans obtain an education.

Lee responded to many letters during his tenure at the university. The majority of the letters written pertained to the condition of African American students on campus. Additionally he constantly wrote to African American elected officials for their support in helping to secure equal accommodations for African American students on campus. He was always concerned with how to improve the experiences of African American students. Moreover, Lee wrote to the president of the university when he felt a situation concerning African American students could be handled more effectively at that level or when he saw the need to compliment the president on a job well done. Publicly he never denounced the university and its practices, but often in his letters to the president he questioned the discrimination that he observed.

He monitored African American students on campus; kept records of their years of attendance as well as their campus affiliations. Apparently, Lee was passionate about and committed to keeping track of the number of African American students on campus. He listed their names, addresses, and campus affiliations (e.g., fraternity or sorority). His papers included several typewritten or handwritten lists of this sort of information.[16] He was very conscientious about recording methods, meticulous to the point of correcting the smallest error. For example, Lee annually took a census of UIUC African American graduates and submitted it to the *Crisis* as part of the magazine's yearly account of black graduates of predominately white universities.[17] Once he made a mistake and he quickly rectified the error in a letter to the editor of the *Crisis*, W.E.B. DuBois. On June 13, 1927 Lee writes to DuBois:

> Dear Doctor:
>
> In my recent letter to you giving the names of graduates from the University of Illinois, I made an omission. Kindly add to the list of graduates that of Ella Madalyne Towles, Piano, School of Music, degree of B. of Music, Harrisburg, Illinois.
>
> Cordially yours
> Albert R. Lee
> Chief Clerk
> Office of the President[18]

As the unofficial Dean of African American students, Lee took responsibility for the experiences of African American students on the UIUC campus. Furthermore, he believed it important to document their experiences on campus.

Enrollment Trends

It was difficult to ascertain the actual enrollment of African American students. Albert R. Lee seemed to be the only one concerned with the actual numbers. In 1936, Carl Stephens of the Alumni Association contacted Lee regarding the number of African American students in the university since the beginning of their enrollment in 1887. Lee was delighted to have the opportunity to conduct this study and did so very diligently. Although very excited about the project, Lee was concerned about the preciseness of his work. He explained in his report that:

> This compilation is in a way a creation. We have made something whereof nothing existed. It is humanly impossible to make a perfect list under the conditions that confronted the compiler. A period of fifty years presents problems in selecting material, methods of work. Yet out of it he by the help of the gods been able to get together over 900 names. As to how complete it is, it may be said that in the period up to 1920 it is fully 98% complete. For the period since that time when there has been such a marked increase of Negro students-their frequent coming in and dropping out, the percent of completeness may drop to 85%.[19]

Lee was very meticulous with his work. He began by consulting the Alumni directories and recorded the names of the students he remembered, after that he referred to city directories that kept names of individuals that he could recognize as African American by the addresses, and then consulted them to determine whether or not they housed students. Finally he checked university catalogues for verification of names, degrees, and courses. All of these sources were then checked against list he had made for 12 years of African American students. He then alphabetized the lists and rechecked his sources for any names that may have been omitted.[20]

To give an example of the scarcity of African American students at UIUC, table 3.1 lists the numbers of students during the first half of the twentieth century. The relevant data is missing for years 1905–1918 and 1920–1924 respectively. It is important to mention that Albert R. Lee compiled the majority of this information voluntarily for the purposes of reporting to W.E.B. DuBois, editor of the journal *Crisis*. DuBois would request this information from all institutions and report the results annually in the *Crisis*. Scholars often utilized this source in lieu of having access to university transcripts. It is unclear as to how DuBois was able to ascertain from whom he should request the information.

Table 3.1 Student enrollment, University of Illinois 1900–1940

Years	Black Enrollment	Total Enrollment
1900	2	2,505
1901	5	2,932
1902	4	3,288
1903	9	—[a]
1904	19	3,729
1919	48	7,157
1925	68	10,710
1926	55	13,731
1927	92	14,071
1929	138	14,594
1930	92	14,986
1931	129	14,569
1933	109	12,122
1934	104	13,067
1935	101	14,036
1936	94	15,831
1937	112	16,865
1938	108	17,500
1939	139	17,212
Total	1,428	208,905

[a] Missing data.

Source: "The University of Illinois Negro Students, Location, History and Administration," Arthur C. Willard Papers, General Correspondence 1934–1946, Series 2/9/1, Box 42 (Folder "Colored Students University of Illinois"), and *Register of the University of Illinois*, University of Illinois Archives, Urbana, Illinois.

Additional names were added to the list after Lee completed his study in 1936. In addition to student enrollment there was also a list of African American graduates from the early years found in University President Willard's files. Table 3.2 displays the approximate number of African American graduates and their degrees between the years of 1904–1934, with data missing for years, 1901–1903, 1905, and 1913 respectively.

Between the years of 1945–1955 the pattern of enrollment increased quite a bit. For the ten year period there was an estimated one thousand fourteen hundred African American students that attended the university. This information was gleaned from Eddie Russell's preliminary look at African American students, in addition to a survey of yearbooks, transcripts, card files and employment records, conducted by the author with the assistance of undergraduate

Table 3.2 Total number of African American graduates, University of Illinois, 1900–1936

	AB	BS	Masters	Ph.D.	Total
1900	1				1
1904		1			1
1906	1				1
1907		1			1
1908	2				2
1909	1				1
1910	2	1	1		4
1911		1			1
1912	1	1	1		3
1914	3	2	1		6
1915	1	1			2
1916	2	1		1	4
1917	1	1		1	3
1918	3	3			6
1919	3		1		4
1920	2	3			5
1921	2	2			4
1922	4	2			6
1923	2				2
1924	2	2			4
1925	8				8
1926	4	4			8
1927	3	5	1		5
1928	4	5			9
1929	11	7	3		21
1930	4	7	3		14
1931	8	8	3		19
1932	8	17	6		31
1933	15	9	5		29
1934	6	14	4		24
Total	104	98	29	2	240

Source: "Negro Students at the University of Illinois, an Outline of their Enrollment? Activities? History, Living Conditions," Arthur Cutts Willard Papers, General Correspondence, 1934–1946, Series 2/9/1, Box 2 (Folder "Colored Students University of Illinois"), University of Illinois, Urbana, Illinois.

students. Table 3.3 displays overall campus enrollment between the years of 1941–1955, with data missing from years 1941–1944.

Black Alumni Ex-Student Project

Eddie Russell, a physical education student in the class of 1969, was very interested in bridging the gap between prospective college

Table 3.3 Urbana campus enrollment trends, University of Illinois, 1941–1955

Year	Men	Women	Black Enrollment	Total Enrollment
1940	9,115	3,243	8	12,358
1945	4,718	4,797	60	7,906
1946	13,938	4,440	96	18,378
1947	15,140	4,251	71	19,391
1948	15,137	3,957	72	19,094
1949	15,231	4,290	67	19,521
1950	13,098	4,064	71	17,162
1951	11,355	3,790	57	15,145
1952	11,452	3,987	69	15,439
1953	11,701	4.075	55	15,776
1954	12,648	4,218	45	16,866
1955	13,869	4,206	17	18,075

Source: Greybook of Enrollment Tables: First Semesters 1945–1955, Annual Report of the Director, Series 25/7/0/5, Box 1, and Student Transcripts Series 25/3/4, University of Illinois Archives, Urbana-Champaign.

students, current students, and former alumni. He desired the black alumni to become more actively involved in the recruitment, retention, and support of young African American college students. Russell conducted a study entitled "Project RECALL" to gather information about African American students at UIUC. In an *Illinois Alumni News* interview he stated:

> The purpose of the project [is] to solicit the support advice and guidance of Negro alumni in the matter of job information, help with recruiting qualified Negro high school graduates for entry into the University, contributions towards scholarship funds and scholarship loans for impoverished Black students, counseling in regard to retention of these students in the University, and community-University coordination.[21]

Although Russell's goals were very noble, they were met with opposition from some university officials.

In a meeting held on October 14, 1968 that involved Eddie Russell, university archivist Maynard Brichford, and Professor Dimitri Shimkin, the issue of opposition was discussed. In meeting notes the three gentlemen described the feeling of one T. Jones, assumed to be a university official, but the record is unclear. Jones adamantly opposed the study for fear that it might actually bring African American Alumni together. According to the meeting notes he was opposed to the study for three reasons: (1) he did not believe an organization was needed, (2) he believed there was no need for the university to interfere in the social affairs of the "Negro" student, and (3) the data collected for such a study would only work to organize African American Alumni and that should not be the goal, as it was unnecessary.[22] This, however, was not the sentiment of other university officials.

Maynard Brichford, university archivist wrote a letter to Dr. Jack W. Petalson, chancellor of the university explaining the importance of the black alumni project:

> For seventy-five years, the University of Illinois has been providing opportunities in higher education to black Americans. Thousands have attended the university and used their education to serve their communities and the nation. Due to the social and political impact of racism, the university has seldom attempted to identify, and has never sought to establish contacts with, black alumni and ex-students.
>
> The establishment of a communications network to compile a directory would establish a pattern of records essential for the study of the role of the Negro in American life and history. The project would provide administrative offices and departments with a reliable base of research data about a most significant group-black Americans who have sought and obtained higher education.[23]

Archival records seem to indicate that Petalson may have been agreeable to the project but was dissuaded by John William Briscoe, Assistant Chancellor for Administration and Professor of Civil Engineering. Briscoe felt that the project would cause more harm than good. He was most concerned with the final results would be used to assemble African American students. He also indicated that African American students preferred to utilize their own established networks. The general idea was that bringing this group together would represent potential harm to the university, although it is not clear what sort of harm would result.[24]

In a field note dated November 12, 1968, there were several reasons for the rejection of the proposal for funding in addition to other ways to go about conducting the project. Briscoe stated the he did not "see value in seeking other university means of support" and went on to say that (1) an individual faculty member may request a research grant from an outside foundation, but this would require university approval, (2) an outside group may request the university to supply this information, (3) a graduate student could undertake the project as a research project or thesis subject and (4) the university administration is afraid of the results of the project and will not support it in its present state.[25]

Brichford was not discouraged by the rejection from the University Research Board. Clearly Brichford and others saw the value in this project and were determined to see it to fruition. In a letter to James Vermette, Brichford further assures Vermette, a member of the University Research Board, that the information will in no way be used to organize or further separate African American Alumni. He goes on the thank him for his support even though his financial proposal was turned down by the University Research Board, and asked if there were any other financial alternatives that existed.[26]

The project did receive some funding although it is unclear as to how much. Russell was the person primarily responsible for the data collection. Russell began by looking through the *Illio*, the university yearbook, and identified African American students by visual sight. He first went through all the traditional African American fraternities and sororities, then housing units, sport teams, groups and senior photos. The next step was to transfer the students' names to a data sheet, which Russell checked against Albert R. Lee's lists, and the alumni directory. He also used the Chicago Alumni Directory as a resource for additional names. As of October 21, 1971, Russell compiled a list of 2, 479 African American students who attended the university from its founding to 1971 and these data are now housed in the university archives.[27]

Social Characteristics of African American Students at Illinois

African American students at UIUC from 1945 to 1955 were not a monolithic group. They came from various social and religious backgrounds and there were significant differences in age. The postwar era, specifically the GI Bill, brought to the campus a much older and more mature black male population. In many categories these students differed as much from each other as they did from the larger student population. The unifying piece that held them together was their shared racial heritage, and the second-class treatment based on that shared characteristic. Beyond these characteristics they were dissimilar in vital respects. Between the years of 1945–1955 there were a reported 1,042 students that had transcripts and of that number 352 were female and 677 were male, and there were 13 students whose gender was not reported, because the information was not present. Both the distribution of birth state and parental home state indicate that the majority of these students were from Illinois or at least had parents living there when they enrolled in college with Missouri being the second largest state to provide UIUC with African American students.

It was not uncommon for the men to outnumber the women due to the increase in male enrollment under the GI Bill. Typically men entered college at age 21 as opposed to the women who entered at age 19, although it typically took them longer to finish their college courses.

Despite the differences in age and time taken to complete the degree there was an overall graduation rate of 58.3 percent for African American students. Given that this rate of graduation occurred within about four years, this figure is most impressive considering the racial climate that was present on campus and in the community. Women may have finished at a faster pace but men outnumbered women in relation to their graduation rates. About 68 percent of the graduates were men as opposed to 32 percent of women.

Among graduates the grade point averages of men compared with women also indicates that men performed slightly better than women and that may be attributed to the fact that women were on the fast track to get in and get out. Also men were older and perhaps more mature. The most interesting aspect of the male–female background is high school percentile rank, which is normally associated with predicting academic success. On average, women did significantly better than men in their overall high school achievement, finishing a full nine percentile points ahead of men (females at the 73rd percentile, men at the 64th).

Another point of analysis was the association of parental occupation in relation to graduation rates of students. Student responses to parental occupational field displayed in table 3.4 were collapsed into seven main categories. The majority of the students' parents worked in the managerial field; however, when all other categories are combined those numbers change and it is discovered that most students'

Table 3.4 Student's parental occupational fields, University of Illinois, 1945–1955

	%	n
Managerial, Professional	22	108
Technical, Sales, Admin.	22	106
Service	18	89
Farming	5	23
Precision, Production, Repair	14	68
Operators, Laborers	18	89
Military	0.4	2
Total	100	485

Source: Student Employment Folders, Series 41/4/5, University of Illinois Archives. The number 485 represents the total number of students that reported parental occupation on their employment folder. The percentages have been rounded to whole numbers when possible.

Table 3.5 Student's religious preference, University of Illinois, 1945–1955

	%	n
Baptist	33.6	101
Catholic	11.3	34
Methodist	29.2	88
Protestant (unspecified)	25.9	78
Total	100.0	301

Source: Student Employment Folders, Series 41/4/5, University of Illinois Archives. The number 301 represents the total number of students, who reported religious preference on their employment application, collapsed into four categories.

parents are involved in administrative support, labor, repair, and production professions.

The farming occupation has the highest high school percentile rank, however, the total number of students (n = 6) with parents in this field is relatively small. The most significant finding here is that students (n = 42) with parents in managerial, professional fields had an average percentile rank of 73 over a ten-year period.

Male enrollment outweighed female enrollment and created a similar pattern in martial status. However, the proportion of men that were married, 22 percent, compared with women, 12 percent, suggests that men were more likely to be married at this time.

Table 3.5 presents the collapsed distribution of religious preferences of students, based on the responses that were available. More work needs to be done in the area of religion. The data here are all suggestive, as there are no clear patterns of association between religion and academic achievement. The highest concentration occurred for Baptists, followed by Methodists. The category Protestant (unspecified) refers to those students that did not list a specific denomination Protestant. For reasons of parsimony I was able to collapse the larger categories into smaller ones. Table 3.5 represents those four categories. Additionally the Baptists and Methodists were excluded from the Protestant unspecified category. On average Protestant (unspecified) did better in high school, and the women within this group appeared to far exceed the men. Women that designated Catholic as their preferred religion did significantly better than men.

Tables 3.6 and 3.7 address the issue of skin color and race. The employment files asked for a response to these questions and there were students that answered them. It is interesting to note that the majority of the reported their skin color as Brown, 46 percent and their race as

Table 3.6 Students self reported skin color, University of Illinois, 1945–1955

	Percent	Frequency
Black	10.8	38
Very Black	0.2	1
Brown	46.4	162
Brown Skin	0.8	3
Light Brown	4.0	14
Medium Brown	1.1	4
Dark Brown	3.1	11
Colored	6.8	24
Color	0.2	1
Fair	0.2	2
Light	2.0	7
Medium	0.2	1
Dark	2.0	7
Copper	0.2	1
Olive	0.5	2
Tan	0.5	2
Negro	12.0	42
Negroid	0.2	1
White	0.5	2
Not Listed	6.8	24
Total	100.0	349

Source: Student Employment Folders Series 41/4/5. The total represents the total number of students that reported color on the employment records.

"Negro." This time period was directly following a time when "colored" was the preferred term. Another interesting finding from the table is the number of people who considered "Negro" to be a color. It is plausible to assume that many African American students did consider it a color because of the Spanish origins of the word. Finally the third highest response for African American student skin color, is Black. The data here are very revealing about the changing tides of skin color and racial designation. The use of the word "Negro" follows the word "colored" and precedes the word "Black" by several years. Table 3.7 displays a small percentage of the African American student population utilizing the outdated "colored" or the word "Black."

Housing Issues for African American Students

At UIUC, housing would become a long battle for the students as well as for the African American community. The inequities related to housing coupled with the racial discrimination that occurred resulted

Table 3.7 Students self reported race, University of Illinois, 1945–1955

	Percent	Frequency
African	0.5	2
Afro-American	0.2	1
American	1.7	7
Am. of African Descent	0.2	1
Black	0.2	1
Colored	2.0	8
Indian-Negro	0.2	1
Indian Irish Negro	0.2	1
Indian White Negro	0.5	2
Irish-Dutch	0.2	1
Irish	0.2	1
Latin American	0.2	1
Mixed	0.2	1
Mulatto	0.2	1
Negro-American Indian	0.2	1
Negro-Brown	0.2	1
Negro-Indian-French	0.2	1
Negro	82.6	325
Negroid	3.3	13
Portuguese	0.2	1
Swedish	0.2	1
White	0.2	1
Not Listed	5.0	20
Total	100.0	393

Source: Student Employment Folders Series 41/4/5. The total represents the total number of students that reported color on the employment records.

in the development of a community network that included UIUC African American students and the African American community. Many members of the community opened their homes to students. According to the Champaign County Housing Authority survey, "110 out of 587 Negro dwelling units were occupied by more than one family group or had lodgers, although 67% had only 1 or 2 bedrooms."[28] During the academic school year 1929–1930, there were 138 African American students, 66 of who had room only and not board, and the remaining 72 received room and board from local African American residents.[29] On woman remembers that,

> we were all poor but the students were poor too. They weren't used to living any better than what they were when they came here. We fed them. I don't think anybody made any money off them but usually if they roomed with us they would eat whatever we would eat, they

would come in, we were eating, and they would eat. We didn't make any money but they were nice and they were good company and they were like family, we took them in as part of the family.[30]

In addition to providing meals for students in their homes, one woman made sure that many African Americans ate through their job. Mrs. Gray was the house manager at the white greek house Alpha Chi, and remembers hiring all African American men to work there. Her rationale was to provide them with a place to eat. As a part of payment they were allowed to eat their meals there. They worked as service and bus boys. At the end of the evening instead of throwing away uneaten food, Mrs. Gray would tell the gentlemen to take the food with them, and feed those that did not have the opportunity to have a meal service job.[31] This was just one of many ways African Americans subverted the forms of discrimination faced in everyday life. This opportunity could have only existed due to the close relationship between the campus and community.

Along with the African American students, African American community members were expected to live in restricted residential areas. A study conducted by the League of Women Voters of Champaign County in 1946 indicated that housing for African Americans was a total disgrace.[32] Many families lived in shacks with no indoor plumbing and had to use outdoor privies. In most cases these privies were very unsanitary and caused many people to contract communicable diseases, such as tuberculosis. Furthermore the shacks' people were living in were previously coal bins.[33]

It is very important to note that many African Americans living in these conditions were able to afford better housing. For example, one woman was reported as saying that her husband made $40 a week and that they were able to live elsewhere, and still have enough money left over for livelihood. Despite having the means to afford better, racial discrimination by the city Realtors and landlords prevented them from finding better housing.[34] As a result, they were forced to live in a racially segregated and impoverished residential area, despite their economic capability to maintain a household in a more inhabitable environment. The housing condition for African Americans in the community affected the majority of Black students, because many of them had to live in the community. To a lesser extent there were Black students who lived in fraternity and sorority housing and others who lived in dormitories.

Many of the homes in the African American community were substandard and considered dangerous to live in, including a lack of indoor plumbing, no toilets, one bedroom to accommodate several people, transformed coal bins and shacks in areas with no sidewalks. These conditions were due to a lack of concern on the part of the city as well as the racism present within the Champaign-Urbana areas. Many of these homes were considered to be health hazards to the residents and the rest of the area. All these factors contributed to the unsanitary conditions present within the African American community. Although the Public Health District "has the authority to condemn dwellings, but considers it impossible to exercise this authority when there is no other place for people to move."[35] Consequently, it was virtually impossibly for African Americans to live outside of this area. This was due in part, if not wholly, to the racially restrictive covenants. It was clearly stated that various properties were not available "to be occupied as owner or tenants by any person not of the Caucasian race."[36] Long time African American residents of this community understood this arrangement, despite their disapproval of it.

As the enrollment of African American students increased, after World War II, so did their housing needs. When a student was admitted to the university it was without the promise of housing. Despite small and cramped accommodations, the community and students made the best of the situation and it became mutually agreeable. The early generation of African American students at Illinois owed a lot to the African American community of Champaign and to Lee. Lee was responsible for making the initial contact between students and potential renters.[37] This informal arrangement lasted for several decades.[38]

Lee would identify members of the African American community that were willing to rent to students. After potential renters were contacted in person and by mail, concerning the possibility of taking in boarders, Lee would compile a list of available housing for new students. Once an African American student decided to attend the university, Lee would provide the student with the housing list and allow them to choose their place of residence. In many cases Lee corresponded with the parents and they requested that he make contact with the potential renter and secure housing for their children, sight unseen. Moreover, Lee would often check on students and send letters to their parents informing them of their children's situation. Many parents responded very positively toward this practice.[39]

Parents and the university were pleased with Lee's work. In fact both entities relied heavily on his assistance over the years. Several meetings and planning sessions with African American students and the community took place concerning the topic of housing. Lee was again at the forefront of addressing the housing situation of African American students. Students and community members met at Lee's church, Bethel African Methodist Episcopal Church (A.M.E.), to discuss strategies in combating the injustice that faced students in housing as well other issues concerning discrimination. The church would be the site for other debates as well. During these meetings minutes were taken and placed in the church file.[40]

> Bethel church was one of the two Negro churches in town and I must say the popular. Students came here all the time and not only to worship. Bethel was a second home. I mean, the students could not go anywhere else. There was a group called Lyceum and they held programs on Sundays, lectures, discussions, and all the students would come here and we would too.[41]

One individual remembers a room at the church called the "Black room." She reported the following:

> The Black room was up in the old deck of the church and they had all of these books for students to come and study, and so they set up study periods and study tines because the students at that time really couldn't go to much on campus to study, so they had study periods, they had Friday night classes for them, and you had to obtain a certain level before you were even allowed upstairs. You know that was for the students that were in high regard. They had a lady who graduated from Tennessee State, Mrs. Martin, who was a scholarly kind of person. You did the elocution kinds of things, we did all those things at that time and we—education was in high regard.[42]

The community commitment to excellence and achievement was exemplary. African Americans were dedicated to the success of the students, and they were willing to participate in spite of the racialized conditions of Champaign-Urbana. Although students were not allowed to eat, live, or interact on campus, the community rallied behind them to support them within the community to ensure academic success and stability.

Academic Achievement

The tables included in this section discuss the characteristics of African Americans who graduated from UIUC. In letters written to Albert Lee, parents asked for his assistance in helping their children to find a "place" in the local African American community. His assistance aided students in a variety of ways, and successful academic achievement was only one of them. For those students that did not complete their degree, their time spent and contributions made in and around the university community were recognized as a sustaining force for all African American students.

Table 3.8 displays the graduation status of African American students by gender. Men out number women in their enrollment as well as graduation rates. There was a total of 774 students with graduation information on their transcripts and of those students 451 graduated and within that number 31.5 percent were women and 68.5 percent were men. During this ten-year time period men graduated at twice the rate of women. Of these graduates table 3.9 displays their marital status. Overwhelmingly most students were single; however, more men than women were married. This is a very critical point of comparison. Living in the Champaign-Urban area in the postwar years men were older and more likely than women to be married. This information sheds a new light on the issue of discrimination at this time. Aside from many men having served in the war and enrolling in college they may have had a family to support. Hence the discrimination that many of them faced was felt not only individually but by their families as well.

Table 3.8 Graduation status of students by gender, University of Illinois, 1945–1955

	Female		Male		Total	
	%	n	%	n	%	n
No	37.5	121	62.5	202	41.7	323
Yes	31.5	142	68.5	309	58.3	451
Total	34.0	263	66.0	511	100.0	774

Source: Student Transcripts, Series 25/3/4, University of Illinois Archives. The number 774 represents those students that had graduation information reported on their transcripts.

Table 3.9 Marital status of graduates, University of Illinois, 1945–1955

	Female		Male	
	%	n	%	n
Single	66	104	63	217
Married	40	5	73	55
Total		109		278

Source: Student Transcripts Series 25/3/4, Student Employment Folders, Series 41/4/5, University of Illinois Archives. The number 109 and 278 represents the total number of female and male students who reported marital status on their employment folder and had graduation information on their transcripts.

Additionally, these male students returning from the war were at a greater distance from the social and academic scene at the university. Many of the veterans were much older than the traditional college age students, therefore bringing a different level of maturity to campus. It was clear in many instances the veterans were at the forefront of racial equality advocacy. In terms of academics they lagged somewhat behind their peers, as the GI Bill offered many of them college access, even if they were not adequately prepared to enter college.

Table 3.10 presents the total distribution of graduates within academic fields. LAS General has a significant representation of African American students that graduated, followed by Education and then Engineering. The total number is small overall; however, it is highly suggestive of a pattern of academic stability. This data when examined within the context of a Jim Crow town and gown clearly demonstrates the stability of academic achievement in spite of discrimination.

Although men graduated at a disproportionately higher rate than women did, when the two groups are compared, the results are revealing. The data suggests that female graduates enrolled at the University of Illinois with a high school percentile rank of 84 compared with a male high school percentile rank of 69. This figure represents an average over a ten-year period. This data suggests that long before

Table 3.10 Total distribution of graduates within academic field, University of Illinois, 1945–1955

	%	n
Agriculture	2.4	9
Ag./Home Econ.	2.6	10
Com./Business	1.3	5
Communications	1.3	5
Education	14.5	55
Engineering	11.6	44
FAA	7.7	29
LAS/General	37.5	142
Life Sciences	1.1	4
Physical Sciences	3.2	12
Social Sciences	2.4	9
Humanities	1.1	4
Medicine	8.2	31
LIR	0.8	3
Library Sciences	0.5	2
Law	4.0	15
Total	100.0	379

Source: Student Transcripts Series, 25/3/4. The total 379 represents the total number of students that had curriculum and graduation information on their transcript.

Affirmative Action there was a record of successful academic achievement for African American students. This point may be viewed as controversial; however, it is clear that African American students were entering the University of Illinois with high marks during the pre-civil rights movement era. This in fact is critical when addressing issues related to academic achievement, one may ponder whether or not the sustaining communities contributed to the success of African American students in this era.

African American students maintained a relatively consistent grade point average over the ten-year period. Table 3.11 presents the overall distribution of grade point averages in relation to parental occupational field. The grade point average is based on a 5.0 scale. With the exception of African American women, with at least one parent in farming, the grade point averages are in the "C" range. There were three women with a parent in farming and their grade point average was 4.0. The sample is too small to make an assumption based on the relationship between farming occupations and academic achievement.

In essence African American students at the University of Illinois experienced varying forms of discrimination. As their enrollment trends increased, so did the discriminatory acts they faced. These students attended school under very antagonistic conditions. Having to find a place to eat and live miles from campus, not being allowed to sit in adequate seats in theaters, or get haircuts without discrimination, to name only a few instances of discrimination, were the harsh conditions they had to live under. These various acts of discrimination had an impact on the educational and social environment of these

Table 3.11 Final GPA of students by parental occupational field, University of Illinois, 1945–1955

	Total		Female		Male	
	GPA	n	GPA	n	GPA	n
Managerial, Professional	3.36	64	3.41	23	3.36	39
Technical, Sales, Adm.	3.24	59	3.46	19	3.14	40
Service	3.34	52	3.45	14	3.03	38
Farming	3.41	14	4.02	3	3.23	10
Precision, Production, Repair	3.37	45	3.41	11	3.36	34
Operators, Laborers	3.27	54	3.11	17	3.35	37
Military	3.00	1	0	0	3.00	1
Total	3.32	289	3.39	87	3.29	199

Source: Student Transcripts, Series 25/3/4 and Student Employment Folders, Series 41/4/5, University of Illinois Archives. The number 289 represents the total number of students that reported parental occupation on their employment folder and had grade point average information on their transcript.

students. Although the social impact was negative, a great number of students accomplished their goals.

The data presented here suggests that African American students were highly motivated to achieve. Their exceptional graduation rates, representation in academic fields and ten-year academic stability indicates that African American students were exemplary in spite of racially hostile circumstances.

Conclusion

UIUC represented an institution of higher learning situated in the "liberal' North, a place that was perceived as some how different from the Jim Crow South. The whole notion of liberalism when applied to the University of Illinois seems a bit bizarre. The term is often loosely used, but it actually does have meaning in the context of higher education in the North generally and specifically at the University of Illinois. Liberalism is an ideal that supposedly positions itself in such a way that it promotes liberty and the pursuits of that liberty. Although those responsible for the notion of liberalism forgot to mention the key element, pursuit of liberty as long as your liberty does not infringe upon mine. The North was not the free place that many expected it to be, in fact it was very much similar to Jim Crow South, full of racism and hatred. The difference was that if anything the North was more genteel. However, what students encountered here was very much the same forms of segregation their Southern counterparts experienced. Despite time spent serving their country, and devoting time to studies so they could compete academically at the university, those things meant nothing. African American students would not be able to change the view of whites in and around the university. The liberal thing to do was to allow African Americans to attend schools in the North that were not segregated by law. Eating in a segregated section of a restaurant or sitting in a special section of a movie theater was considered very liberal. These were freedoms and privileges that Southern African Americans were not afforded. Liberals believed very much in the notion of education, because that brings about a better society, but how far is one to go in education and how that individual will be treated once admitted to an institution of higher learning is a very different question. It was never a question of access to higher education but more appropriately a question of treatment while in higher education. After all African Americans were admitted to the University of Illinois, that in and of itself was a very liberal ideal.

It is apparent from the information provided here, that African Americans were discriminated against in all aspects of their lives.

These students attended school under hostile and difficult living conditions. It was not until 1941, with the help of Albert R. Lee that African American students were allowed to dine on campus. Lee wrote to the president of the university and explained the hardship that African American students endured due to the lack of eating facilities available to African Americans. The year the Illini Union was built, and African American students were allowed to eat there.[43]

The cohorts of University of Illinois African American students changed every four to five years. However, patterns of contending with difficulties, stability and continuity were provided by the ongoing presence of Albert R. Lee, African American elected officials, Interracial Committee, some university officials, and by the Champaign African American community. These individuals were the backbone to the growth and development of the students during the days of segregation.

Liberalism was not about changing the views of a white dominated society. It was more about contending with a group of people that now coexisted with the larger society and considering what to do with them. Liberals believed in education, and the power of that education to transform society, one that was very separate and very unequal. When reflecting on the comments made concerning the importance of the Black Alumni and Ex-Student Project, those liberal ideals come to mind. The purpose of this project was to develop a network of African American students so that future, current and past students have a way to connect and provide financial assistance, encouragement, and information for people within their group. That is a very liberal ideal and one that does not infringe upon the larger society to play a role.

The complexity of African American student life at the University of Illinois was very difficult to comprehend, if it was examined in the context of education above the Mason-Dixon Line. These students lived in an area that was perceived liberal, but in actuality a place where racism was of the most dangerous form. Living in the South provided African Americans with a set of guidelines by which to live. Racism, Jim Crow laws and lynching made it plain. Indeed there was a set of rules that applied to African Americans, and policies that called for equal treatment and protection under the law. Unfortunately students at the university rarely had the privilege of being treated fairly or as first-class citizens. They lived by the Jim Crow laws of the North, a set of laws that boasted the inferiority of African Americans.

In spite of these less than comfortable surroundings veiled with discrimination, African American students were able to succeed. The 58.3 percent graduation rate tells a remarkable story. These students were able to achieve success. African American students came with a determination to succeed and left well prepared to serve in their professions. Although many of the students came from working-class backgrounds, their career aspirations far exceeded the occupations of their parents. These students were involved in a variety of academic fields. Many students became doctors, lawyers, scientists, and educators. They did believe in giving back to their community, which is evidenced by their bonds with each other and the fact that many of them returned to the communities that produced them, in addition to maintaining contact with some of the families that cared for them while attending the UIUC.

It is very important to recognize the importance of the Black community in the lives of African American students. The kind of segregation that existed created a sense of community that was not all bad. In fact it was one where there was a strong sense of family, community and a place to fit in, in essence a nurturing environment. African American students lived with families, ate with them, attended church with them, they were family. It was that sense of family that sustained them during their academic years at the university. In a town steeped with racism and discrimination emerged a class of African American students that graduated from the university at remarkable rates in spite of the segregationist traditions. That is the contradictory side of Jim Crow.

Jim Crow and the crucible of excellence was the theme from African American students in the postwar years. Students did not have any other alternatives but to be an active part of the community, as it was all that was available to them. This phenomenon created community student relationships that were shaped and refined in spite of the insidious nature of racism. Race and racism operated as an organizing principle in the lives of African American students.

The strange career of Jim Crow may have impeded them but it did not stop them. The isolation that existed for these students was difficult to comprehend. African American students for several years represented less than 1 percent of the total student population. During the postwar years, specifically 1945–1955, in any given year there was an average of 140 students that encountered Jim Crow laws of the North. It is difficult to imagine having attended school without the negative influences around them, but without the racism, perhaps their graduation rates would have been even more impressive. Despite the less than pleasant or inviting instances, African American students were able to matriculate, persevere, and achieve, under extremely rigid segregation.

The most puzzling aspect of their experiences is the loyalty that exists between the students and the university. The people that were interviewed were very candid in their discussions and vivid in their recollections, but despite the obvious denial of equality these students in addition to a group who refers to themselves as the FBI (Fifties Black Alumni), still hold strong loyalty to the university. This is not to say that there are those who have placed the university years behind them and care not to revisit the memories. There are still those that are inextricably linked to the University of Illinois. One has to wonder whether it is a blind loyalty or one that grew in the face of adversity. Adversity is often known to make the heart grow fonder and the idea of succeeding in an institution such as the University of Illinois is enough to foster a sense of pride and loyalty, not so much to the institution but to those coming after them. The final analysis of the university's history of African American students can be best summed up as a rewarding experience. Lessons in the fundamentals of surviving the intricacies of racism and discrimination and leaving with what most would consider an excellent education and perhaps an even better experience in the reality of a racialized society. Regardless of their high school rank, grade point average, intellect or character, they could not eat in local restaurants, see a movie without discrimination or live in campus residence halls. Academic excellence and social inequality were the pillars of their experience at UIUC.

Notes

1. James D. Anderson, *The Education of Blacks in the South, 1860–1935* (Chapel Hill: University of North Carolina Press, 1988), 164.
2. Linda M. Perkins, "The Impact of the 'Cult of True Womanhood' on the Education of Black Women," *Journal of Social Issues* 39, 3 (1983): 18.
3. Jeanne L. Noble, "Negro Women Today and Their Education," *The Journal of Negro Education* 26, 1 (Winter 1957): 17.
4. Rosalyn Terborg-Penn, "Discrimination Against Afro-American Women In The Women's Movement, 1830–1920," Sharon Harley and Rosalyn Terborg-Penn, eds., *The Afro American Woman On Race And Sex In America* (Port Washington: Kennikat Press, 1978), 21.
5. Winton U. Solberg, *The University of Illinois, 1867–1894: An Intellectual and Cultural History* (Urbana: University of Illinois Press, 1968), 57. See U. S. Statutes at Large, 37 Cong., 2 Sess. (1861–1862), chs. 130, 504 on that page.
6. "The University of Illinois Negro Students: Location, History and Administration," President Arthur Cutts Willard Papers, General Correspondence 1934–1946, Record Series 2/9/1, Box 42 (Folder "Colored Students of Illinois"), University of Illinois Archives, Urbana, Illinois.

7. "The University of Illinois Negro Students Location, History and Administration," President A.C. Willard Papers, Record Series 2/9/1 Box 42, University of Illinois Archives, Urbana, Illinois.
8. "The University of Illinois Negro Students Location, History and Administration," Willard Papers.
9. "Negro Students at the University of Illinois, An Outline of Their enrollment, Graduates, Activities, History, Living conditions," Willard papers, Box 2.
10. Brisbane Rouzan, unpublished chapter.
11. Lucy J. Gray, interview by author, tape recording, Champaign, Illinois, June 12, 1997, "He was the Dean of Negro students."
12. Lucy J. Gray, interview.
13. L.C. Hamilton to Albert R. Lee, September 20, 1922, Albert R. Lee Papers, Record Series 2/6/21, Box 1, University of Illinois Archives, Urbana, Illinois.
14. Lee to Mrs. Harrier Anderson, January 7, 1928, Lee Papers.
15. Lee to Ollie Brown, August 31, 1928, Albert R. Lee, 1912, 1917–1928, Series 2/6/21, Box 1 (Folder "Personal, Financial, University and Eastern Star"), University of Illinois Archives, Urbana, Illinois.
16. "Negro Matriculants List," 1919–1937, Lee Papers.
17. *Crisis.*
18. A.R. Lee to W.E.B. DuBois, June 13, 1927, Lee Papers.
19. "Memorandum in Re Compilation of Names of Negro Students Who Have Attended the University of Illinois During the Past Fifty Years," Arthur C. Willard Papers, Record Series 2/9/16, Box 1, University of Illinois Archives, Urbana, Illinois.
20. "Memorandum in Re Compilation of Names of Negro Students Who Have Attended the University of Illinois During The Past Fifty Years," Willard Papers, Box 1.
21. "*Illinois Alumni News*, 'Project Seeking Negro Alumni To Aid Students,' " Black Alumni and Ex-Student Project File, 1967–1973, Series 35/5/50, Box 1, University of Illinois Archives, Champaign, Illinois.
22 "Meeting Notes, 10/14/68," Black Alumni Ex-Student Project File, 1967–1973, Series 35/3/50, University of Illinois Archives, Urbana, Illinois.
23. Maynard Brichford to Jack W. Petalson, 30 October 1968, Black Alumni Ex-Student Project File, 1967–1973, Series 35/3/50, University of Illinois, Urbana, Illinois.
24. Field Note, November 12, 1968, Black Alumni and Ex-Student Project File, 1967–1973, Series 35/3/50, University of Illinois Archives, Urbana, Illinois.
25. Field Note, November 12, 1968, Black Alumni and Ex-Student Project File, 1967–1973, Series 35/3/50, University of Illinois Archives, Urbana, Illinois.

26. Maynard Brichford to James Vermette, Black Alumni and Ex-Student Project File, 1967–1973, Series 35/3/50, University of Illinois Archives, Urbana, Illinois.
27. "Untitled List of Procedures for Data Collection," Black Alumni and Ex-Student Project File, 1967–1973, Series 35/3/50, University of Illinois Archives, Urbana, Illinois.
28. "A Community Report" League of Women Voters, Champaign County, 1946–1948, YWCA Subject File, 1906—Anniversary Tea—Policy Statement, 1930–1971, Record Series 41/69/331, Box 34, University of Illinois Archives, Urbana, Illinois.
29. "Boarding and Housing Conditions of Colored Students of the University Of Illinois, 1929–1930," Dean of Students, Dean of women Subject File.
30. Lucy J. Gray, interview.
31. Lucy J. Gray, interview.
32. "A Community Report" League of Women Voters.
33. "A Community Report" League of Women Voters, Champaign County 1946–1948, YWCA Subject File.
34. "A Community Report" League of Women Voters.
35. "A Community Report" League of Women Voters.
36. "A Community Report" League of Women Voters.
37. Lee to Richards, July 22, 1920, Lee Papers.
38. "A. R. Lee general Correspondence," Lee Papers.
39. Edward Jacobs to Lee, August 17, 1928, Lee Papers.
40. "University of Illinois Presidents I Have Known," Lee Papers.
41. Lucy J. Gray, interview.
42. Hester Suggs, interview by author, tape recording, Champaign, Illinois, October 14, 1996.
43. "History of SCIC, 1945–1951," Tiebout Papers.

Chapter 4

From Isolation to Imagined Communities of LGBT School Workers: Activism in the 1970s

Jackie M. Blount

These days, one effective way to shatter the notion that schools are cohesive, friendly, trouble-free, and even family-like entities is to confront them with lesbian, gay, bisexual, and transgender (LGBT) issues, particularly those faced everyday by LGBT school workers and students. Once relegated to the margins or deemed as other schools' problems, today *all* schools must wrestle with a wide variety of issues concerning sexual identity and/or gender presentation. Should two young women be punished for kissing—purportedly because it causes a disruption—while male/female couples kiss with no administrative attention? What should teachers and school administrators do when they learn that students are harassing others on the basis of supposed sexual or gender identity? Will school officials support a teacher who includes LGBT-themed materials in the curriculum, especially when vocal parents complain? Will the school board seek dismissal of a school worker who undergoes sex-change surgery? Will parents and fellow teachers welcome the news when a colleague "comes out"? Will children of lesbian and gay couples be treated with respect by teachers and other students—or, as recently was the case, will a young student be punished for mentioning that his mothers are "gay"? Will teachers work as respectfully with parents who identify as LGBT as they do with those who appear heterosexual? Will high schools not only tolerate, but also celebrate students who attend school-sponsored functions with their same-sex dates? Will schools ever fully welcome females who pursue traditionally male activities, classes, or fashions? Or males who seek those usually reserved for females?

The contentiousness that usually surrounds such issues reveals deep schisms in social understandings of what it means to be women and men. It also suggests the powerful role that schools play in regulating the sexuality and gender of their charges. Though not explicitly tasked with assuring the normative heterosexuality and gender conformity of students, school workers face serious conflict when their actions—or identities—run afoul of such tacit expectations.

Although schools long have been expected to influence the normative gender and sexual development of youth, this typically unspoken demand became particularly explicit during the 1970s. During this tumultuous decade, scattered media reports of a gay riot in Greenwich Village eventually became the stuff of legend as a grass-roots gay liberation movement grew in its wake. Self-identified LGBT persons around the country, but particularly in urban areas, organized a series of events that rapidly thrust the nascent movement into the public eye. LGBT school workers, too, sought to increase their visibility; however, the emergence of this specific group sparked a powerful backlash movement among religious and political conservatives who wished to quash what they regarded as a concerted effort among militant homosexual teachers to corrupt the nation's youth. Throughout the 1970s, they conjured notions of community for rhetorical effect and political impact. The emotions aroused in these often-bitter exchanges galvanized otherwise motley and unconnected individuals into cohesive groups united by their animus for the foes they imagined.

In this chapter, I explore notions of community that surfaced during early gay liberation era skirmishes over the rights of LGBT school workers. I begin by describing the Cold War contexts in which the larger movement emerged. Then I highlight the individual and then collective efforts of LGBT school workers to confront discriminatory school policies and practices. Finally, I examine the degree to which "community" existed among LGBT school workers during these pitched battles.

Cold War Contexts

As World War II drew to a close, men and women desiring others of the same sex gravitated to growing homosexual enclaves in urban areas around the country. War-related industries and military installations created de facto homosocial environments as men lived and worked for long stretches with other men, and women with women. Although military recruiters instituted screening mechanisms intended to weed out homosexuals, potential enlistees found these procedures, which included asking about recruits' sexual habits and watching their mannerisms, relatively easy to circumvent. Consequently, untold numbers of men and women who desired others of the same sex found themselves in close proximity to many others like themselves. In his seminal work on the rise of homosexual communities in the United States, John D'Emilio describes how eventually a variety of establishments catered to what had become a critical mass of persons desiring others of the same sex. Mutual recognition and these new and relatively safe spaces helped foster what D'Emilio and Freedman have called a nationwide "coming out" experience.[1]

Then in 1948, when Kinsey and his research team published their landmark study, *Sexual Behavior in the Human Male*, not only did public awareness of a range of sexualities increase, but also in particular, the unexpectedly high incidence of same-sex desire and behavior among men captivated the attention of many. The study frankly reported that nearly half of the adult male population indicated some degree of arousal in connection with other men. Of these, many had reached orgasm with other men. Kinsey carefully avoided calling such individuals homosexual, opting instead to place their activities along a continuum of sexual experiences ranging from exclusively heterosexual to exclusively homosexual.[2] The 1953 volume, *Sexual Behavior in the Human Female*, similarly described a higher than expected incidence of same-sex desire and behaviors among women, though not as high as for men. Although initial reaction to these widely discussed studies was positive, critics soon attacked Kinsey and his team purportedly for *promoting*, rather than merely *describing*, same-sex sexual behavior. And in an increasingly fearful and polarized Cold War climate where Communist enemies supposedly lurked in the shadows, ready to infiltrate the weak and unprepared, homosexuals quickly became nearly as feared.

Throughout the 1950s and 1960s, hostilities directed at homosexuals increased dramatically. Sodomy laws changed so that they applied specifically to homosexual activity.[3] California required law enforcement officials to notify school administrators of any teachers arrested on morals charges, which often happened during stakeouts of public washrooms. Police frequently raided gay bars, arresting patrons present, particularly those who cross-dressed. In Idaho and Florida, extensive and very public investigations pressured supposed homosexuals for the names of others until sizeable numbers could be identified. The Florida Legislative Investigation Committee, after several years of work and the close investigation of many public school teachers and university professors, announced that the state finally was free of homosexuals in sensitive instructional positions. Around the country, individuals identified as homosexuals, regardless of the truth or the relevance of such charges to their professional efforts, typically lost their jobs immediately. Some disappeared to start new lives elsewhere. In places such as Sioux City, Iowa, officials incarcerated some in mental institutions. And a few committed suicide rather than face the enormous social consequences that accompanied supposedly homosexual identity at the time.

A few individuals began organizing small groups to support and affirm homosexuality in this chilly climate. In California, organizations such as the Daughters of Bilitis, the Mattachine Society, and One held regular meetings announced through word-of-mouth networks. Members published newsletters filled with pseudonyms— and recipients cautiously circulated their copies among their most trusted friends. Membership in these groups, while important because of the intellectual, leadership, and organizational work done, remained quite small, numbering from a few handfuls to hundreds by the mid-1960s. The overwhelming majority of persons who desired others of the same sex did not dare join such organizations for fear of discovery, job loss, social sanction, and arrest. Many such men and women lived daily with the terror that a trusted friend, a suspicious acquaintance, or a slip of the tongue would reveal one's homosexual identity. Rather than organize, women and men who desired others of the same sex chose their friends carefully. They developed elaborate means of disguising their desires/identities such as adopting conventional dress and mastering the art of pronoun switching as they described their romantic attachments. In addition, they studiously avoided other social contact with persons who might place them at risk. Most proved so adept at such deception that years later, long time coworkers would be surprised to learn of each other's homosexual identities. Although community may have existed among small clusters of friends, clientele of certain establishments such as bars, or members of rare "homophile," or homosexuality-affirming organizations, efforts at bringing together persons desiring others of the same sex were fraught with terrible dangers that most simply avoided.

It is against this backdrop of continual harassment by police, discrimination in the workplace, and constant fear of discovery that the patrons of the Stonewall Inn in Greenwich Village believed they had endured enough. In June of 1969, police attempted one of their usual raids of suspected homosexual haunts. Instead of acquiescence, however, the bar's patrons resisted aggressively, pelting police with anything that could be thrown. When officers called in reinforcements, the rapidly growing crow greeted them with taunts and chants for "Gay Power." The underground press published extensive coverage of this groundbreaking spectacle, announcing that indeed, some new spirit of resistance seemed to have emerged. The Stonewall rebellion would grow in significance in the years to come as it increasingly symbolized a shift from accepting the oppression of homosexuals toward actively resisting it. Annual parades would mark the event as pivotal in the emergence of a gay liberation movement.

LGBT School Workers in the 1970s

It is in this context that a small number of self-identified lesbian and gay school workers began to work toward improved conditions for LGBT persons in schools. In 1969, Morgan Pinney and some students from San Francisco State University lobbied the California Federation of Teachers to support what may have been the first organizational resolution on behalf of homosexual teachers. Initially, some of the 250 delegates in attendance were incredulous at the boldness of the resolution—and a few snickered. However, Pinney proceeded to explain that "homosexuals are harassed and intimidated by the police," and that "the government's anti-homosexual policies set the tone of homosexual oppression as national policy." Worse still, he argued, was the consequent self-loathing that many homosexuals developed. To the surprise of many, Pinney's remarks garnered a standing ovation and overwhelming support for the resolution, which then passed.[4] This influential organization later would prove vital in the effort to protect the rights of LGBT school workers.

In the spirit of Pinney's courageous bid for support, John Gish, a high school English teacher in New Jersey, organized the Gay Teachers Caucus of the NEA right before the 1972 Representative Assembly. Prior to this, Gish had assumed important leadership in the New Jersey Gay Activists Alliance (GAA). In this work, he had developed deep knowledge of the tenets of gay liberation. He also had demonstrated particular organizational and leadership gifts, all of which would be necessary in the months ahead as his activism shifted from the GAA to fighting specifically for the rights of lesbian and gay teachers. He believed that organizing the NEA's Gay Teachers Caucus made sense. Despite his efforts, however, Gish and the Caucus could not persuade the NEA Representative Assembly to pass a resolution supporting the rights of lesbian and gay teachers that year.

When Gish returned to his job that fall, his school board ordered him to undergo psychiatric examination—and they assigned him an administrative, "make-work" job in the central office where he had no contact with students. For the remainder of the 1970s, Gish pursued a lengthy legal battle eventually joined by the NEA after it finally passed a resolution in support of lesbian and gay teachers in 1974. The networks that Gish had managed to create proved central in his high-profile legal defense. In the end, however, he would not be allowed to resume his teaching position, even though his case resulted in expanded rights for all lesbian, gay, and bisexual teachers.[5] Through the years, the Gay Teachers Caucus of the NEA would serve as a steady, ongoing national voice in the larger effort to support the rights of LGBT school workers.

Shortly after the NEA passed its resolution adding sexual orientation to its nondiscrimination policy, a small group of teachers in New York City who, like Gish, had worked in the gay liberation movement, organized what may have been the first local association for LGBT school workers. After placing an ad in the *Village Voice* announcing a meeting of gay and lesbian teachers, over four dozen people came to the first meeting, many more than organizers had anticipated. The lesbian and gay cochairs of this new organization, dubbed the Gay Teachers Association, quickly demonstrated impressive leadership abilities. In short order, the Gay Teachers Association successfully agitated for political gains in the New York City schools and teachers union, educated members about their unique circumstances and issues, and reduced the social isolation that such educators routinely experienced. As further testament to the vision possessed by early members, the Gay Teachers Association consciously sought to avoid the "political factionalism," "power struggles," and "women/men discord that has struck so many other sexually integrated gay organizations," as one early leader wrote in a retrospective newsletter article. Lesbian and gay teacher organizations typically stumbled around gender issues and many eventually segregated.

An issue of prime importance to LGBT educators at the time was, not surprisingly, secrecy. The Gay Teachers Association needed to address this powerful concern to expand membership. Consequently, meeting announcements prominently carried the reassuring message: "closet rights respected." Marc Rubin, one of the first cochairs, explained the problem:

> Gay teachers are, on the whole, an incredibly paranoid group of people. Smeared for years by the pre-Stonewall image of gays, and feeling intensely vulnerable to the vicious myth of child molestation, now masquerading under the more sophisticated label of "undesirable role model" or "threat to the family," most of the gay teachers that we have met are simply afraid that they will lose their jobs if *anyone* finds out their secret. We still have people who are afraid to be on our mailing list. Three-quarters of the teachers who call us, ask for information, and say they will come to our meetings, never appear.[6]

One of the most powerful gestures that members of the Gay Teachers Association could make was to "come out" in their districts and the city. For years, members of the Association marched in the annual Christopher Street parade with a large banner that read, "Gay Teachers Association—New York City." Rubin explained that this proclaimed, "not only that there are gay teachers, but that there are gay teachers who stand proud and united with their gay sisters and brothers. That, in itself, is our most powerful political statement."[7]

In 1975, a year after New York City teachers organized the Gay Teachers Association, several teachers in San Francisco started the Gay Teachers and School Workers Coalition. One teacher, fresh with inspiration from having watched a Christopher Street West parade, decided that the time had come for such a group. For their first action, they planned a demonstration at the next San Francisco Board of Education meeting to pressure members to pass a resolution to include sexual orientation in the district's nondiscrimination policy. The raucous and sizable crowd that rallied outside an hour before the meeting then filed inside loudly chanting and singing "When the Gays Go Marching In." Board members, stunned both by the overwhelming numbers of demonstrators as well as by their display, addressed the crowd with politeness and deference. Then after one board member recounted the story of how some high school students had started a "queer hunters club" whose members eventually murdered a suspected gay teacher, the board approved without dissent the inclusion of sexual orientation in the district's nondiscrimination ordinance Immediately, the crowd exploded into cheers and two minutes of applause.[8]

Among other actions, members of the Gay Teachers and Schoolworkers Coalition also marched in gay pride parades. One teacher described her experience, "There I was marching down Market Street carrying a giant red-apple, support gay teachers banner and hundreds of people clapped and shouted their support! It would be impossible to explain the feeling that filled my insides as I walked that one mile but I know that it was entirely new."[9]

LGBT educators in other cities quickly followed the examples of the New York and San Francisco groups. One year after the San Francisco school board added sexual orientation to the district's nondiscrimination policy, teachers in Los Angeles met to consider forming their own organization. The small group of eight quickly grew in number and influence.[10] Soon the Gay Teachers of Los Angeles had managed a delicate balance of social and political functions. Several members were elected to the House of Representatives of their local union. They successfully pushed for a resolution that added sexual orientation to the union's nondiscrimination statement, winning 95 percent of the vote. Through parties, potlucks, and marches in gay pride parades, word of the organization spread—and the newsletter proudly boasted of a rapidly swelling membership roster.[11]

A year after the Gay Teachers of Los Angeles organized, teachers in Boston and Philadelphia quickly followed suit. Soon, organizations of LGBT educators had sprouted around the country in places such as Denver, Oregon, Texas, and Maryland. These groups revolved around several main activities. First, each organized a number of social functions because lesbian and gay school workers otherwise reported feelings of deep and ongoing isolation. Thus, these associations offered some semblance of community. Second, each engaged in political strategizing and activism geared toward increasing the rights of LGBT school workers. Third, each endeavored to educate their colleagues and school districts about issues confronting LGBT school workers. All three aims were accomplished when these organizations of LGBT school workers formed a visible unit in their local gay pride parades. Marchers uniformly reported their feelings of exhilaration at becoming visible—and thereby contradicting their isolation, by being part of a group of professional and social peers, by receiving the overwhelming support of parade audiences, and by showing city residents their human faces. As empowering as participants found these parade appearances, however, religious and political conservatives found them powerfully objectionable. In reaction, they specifically targeted LGBT school workers in a backlash movement of breathtaking scope.[12]

Backlash

By early 1977, Anita Bryant had organized her "Save Our Children" campaign in Miami, Florida to overturn the recent inclusion of sexual orientation in the local nondiscrimination ordinance. Bryant, however, did not focus her campaign on the broad ordinance issues of assuring freedom from discrimination on account of sexual orientation in the realms of housing, public accommodations, and employment. Instead, she focused her wrath on what she considered the profound problem of "homosexual" and gender-nonconforming teachers in schools. By alleging that lesbian and gay teachers recruited children or otherwise molested them, she effectively whipped up the passions of local and then national conservatives. She explained her views: "First, public approval of admitted homosexual teachers could encourage more homosexuality by inducing pupils into looking upon it as an acceptable life-style. And second, a particularly deviant-minded teacher could sexually molest children."[13]

Bryant and her fellow "Save Our Children" campaigners gained extraordinary financial and political support by evoking images of organized and dangerous homosexual teachers. She argued that high on the agenda of a faceless but powerful homosexual lobby was a "national homosexual bill." In her book, *The Anita Bryant Story*, she recounts: "The hurt in my heart and the agony in my soul were of such intensity that when I heard . . . the news of a national homosexual bill similar to the one in [Miami] Dade County, all I could do was cry. This bill . . . would have the effect of making it mandatory nationwide to hire known practicing homosexuals in public schools and in other areas."[14] She characterized her opponents as "militant homosexuals," working in concert to destroy the moral fiber of the country. And in the final days of the campaign to defeat the ordinance, money she had raised from appearances on nationally syndicated religious broadcasts such as the *PTL Club* and *700 Club*, was used to finance television commercials. One such spot featured wholesome, apple-pie images of the Orange Bowl parade, complete with marching bands, majorettes, and beauty queens. Then in a stark cutaway, images of a gay pride parade filled the screen. The grave voice of the narrator intoned: "In San Francisco, when they take to the streets, it's a parade of homosexuals. Men hugging other men. Cavorting with little boys. Wearing dresses and makeup. The same people who turned San Francisco into a hotbed of homosexuality . . . want to do the same thing to Dade." Bryant's campaign employed such fear-mongering tactics in newspaper ads as well. One read: "This recruitment of our children is absolutely necessary for the survival and growth of homosexuality—for since homosexuals cannot reproduce, they must recruit, must freshen their ranks. . . . And who qualifies as a likely recruit: a 35-year-old father or mother of two . . . or a teenage boy or girl who is surging with sexual awareness?"[15] Through all of these appeals, Bryant and her supporters created an image of lesbian and gay men as a unified, surging threat, particularly those who sought to teach.

After Bryant succeeded in her efforts and the Miami nondiscrimination ordinance went down in defeat, California Senator John Briggs joined her in celebrating. During the weeks after the Miami vote, Bryant then flew to California to help Briggs kick off his bid to rid California schools of homosexual teachers and their supporters. Briggs, who wished to run for governor, reasoned that by introducing a measure to this effect, he could capitalize on the intense public sentiment against lesbian and gay teachers, raise significant funds as Bryant had, and bolster his political image. After all, lesbian and gay activists had misjudged Bryant's ability to mobilize an effective campaign in Miami. Briggs also decided against introducing a measure against *all* lesbian and gay persons and instead only targeted school workers. To this point, many gay activists were ambivalent about supporting the rights of teachers. Some remembered their own trying experiences in schools. A few, burdened with their own internalized homophobia, hesitated to support lesbians and gay men in the classroom. Others believed it inappropriate to rally behind a whole segment of the LGBT population that resisted so profoundly the politically important act of "coming out." Briggs's strategy, then, might have driven a wedge among LGBT activists.

Another factor considerably in Briggs's favor was that the still-young gay liberation movement hardly was unified, much less did it resemble a community. Self-identified bisexuals often encountered resistance in the movement because lesbians and gay men typically considered bisexuals either to be homosexual—but really afraid to admit it, or sellouts who desired same-sex sexual relationships while maintaining heterosexual privilege. On the other hand, religious and political conservatives tended to regard anyone who desired or engaged in same-sex sexual activities to be homosexual, even if they sometimes had heterosexual relationships. Not only were bisexuals greeted with ambivalence by gay activists, but so too were transgender individuals. The deeply complex issues confronted daily by transgender persons were difficult for most to understand. When it came down to it, many activists believed that lesbian and gay rights came first, or, erroneously, that winning lesbian and gay rights automatically would take care of rights for transgender persons. Even between lesbians and gay men, tensions often ran high. Lesbian separatists, who accounted for an important part of the larger lesbian movement, wanted nothing to do with men. Lesbians who were willing to join gay men in organizing often found their voices ignored, their presence unacknowledged, and their unique gender-related concerns dismissed.

Most grassroots gay liberation groups also ignored the important and unique experiences of LGBT persons of color, who uniformly endured multiple forms of oppression. All-too-often, European American organizers mistakenly assumed that LGBT identity outweighed racial/ethnic identity. They typically ignored the second-class status that LGBT persons of color routinely experienced in the larger gay movement. Age proved to be a confounding factor as well. Older men found their appeal limited in organizations that idealized the beauty of young men. LGBT adults all understood, too, that socializing with LGBT teenagers carried profound risks. Efforts to mentor or organize social support groups for LGBT youth brought the risk that LGBT adults would be seen as pedophiles.

Finally, LGBT persons typically come to their identities in their own ways, with no standard script available. LGBT persons have very little background in common—because they come from all economic and social strata, all races and ethnicities, all religions.... In fact, there is very little that holds LGBT persons together except for: (1) the common experience of struggle in a heterosexually dominant, gender-ordered society; and (2) whatever common experiences LGBT persons have managed to create, such as political organizations, bars, bookstores, restaurants, neighborhoods, symbols, styles, music, events.... When Briggs began campaigning against the rights of LGBT school workers, LGBT persons and their allies needed to overcome these substantial obstacles, as well as many others, to rally sufficient numbers of California voters to their side.

On May 1, 1978, Briggs produced over 500,000 signatures calling for a public referendum to ease the dismissal of LGBT school workers and their allies, thus placing the measure on the November ballot. The official wording read:

> As a result of continued close and prolonged contact with schoolchildren, a teacher, teacher's aide, school administrator or counselor becomes a role model whose words, behavior and actions are likely to be emulated by students coming under his or her care, instruction, supervision, administration, guidance and protection.
>
> For these reasons the state finds a compelling interest in refusing to employ and in terminating the employment of a schoolteacher, a teacher's aide, a school administrator or a counselor, subject to reasonable restrictions and qualifications who engages in public homosexual activity and/or public homosexual conduct directed at, or likely to come to the attention of, schoolchildren or other school employees.[16]

The seeming groundswell of public sentiment that had produced the signatures for this referendum overwhelmed some LGBT activists, such as the editor of *The Advocate*, the influential gay news magazine, who wrote: "The bottom line is that it is most unlikely that the Briggs initiative can be defeated in this November's election."[17] However, the referendum contained language that contributed to its eventual demise. "Homosexual conduct" or "homosexual activity," for which school workers might be dismissed, included expressing support for the rights of LGBT persons. Theoretically, then, heterosexual school workers who indicated any degree of support for LGBT rights or persons could lose their jobs just as surely as self-identified LGBT persons. This considerably broadened the potential impact of the measure.

As LGBT activists began strategizing how they would mobilize a credible campaign against the Briggs Initiative, problems quickly surfaced. First and foremost, leaders needed to address the lack of cohesiveness of the state's LGBT population. Most resolved to build coalitions and to break down barriers between subgroups. A group of activists organized a state conference where participants deliberated and reached agreement on their central arguments against Briggs's initiative. Chief among these was the notion that all forms of oppression are linked; that persons of color, women, lesbians, and gay men, and other persons experience different, but related kinds of discrimination; and that activism against all oppressions ultimately would be more effective than waging battles in isolation. Conference attendees agreed that they would commit to fighting all forms of discrimination, not just those directed at lesbians and gay men. One participant reported that "It was encouraging to hear that most people at the conference agreed that there is a connection between all these oppressions and that it's important not to treat the oppression of Gay people as a single isolated issue; we need to support other struggles."[18]

Though some activists despaired that the unity of the moment might only be superficial and therefore temporary, a reporter for the *Lesbian Tide* wrote that most made serious efforts at coalition-building nonetheless. One lesbian was quoted: "I'm a separatist" who agrees with the necessity of working with gay men "on limited projects of mutual benefit. . . . After all, if we're all put in concentration camps, there can't be Lesbian Nation." In the spirit of cooperation, conference participants enacted a variety of policies including casting their support for the Equal Rights Amendment, advocating full custody rights for lesbian mothers, insisting on lesbian and gay representatives in media and other public events where possible—or only lesbians if only one representative were permitted, and both male and female conveners at meetings.[19]

Despite efforts by activists to build coalitions and campaign against other oppressions such as racism and sexism, Briggs and sometimes members of various media effectively exacerbated divisions within the LGBT movement. As the referendum approached, Briggs debated opponents in highly publicized media events around the state. However, the media tended to downplay the substantial presence of lesbians among activists fighting the initiative. One television station kept the camera off of a lesbian who formally debated Briggs, focusing instead on the silent gay man seated beside her. After this event, Briggs chose only to debate gay men.[20]

These divisive actions did not discourage LGBT activists and their allies, however. Many continued forging ties with labor unions, civil rights activists, women's groups, entertainers, and numerous other organized entities. Such efforts slowly paid off as polls close to the referendum indicated that the Briggs Initiative was losing support. Then on November 7, as voters packed their precincts, gay activists began celebrating. The local evening news carried reports that California voters had rejected the Briggs Initiative by a convincing margin of 58 percent to 42 percent. Shortly afterward, Briggs conceded defeat. At a hastily organized rally, Los Angeles Mayor Tom Bradley, himself a masterful coalition builder, told the large, cheering crowd, "How sweet it is! You have put on the greatest campaign ever seen in California, uniting all religions, all parties, all minorities. You have carried the message to all. May this be a lesson that Briggs will never forget. The spirit of Justice lives in California because of you."[21]

Activists who resisted the Briggs Initiative had hoped that in a narrow sense, educators could win unquestioned freedom from employment discrimination on the basis of sexual orientation. More broadly, they wanted greater public recognition of social rights of all LGBT persons. A few wished that the campaign against the Briggs Initiative centrally would provoke a larger public discussion about the typically unarticulated, irrational fears many have around sexuality in general. In the end, though, most voters simply rejected the initiative because it was perceived as a possible first step in a potential decline of basic rights, such as free speech. Many voters who rejected the initiative had no special regard for LGBT educators, but they did not want to see one group targeted for denial of rights.

In the final analysis, the battle over the Briggs Initiative provoked a public reconsideration of persons who desire others of the same sex. And ironically, even though Briggs purportedly introduced the measure to protect students from exposure to homosexuality, the vigorous and very public discussions provoked by the referendum dramatically increased students' knowledge about LGBT persons.[22]

Conclusion

Although Briggs, Bryant, and their supporters typically maligned LGBT activists, accused them of conspiring to seduce younger generations into acquiring LGBT identities and agitating in concert for the "militant homosexual agenda," in fact, LGBT activists faced extraordinary difficulties in forming coherent and inclusive communities. Lesbians, gay men, bisexuals, and transgender individuals struggled to find common ground in their experiences and aims. Furthermore, some LGBT persons initially experienced ambivalence about supporting school workers, who rarely chose to "come out."

However, as LGBT school worker organizations formed and grew, providing some modest feeling of community for individuals who previously had experienced only isolation and fear, then growing numbers of other LGBT school workers became emboldened to join, "come out," and become politically active. Marching together in gay pride parades effectively strengthened their sense of community. In such a symbolic act, LGBT school workers also joined the larger gay liberation movement, composed of motley individuals and organizations united by the particular oppression they experienced, their determination to resist that oppression, and their desire to be part of something bigger.

The Briggs Initiative put the issue of LGBT school workers squarely in the center of public attention in California as well as throughout the country as national media provided ongoing coverage of the story. Jubilation filled the ranks of LGBT activists who believed that the campaign against the initiative was not just about school workers, but also about the rights of *all* LGBT persons and their allies. LGBT school workers in California felt some slight relief as the threatening measure disappeared, and furthermore, as unexpectedly high numbers of voters had demonstrated their disapproval of Briggs's handiwork. However, over 1980s and 1990s, while voters in California were willing to oppose a hostile measure such as Briggs's, the national citizenry generally was unlikely to show much overt support for the employment rights of LGBT school workers. Such employees continued to fear for their jobs with the rise of the political and religious right, which often targeted LGBT school workers and LGBT issues in school districts everywhere, effectively driving a wedge between previously united political factions.

Even today, as a variety of LGBT issues confront *every* school, many LGBT school workers continue to feel isolated and vulnerable, unable to educate their colleagues, students, and parents about their experiences. As this brief examination of LGBT school worker activism has described, though, when such educators have been willing to resist their oppression and join together, no matter how difficult and complex the effort, they have made strides in winning employment rights—and sometimes even a fleeting sense of community.

Notes

1. John D'Emilio, *Sexual Politics, Sexual Communities: The Making of a Homosexual Minority in the United States, 1940–1970*, 2nd ed.

(Chicago: University of Chicago Press, 1998); and John D'Emilio and Estelle B. Freedman, *Intimate Matters: A History of Sexuality in America*, 2nd ed. (Chicago: University of Chicago Press, 1997), 288–289.
2. Alfred C. Kinsey, Wardell B. Pomeroy, and Clyde E. Martin, *Sexual Behavior in the Human Male* (Philadelphia: W. B. Saunders Company, 1948), 621–622.
3. John D'Emilio, *Sexual Politics, Sexual Communities: The Making of a Homosexual Minority in the United States, 1940–1970*, 2nd ed. (Chicago: University of Chicago Press, 1998), 14.
4. "Teachers Favor Freedom for Gays," *The Advocate*, March 1970, 10.
5. "Gay Teachers Organizing," *The Advocate*, July 5, 1972, 17; "Gay Teacher Wins Fight against Mental Exam," *The Advocate*, October 11, 1972, 17; Karen Harbeck, *Gay and Lesbian Educators, Personal Freedoms, Public Constraints* (Maulden, MA: Amethyst Press, 1997), 66–68.
6. Marc Rubin, "History of the Gay Teachers Association," *Gay Teachers Association Newsletter*, January 1978, 1–4, Eric Rofes's private collection.
7. Rubin, "History."
8. David Lamble, "10th Anniversary: Gay Teachers Struggle for Right to Teach; Take on the City's School Board," *Coming Up!*, June 1985, 5–6; "School Board Approves a Gay Anti-Bias Policy," *San Francisco Chronicle*, June 18, 1975, n.p.; and Jim Wood, "Gay, Gifted Yet Closeted in City's Classrooms," *San Francisco Examiner*, June 12, 1975, n.p.
9. "Apple Banner Energy Transformed," *Gay Teachers and School Workers Coalition*, August/September 1977, 2, located in "Briggs" file, June Mazer Collection.
10. "Minutes of June 17, 1976 Meeting," *Gay Teachers of Los Angeles*, June 26, 1976, Eric Rofes's private collection.
11. "Minutes of September 30, 1976 Meeting," *Gay Teachers of Los Angeles Newsletter*, Eric Rofes's private collection; "Next Week the World," *Gay Teachers of Los Angeles Newsletter*, Eric Rofes's private collection; "United Teachers of Los Angeles," *Gay Teachers of Los Angeles Newsletter*, April 11, 1977, 2, Eric Rofes's private collection; and "The Gay Pride Parade," *Cheery Chalkboard*, Gay Teachers of Los Angeles, July 1977, 2, Eric Rofes's private collection.
12. "Political News," *Cheery Chalkboard*, Gay Teachers of Los Angeles, July 1978, 3, Eric Rofes's private collection.
13. Anita Bryant, *The Anita Bryant Story: The Survival of Our Nation's Families and the Threat of Militant Homosexuality* (Old Tappan, NJ: Fleming H. Revell Co., 1977), 114–115.
14. Bryant, *The Anita Bryant Story*, 53.
15. Dudley Clendinen and Adam Nagourney, *Out for Good: The Struggle to Build a Gay Rights Movement in America* (New York: Simon & Schuster, 1999), 303.

16. Pat Donohue, "Initiative Measure to Be Submitted Directly to the Voters with Analysis," "Briggs" file, June Mazer Collection.
17. David Goodstein, "Fighting the Briggs Brigade," *The Advocate*, June 1978, 6.
18. Marilyn Gode-von Aesch, "Statewide Network Fights Briggs Initiative," *Unlearning the Lie/Gay Teachers and School Workers Coalition*, April 1978, 3, "Briggs" file, June Mazer Collection.
19. Lin Duke, "California Goes on Orange Alert!" *Lesbian Tide*, November/December 1977, 12–14.
20. Cindy Riggs, "Sexist Bias Distorts Prop 6 Campaign," *Sonoma SCLGA*, October 1978, n.p.
21. "How Sweet It Is!" *Lesbian Tide*, January/February 1979, 10–12.
22. Amber Hollibaugh, *My Dangerous Desires: A Queer Girl Dreaming Her Way Home* (Durham, NC: Duke University Press, 2000), 43–61.

Chapter 5

School and Community Loss, Yet Still Imagined in the Oral History of School Segregation in Tampa, Florida

Barbara J. Shircliffe

> ... *Remember* ...
> *the black giants*
> *our principals and coaches*
> *who all were always bigger than life*
> *and discipline was such*
> *that you got whipped at school*
> *for doing wrong, and then*
> *your momma would meet you*
> *at the door with a whipping,*
> *because everybody knew everybody*
> *and cared about everybody.*
> *Remember* ...
> *how sweet and communal it was*
> *to be black on black*
> *in black, with black,*
> *around black, being black*
> *such a delight*
> *Remember* ...
> *how it was before desegregation*
> (Excerpt from *Remember* by Otis Anthony, 1969
> Blake High School graduate)

This chapter examines how former students remember Middleton and Blake, two historically Black high schools in Tampa, as communities prior to desegregation. In 1971, the local school board closed Middleton and Blake as high schools as part of a court-ordered desegregation plan in Hillsborough County where Tampa is located.

Reflecting this longstanding resentment, in 1991, alumni from Blake, Middleton, and other historically Black high schools successfully advocated that Hillsborough County school board rebuild Middleton and Blake high schools in their former neighborhoods. In 1997, Blake High School, with a Performing Arts Magnet, opened in the west Tampa. In 2002, Middleton High School opened in east Tampa. As former teachers and students celebrate the opening of the new high schools, they construct idealized portraits of a school community prior to desegregation. Yet the increasing segregation among schools in the district raises concern about educational inequalities, particularly between urban and suburban schools.

This exploration focuses on the tension between African Americans' yearning for community schools and desegregation policies that equated community schooling with inferior schooling for Black children. For many, the downgrading of historically Black schools demonstrates the persistence of White privilege in the desegregation process. In the post–desegregation era, African Americans attempt to revitalize the relationship between school and community they believe as necessary for school success. In the pages that follow, I describe how former students of Middleton and Blake imagine school communities of the past as a way of reckoning with the devaluation and marginalization of the Black community and its schools during the desegregation process. I argue that the sense of community loss associated with the closing of the all-Black high schools has roots in changes in the economic and social landscape brought by larger public policy decisions promoting suburbanization, economic restructuring, and urban renewal. Furthermore, the discriminatory aspects of the 1971 desegregation order transformed school–community relations in Black neighborhoods to a greater degree than White neighborhoods and heightened the isolation of low-income neighborhoods in the inner city. Confronted with these challenges, it is not surprising that many former students turn to the past for answers. In a desegregated system, African Americans struggle to form new ways to remain involved with their children's education, as Marlena Baber has shown, many African American parents in Tampa have become less likely to view schools as community resources, and see historically Black schools of the segregation era as models for "how schools and education should be handled."[1]

Segregated Schools as Imagined Communities

The nostalgia for segregated schools has sparked debates among historians about the credibility of oral history because it seemingly neglects the gross inequalities imposed by segregation, which had devastating consequences for African Americans.[2] In addition, the yearning for the all-Black school experience can be used to suggest that desegregation has failed.[3] In their book *Dismantling Desegregation*, Gary Orfield and Susan Eaton argue that critics of desegregation often "compare their memory of the best of the old Black schools with the worst problems in the desegregated schools and assume a decline" in Black achievement without looking at evidence that reports otherwise.[4] As schools are resegregating, scholars fear that the nostalgia for segregated schools diverts attention from the sources of educational failure in poor, isolated, and racially segregated communities, creating what Stephanie Coontz eloquently describes as the "nostalgia trap."[5] Any reading of the history of segregation demonstrates the gross inequalities between Black and White schools, which had devastating consequences for African American educational attainment.

Despite the fragmented relationship between memory and history, the notion of community loss emerging from oral history narratives is overwhelming and demands analysis. For one, in many communities African Americans protested desegregation plans that resulted in the closing and downgrading of Black schools, and the disproportionate busing of African American children to schools outside their neighborhoods. Recent studies indicate that the perspectives of African American educators, parents, and community leaders toward desegregation were often silenced and marginalized during desegregation planning, which was worked out to accommodate and support the interests of the White middle class. In addition recent oral histories document that former students and teachers of historically Black schools from both urban and rural areas, north and south, recall fond memories of growing up and going to school and contrast their school experience with what they see as a break down in school and community relations today.

Although fond memories of segregated schooling are often dismissed and viewed as a dangerous affront to valid historical documentation, these constructions of an idealized community reflect critical perspectives on racist assumptions embedded in the desegregation process; namely, the categorical inferiority of Black institutions, teachers, parents, and children.[6] As Elgin Klugh discusses later in this volume, the growing movement in cities and small towns throughout the United States to restore historically Black schools into community centers, museums, or public schools, in part, represents one manifestation of this critique.[7] To dismiss the perspectives of alumni and former teachers as misguided nostalgia neglects, therefore, the more interesting questions about how and why people imagine schools as communities.

Importantly, it neglects the prevalence of White privilege and interests that shaped desegregation policy in ways that opposed community schooling for African Americans to integration with Whites.

This chapter explores the tensions involved with imagining schools as communities. As with the other case studies in this anthology, this analysis extends Benedict Anderson's discussion of nations as imagined communities to consider how schools are imagined as communities, or in the case of Otis Anthony's poem about Blake High School, how schools are *remembered* as communities in oral history. To understand nations as imagined communities, as Anderson instructs, does not imply they are fictive. Rather, Anderson states: "communities are not to be distinguished by their falsity/genuineness, but by the style which they are imagined."[8] Bracketing the notion of an authentic community, we can ask questions about how people imagine schools as communities, and what those images tell us about their understanding of the past and present. Understanding how schools are imagined communities is particularly relevant when considering oral histories about all-Black schools in the South during state mandated segregation. Former students and teachers remember all-Black schools, despite public neglect, as important centers of community life.[9] Former students and teachers often speak nostalgically about the Black community and associate a sense of community loss with the closing of schools in Black neighborhoods and the busing of Black children to schools outside these areas during desegregation.

Method

The data collected for this paper is part of larger study that examines the history and fate of historically Black high schools in Hillsborough County, Florida. I gathered data on the history of historically Black high schools, the desegregation process, and the African American communities' reaction to the closing of these institutions through analysis of newspaper reports, school records and school board minutes, yearbooks, school plant surveys, court documents and other relevant written sources, and tape-recorded interviews with 31 individuals in Hillsborough County. The majority of those interviewed were former students of Middleton and Blake, several of whom are still active in their alumni groups and public education in Tampa.

Middleton and Blake School Communities

Established in 1934, Middleton was the first senior high school for African Americans in Tampa.[10] According to school board records, the school burned down in 1939, and its students attended Middleton at alternative school locations until 1943, when school officials rebuilt the high school, assisted, in part, by the Works Progress Administration. Despite this troubled start, Middleton Senior High School became a key college preparatory institution in the county for African Americans. According to the 1946 survey, Middleton "was principally a literary college preparatory school, even though not more than 20% of the graduates attend colleges of any kind."[11] The survey of school plants, which in general, described the conditions of Black schools as substandard, rated Middleton highest of all Black schools with a score of 673 (500–700 indicates the building is usable but needs improvements).

In 1946, demonstrating the gross inequities under the segregated system, except for Middleton, none of the county's 19 Black schools surveyed scored higher than 500, and 11 schools scored under 300, indicating that they should be abandoned and/or replaced within the next three years. The average score of the 66 White schools surveyed was 524 (compared to 292 for Black schools), with only six White schools scoring 300 or below. State and district funding of Black and White schools in Florida mirror the gross inequalities of segregation throughout the south. In 1940, Florida African Americans received 44 percent for educational funds granted to Whites.[12] Following World War II, despite efforts to equalize per pupil expenditures between Black and White citizens, disparities remain. In 1952, per pupil expenditures for African Americans were 88 percent of expenditures that the Whites received in Florida's metropolitan school districts.[13]

Following World War II, with increasing demands for secondary and vocational education, Hillsborough County established Don Thompson Vocational High School in Tampa. Located in a two-story warehouse in west Tampa, Don Thompson offered vocational and general secondary courses to African American veterans of World War II and the Korean conflict. Local children could also take high school and vocational courses there. As a permanent vocational school for adults and senior high school pupils, Don Thompson was limited in space and facilities. The plant lacked a gymnasium-auditorium, a library, a cafeteria, a health unit, and a main office.[14]

In 1956, two years following the *Brown* desegregation decision by the United States Supreme Court, school officials opened Blake Senior High School to replace Don Thompson Vocational School. Local African American leaders petitioned that the new high school be named after Howard W. Blake, the former principal of Booker T. Washington (considered the first high school in the county by some), who died in 1954. Local African Americans considered

Howard W. Blake a great advocate for expanding higher educational opportunities for African Americans. Located in a two-story building, which now housed both a cafeteria and library, Blake Senior High School greatly surpassed Don Thompson's facilities.[15] In retrospect, a former student of Don Thompson, Roy Robinson speculates that the school board saw building Blake as a way to avoid integration. It was a way to appease local African Americans who were denied access to secondary education and were dissatisfied with the quality of secondary educational facilities available to Black youth.[16]

Despite these inequalities, Middleton and Blake Senior High Schools quickly became sources of pride for Tampa's Black communities. Middleton and Blake high schools were centrally located in east and west Tampa respectfully, and in walking distance of public housing, working class, and middle-class residential blocks. In addition to regular day class, both schools offered evening courses for adults and youths who left high school prior to graduation. Middleton and Blake were important sources of employment for college educated African Americans as teachers, principals, and secretaries. Educators at Middleton and Blake lived in the same neighborhoods and often attended the same churches as the families of their students. Linking adults and young people across social class lines, the high schools' theatrical, musical, and athletic events were spirited occasions. Football and basketball competitions between the two schools regularly drew crowds in the thousands, as each school became a rallying focus of its community.

In 1971, when the school board announced plans to close Middleton and Blake as high schools, the African American community protested. At the time, Black leaders and parents argued that this policy disproportionately burdened Black children through busing, which threatened opportunities for parental and community involvement in public education. Prior to the 1971 court order, Lavern Jean Hill Brown, who, at the time, was both a school and public housing activist, became involved with the movement to "Save Blake." When asked why she and other parents wanted Blake to remain a high school, Brown explained:

> It was centrally located. Our children would just leave our public housing and go right across the street to school. It was easier for the parent, knowing your child is right across the street. I walked over to the school. I'm going to see about my child, you don't have to worry about bus fare, about getting a ride because we didn't have cars back then in those times. We were welcome when we would go over there to check on our child. But when we went, when the integration comes about, we could feel it, we could see it. You were not wanted there, they say "What do you want?" "Why are you here, you people?" We were always "you people."[17]

Brown does value Blake as a community school because of its proximity. However, a neighborhood location perhaps is not a very important characteristic of a community school when compared with the characteristic that parents are always welcomed. Former students of both high schools linked the idea of a community school with a sense of ownership and belonging shared by its members, a quality Brown does not associate with integrated schools, where Black parents felt or were treated as outsiders.

Examining oral history narratives, former students of Middleton and Blake imagine these schools as communities in three interdependent ways. First, the schools were places where everybody knew, and thus, cared for each other. Second, the schools served as sites for communal gathering. And finally, the schools provided rallying points for members of the community to identify. Structural components associated with these characteristics relate to the relatively small size of the schools, their location in east and west Tampa, and the local residence of the teachers and principals. The following highlights these three interdependent dimensions.

"Everybody Knew Everybody and Cared about Everybody"

A common theme in oral histories of segregated schools is the idea of community discipline. George Noblit and Van Dempsey comment that narratives about the mutual discipline of teachers and parents ("if you got spank by a teacher, you could also expect a spanking when you got home") reflect a community where beliefs are shared and "enforced universally."[18] This theme of shared community values emerges from oral history testimonies of former students and teachers of Middleton and Blake as well. This shared discipline becomes a key trope in these schools as imagined communities because it reveals how "everybody knew everybody." In this sense, the school and community functions as family. Consider the following narratives.

Betty Jo Hayes graduated from Middleton in 1945, and after attending college at Clark University in Atlanta, Georgia, returned to Middleton in 1947 as a teacher. Hayes taught at Middleton until she was transferred to Hillsborough High School, a former White school, to integrate the faculty there. Hayes describes being a student at Middleton:

> You had the cooperation of your family and your school. This is what it was at that time. If I had done something that I needed to have corrected or if I had done something good, the community knew about it.

> My mother knew it immediately, not to punish, but just to make sure that you were walking a straight line so that you could get into what you were expected to do in this world. And our objective in the Black communities [is] that we do it through education because many of our grandparents didn't even read. So our exit out of this thing was through education, which is absolutely true.[19]

In her discussion of family school relations, Hayes connects parent and teacher cooperation that links education with social advancement. Parents and teachers cooperated to ensure children would not stray as Hayes explains and become productive adults.

Other former students describe how teachers would call parents or visit the home if a student was not performing well in school. Disciplinary actions as well as rewards for good deeds were taken as evidence that "everybody cared." Yvette Ballard Sims, who was a student at Blake during the late 1960s, and the daughter of a Blake teacher describes how teachers and parents united, making it difficult for children to get away with anything. Sims and other students tell stories about how teachers would call before the end of the day, or, amazingly, beat the student home, to report on the child. Sims explains:

> That's the way it was, they really cared beyond the classroom. They cared about you as an individual, about your growth. I think that is something that is missing now and it may be because we were such a family, and we all lived in the same neighborhood. And teachers lived in the neighborhood where we lived. We went to church together. When you got out, you were waving at one of the teachers down the street.

The fact that the teachers lived in the same neighborhoods and attended the same churches as their students' families increased the sense of community and that family-like atmosphere of the school.[20]

The idea of surrogate family system involving communities is a common theme in the research on all-Black schools.[21] Alvin Hamilton, who graduated from Blake in 1969, recalled that when he was growing up that his neighbors had unwritten permission from his mother to punish him if he was misbehaving. Parents reportedly extended this unwritten permission to the teachers as Blake graduate Laura Williams comments: "If you did something wrong, [teachers] they would pull up in front of your door to tell your parents about it. You didn't wait until you got a report card for the parents to find out that you did something wrong." For those interviewed, the mutual discipline of teachers and parents and the larger community reinforced values and school success, and above all the authority of the teacher. Importantly, a parent would not take the word of a child over the word of the teacher. Those interviewed contrast this experience with what they see characterizing family–school relations today: distrust and disrespect among teachers, students and parents.

Schools as Sites for Communal Gathering

Middleton and Blake high schools also served as sites for communal gathering. Former students recall how the neighborhood streets were filled with the sounds of the Middleton marching band. They also remember the excitement throughout the neighborhood the week before the "Soul Bowl," when Middleton's Fighting Tigers would meet the Blake Yellow Jackets in the football game of the year. Reverend Abraham Brown, former head coach of Blake, community leader, and minister, reported that Friday night games between the two schools always drew crowds in the thousands.[22] Others interviewed stated that local residents not only gathered for sports events, but also for practice, dances, school plays, and other school activities.

Alvin Hamilton, who graduated from Blake in 1969, describes how high school events were community events. In so doing, he compares the community atmosphere around the Black high schools with what he sees as the separateness between the school and community today:

> Those were beautiful days Barbara, I remember. See everything socially revolved around the school. You had your pep rallies, you had your dances on Friday nights, you had your football games, and when you wanted to play, the playground was right there at the school. Now it's different, when kids get out of school, they jump on the bus, and they don't see the school again until the next day. So you lose that type of bondage. Everything was centered around the school.[23]

Hamilton's description of the school as the center of the community was echoed by others interviewed.

Football as with most high schools was the main sports event. Until 1966 teams from Black and White schools did not compete with one another. Former students recall traveling to other towns across the state to compete with other teams and bands of historically Black schools. Blake won the state championship in 1969, the last Hillsborough County high school to do so until the Armwood Hawks won the title in 2003. In 1970, 10,000 fans gathered to watch Coach Billy Reed lead the undefeated Middleton against undefeated Blake. Middleton won 23-0.[24] Sports and band competitions among schools provided a source of community identity as well as evidence by the rivalry between Middleton and Blake.

Schools as Sources of Community Identity

Middleton and Blake served as sources of community identity. Blake primarily served west Tampa, while Middleton, located in east Tampa, primarily served those neighborhoods. The rivalry between Middleton and Blake was intense but by all accounts healthy. Although some particularly older residents saw Blake more as a vocational school because it replaced Don Thompson, and Middleton as the college prep school, most discussions of the rivalry centered on football games and band competitions. Students and parents saw the bands and the athletic teams as representatives of their communities.

Interestingly, membership to the school was not simply contingent on one's residence. It was not uncommon for a student who lived in west Tampa to attend Middleton and an east Tampa child to go to Blake. However, Middleton and Blake remained sources of community identity for the different areas of Black Tampa. Sims explains:

> It just and it had always been like a friendly rivalry from way back. My mother was raised here in Tampa, and she attended Middleton, but she graduated from [Jones High School in Orlando]. But she had gone to Middleton all of her life. It was just the rivalry. It had always been there when Don Thompson was the original version of Blake, and then when Blake opened in 1956 over on Spruce Street, and everybody got absorbed in there and that became like the west Tampa school and Middleton was the east Tampa School. Really, you could go to either school you wanted to go to. It was open for you to go to anyone of those schools you wanted to attend.

The only other high school in Hillsborough County serving African Americans was Marshall High School in Plant City, a small farming town northeast of Tampa. Like Middleton and Blake former students of Marshall commented on the spirited competitions between high schools, in which as a small rural school, Marshall generally lost.

Not surprising, alumni still pride themselves on school spirit and one can still see the intense rivalry in their comments. Carlton Williams, who graduated from Middleton in 1962, recalled:

> We saw ourselves as little A&M and Blake saw themselves as little Michigan, or Michigan State. Just two distinct styles, the two cultures that got expressed in the clothing, the jewelry, and the style of the performance of the bands. Now, I have always accused Blake of having releases from Marianna, which used to be the old reform school—they beat us a lot in football. I mean this tongue and cheek. The three years that I was there, they beat us twice, we beat them once.[25]

Otis Anthony who graduated from Blake around the same time, recalled Middleton and Blake had distinct styles, though he qualifies that everybody was trying to imitate Florida A&M's band.

The Closing of Middleton and Blake

In 1971, the school board implemented a court-ordered desegregation plan that closed Middleton and Blake as high schools. School officials and local leaders who crafted the 1971 plan were primarily concerned with satisfying the federal judge overseeing the case who recommended a Black/White ratio of 20 : 80 in each school, while not alienating the White community who publicly resisted sending children to schools in Black neighborhoods. To this end, the 1971 desegregation plan, like other plans in southern metropolitan areas, placed a disproportionate burden on Black pupils and parents to desegregate the school system, while greatly limiting the busing of White children.[26] School officials converted most schools in Black communities into sixth or seventh grade centers. In those communities, many first through fifth and eighth through twelfth grade students would be transported to the suburbs to attend former all-White schools. In turn, White suburban children would be bussed to sixth and seventh grade centers in the city.

For many local African Americans, the plan fully displayed the power of white privilege. Schools in White communities, for the most part, remained intact, and White children were exempt from busing during most of their school careers. Following the announcement of the closing of the high schools in 1971, hundreds of parents and students demonstrated at school board meetings in protest. Otha Favor, leader of the activist group Black Youth for Peace and Power, organized rallies to protest the dismantling of Black schools, arguing integration was harmful to the preservation of Black culture and self-determination. Parents and community activists argued the closing of Blake and Middleton as high schools and the disproportionate busing of Black children threatened community identity and parental participation in public education. Lawyers for the Legal Defense Fund for the National Advancement for the Association of Colored People (NAACP) tried to convince the federal judge to revise the plan so Middleton and Blake would remain high schools.

School officials argued that the plan was the most effective way to desegregate the school system, while minimizing the use of transportation for the county as a whole. In addition, they argued Blake and Middleton failed to meet state facility standards for senior high schools. In his order and opinion approving the school board plan,

Judge Krentzman agreed with school officials, asserting that without grade reorganization, more students would have to be transported to create racial balance in every school. He found that such a desegregation plan "would provide an invitation to either 'white flight' or 'black flight' or both."[27] In reference to the historically Black high schools, Krentzman stated that Blake and Middleton did not have the same student capacity as other high schools in the state. He also noted the failure of previous efforts to zone White students into the two high schools. Furthermore, Krentzman stated that the school board was operating in good faith, and that relocating or closing former Black schools "did not constitute invidious discrimination as proscribed by the Fourteenth Amendment."[28]

School official assertions' that Blake and Middleton were substandard and unappealing to White parents only embittered African Americans, who pointed out school officials were responsible for the inadequacies at these schools. In addition, former students and teachers recall that school officials only became concerned about the physical characteristics of the schools when it became probable that White students would attend. This assessment appeared to be supported when following the implementation of the desegregation plan, school officials began ordering long-needed repairs and improvements to historically Black schools. In oral history testimonies, a constant theme emerges how the desegregation plan severed the relationships between the Black community and schools in the interests of Whites.

Altamese Hamilton grew up near Middleton and attended high school there until eleventh grade when she enrolled in Fisk University. After college she returned to Middleton as a teacher, and was teaching there at the time of desegregation. She recalls how when she was a child Middleton was opened to the community. Local residents' accessibility to the school changed following desegregation when school officials decided to block off a street limiting traffic to the school. Hamilton remembers a community meeting with school officials when she voiced her concerns about school administration's decision:

> Remember how I told you we use to roam in and out of the campus and everything. They [school officials] were closing the campus off to the immediate community and so I can vividly remember standing up and speaking to the fact that I thought that was a travesty; our community was not posing a threat to the White children attending the school. And that people used that thoroughfare to get back and forth, and that it was ridiculous and money wasted. And nobody was paying attention to me or anybody else, and this one man said, "You're wasting your breath, the decision has been already made, this is window dressing." . . . The school was like a fortress. People who lived in the

community sort of resented the fact that all of our lives the school had been part of the community, they put fences and things to insulate the students from the community and I think they probably wanted to ensure White parents that their children would be safe in this Black community.[29]

Others interviewed stated that school officials constructed fences around historically Black schools to prepare for the enrollment of White children. Betty Jo Hayes discusses how the suggestion that White children needed to be fenced in and protected from the Black community was both insulting and painful. Richard Pride, the former principal of Blake High School, remembered how he tried to get school officials to fence a ditch near an elementary school he administered to no avail. Pride recalled "when they integrated they put in a fence, they put another building in there, they spruced up everything." Following desegregation school officials began ordering long-needed repairs and improvements to historically Black schools.[30]

The construction of fences in these narratives is symbolic of the sense of community loss associated with desegregation; these memories illustrate the separation of the school from the Black community, which was positioned as a threat to entering White school children. These stories reveal the pain caused by school officials' apparent zeal to cater to the needs of White students, while they had long ignored the interests of Black children. Here, from the standpoint of the Black community, desegregated schools are no longer imagined as communities but fortresses.

The Restoration of Middleton and Blake

As mentioned previously, in 1990, when school officials announced plans to reorganize the grade structure, eliminating sixth and seventh grade centers and creating middle schools, alumni of Blake and Middleton and several community leaders advocated that Blake and Middleton be restored as high schools. Howard W. Blake High School (Performing Arts Magnet) opened in the fall of 1997 in west Tampa. Middleton opened its door in the fall of 2002.[31] Many community leaders, school alumni, and former teachers see the reestablishment of the high schools as a righting of past wrongs, and a means to revitalize community pride and business interests in Tampa's predominately Black neighborhoods.

During the establishment of Blake high school, controversy surfaced over the status of the school as a Performing Arts Magnet, its location, and its attendance zone, which excluded many neighborhood children.

Tensions existed between school administrators and school alumni who held different visions for the new high schools. School officials wanted a high school focused on performing arts curriculum that would also attract students throughout the county, particularly White suburban youth. School alumni wanted a community school with comprehensive academic, vocational, and extracurricular programs, primarily serving children in nearby neighborhoods. Blake alumni were successful persuading the school board to locate the new Blake near the former school and offer a comprehensive high school program along with the magnet component. However, school officials limited the enrollment of children from nearby neighborhoods in an effort to keep Blake more racially balanced.

With the experience of Blake, Middleton alumni and school officials have worked closely in planning the establishment of the new Middleton high school. Like Blake, the new Middleton will be located near the former Middleton, and will house magnet programs centered on technology to attract children throughout the county. Fred Hearns, president of the Middleton Alumni Association, says the school will draw 900 "walkers," children from local neighborhoods, and about a thousand from the county as a whole.

Reestablishing Blake and Middleton High Schools are positive steps to attempt to equalize the desegregation burden while increasing educational opportunities to youth in the city. Nevertheless, school officials and community leaders must grapple with ways to achieve equity and quality education despite trends toward resegregation. In 2000, there were 26 racially imbalanced schools in Hillsborough County (more than 40 percent Black), with most located in the inner city or the northern edge where neighborhoods are experiencing racial turnover. If one includes schools with 90 percent or more White student bodies, Hillsborough County has 50 racially identifiable schools. Fears that segregated schools will lead to low educational gains among poor and minority students seemed to be confirmed when the state Florida instituted an unpopular system of grading schools based on achievement test scores in 1999. For instance, of the 26 schools (grades were not available for 2 schools) considered identifiably Black, 17 received "Ds," 6 received "Cs" and none received "Bs" or "As." Of the 24 schools considered identifiably White, 3 received "Ds," 13 received "Cs," 7 received "Bs" and 1 received an "A." Notably the three White schools that received "Ds" had large "Hispanic" populations (Wimauma, 81.2 percent; Cypress Creek, 62.5 percent; and Ruskin, 64.11 percent). The following year, several schools improved their student achievement on test scores, but the disparity remained. Of the identifiably Black schools graded, 12 received "Ds," 11 received "Cs," 1 received a "B," and 1 received an "A." Of the identifiably White schools, none received "Ds," 11 received "Cs," 5 received "Bs," and 8 received "As."

Some believe that the longing for the imagined community of the past will legitimate resegregation already occurring in the county. Recognizing the limitation of what some see as the "restoration" of Middleton and Blake, several alumni express concerns about the fate of Black children in a desegregated school system that is rapidly resegregating. Some former students contend the plight of Black children as evidence that the White system failed to maximize educational opportunities and achievement. Others, however, fear that over romanticizing the Middleton and Blake experience may lead to what Anthony describes as a "political trap that has been set for us where we get locked out of real quality educational opportunities again."

The nostalgia for Middleton and Blake symbolizes the community loss associated with desegregation and the increasing social isolation and economic decline of inner city neighborhoods in Tampa. Since desegregation, Black students are over represented in many special needs categories except "gifted," and in school suspension and disciplinary actions. In addition economic restructuring, ill-fated plans for urban renewal, and suburbanization has also contributed to the sense of community loss. In most cities, supermarkets and chain stores have replaced corner groceries and local drug stores. Such patterns, coupled with racial residential segregation, tend to concentrate low income African Americans in poor neighborhoods with few employment opportunities.

Demonstrating the prevalence of White privilege in what some see as the post desegregation era, the tensions over resegregation and community schools are not typically noted as problems in White communities. Racial segregation does not lead to low education achievement in White suburban schools as it does in urban schools. This pattern, as Gary Orfield and others point out, is largely due to social economics.[32] Just as Massey and Denton argue that residential segregation concentrates poverty in predominately Black housing markets,[33] school segregation concentrates poverty in schools serving predominately Black and Latino student bodies. As a result, White parents, despite socioeconomic differences, do not have to make a choice between community schooling and quality education. They often can strive for both. African American and Latino/a parents often are confronted with a quandary when striving for community schooling and quality education.

The need to regain a sense of community in face of the sprawling metropolitan environment, with its car-centered, consumer oriented, postindustrial economy is keenly articulated in the stories of school and community among African Americans living in Tampa. Children in poor neighborhoods with high rates of unemployment and welfare dependency, face bleak futures unless educational opportunities and attainment can be raised on par with children of suburban areas. Not only are African Americans in Tampa witnessing the increasing gap between the rich and poor, but also between those who complete formal schooling and those who do not. It is in the context of these contemporary concerns that both former teachers and students speak fondly of their memories of Middleton and Blake, and tragically of their closings. And so doing, imagine a school-community where everybody knows everyone, teachers care beyond the classroom, and parents are always welcomed.

Notes

1. Marlena Yvette Baber, *Parent Involvement Perceptions and Practices in East Tampa: The Impact of Court-Ordered Desegregation in Hillsborough County, Florida* (Ph.D. diss., University of South Florida, Tampa Florida, 1999), x, 66–68.
2. Vanessa S. Walker discusses the problem with nostalgia in *Their Highest Potential*.
3. In what was deemed in the local media as a surprising twist of events, in October 1998, the federal district judge issued an order to continue court oversight of the Hillsborough County School District, stating that the school board had not made every practical effort to eliminate school segregation. See Linda Chion-Kenney, "Desegregation order Stands," *St. Petersburg Times* (October 27, 1998), 1A. In 2001, the US Court of Appeals for the Eleventh Circuit District overturned the district court's decision and asked the district judge to declare the Hillsborough County school system unitary. "Ending Forced Busing in Hillsborough," *Tampa Tribune* (March 20, 2001), 8.
4. Gary Orfield and Susan E. Eaton, *Dismantling Desegregation: The Quiet Reversal of Brown v. Board of Education* (New York: The New Press, 1996), 82.
5. Stephanie Coontz, *The Way We Never Were: American Families and the Nostalgia Trap* (New York: Basic Books, 1992).
6. See Jerome Morris, "Forgotten Voices of Black Educators: Critical Race Perspectives on the Implementation of a Desegregation Plan." *Educational Policy* 15, 4 (September 2001), 575–600; Derrick Bell, *Faces at the Bottom of the Well: The Permanence of Racism* (New York: Basic Books, 1992).

7. Elgin Klugh, "The Glover School Historic Site: Preserving Schools as a Strategy for Community Building," unpublished. Presented at the History of Education Society Annual Meeting, New Haven, Conn., October 18, 2001.
8. Anderson, Benedict. *Imagined Communities: Reflections on the Origin and Spread of Nationalism* (London: Verso, 1991), 6.
9. See David Cecelski, *Along Freedom Road: Hyde County North Carolina and the Fate of Black Schools in the South* (Chapel Hill: The University of North Carolina Press, 1994); George Noblit and Van Dempsey, *The Social Construction of Virtue: The Moral Life of Schools* (Albany, NY: SUNY Press, 1996); and Vanessa S. Walker, *Their Highest Potential: An African American School Community in the Segregated South* (Chapel Hill: The University of North Carolina Press, 1997).
10. Middletonian, yearbook, Tampa, Florida, 1945.
11. Florida State Department of Education, School Building Survey, Hillsborough County Florida (Tallahassee, FL: State Department of Education, 1946), 138.
12. Harry S. Ashmore, *The Negro and the Schools* (Chapel Hill, NC: University of North Carolina Press, 1954), 153.
13. Florida State Department, *School Plant Survey*, 155.
14. Ibid., 136.
15. Teachers Handbook, Blake High School, Tampa, Florida 1996.
16. Roy Robinson, interview with the author (October 14, 1998).
17. Laverne Jean Hill Barron, interview with the author (November 13, 1998).
18. Noblit and Dempsey, *The Social Construction of Virtue*, 8.
19. Betty Jo Hayes, interview with the author (September 14, 1998).
20. Yvette Ballard Sims and Yvonne Glasgow, interview with the author (October 16, 1998).
21. George Noblit and Van Dempsey discuss discipline as a community endeavor that is not seen as an imposition but as part of the construction of virtue.
22. Jim Henderson, "Soulful Era Ends in Tampa, *Tampa Tribune* (July 4, 1971), 1.
23. Alvin Hamilton, interview with the author (October 23, 1998).
24. Henderson, Jim. Middleton Stops Blake Cold 23–0. *Tampa Tribune* (November 21, 1970), 1, 4.
25. Carlton Williams, interview with the author (February 24, 2000).
26. Janet Hall, *School Desegregation in Hillsborough County, Florida*. (Master's Thesis. Tampa, Fl: History Department, University of South Florida, 1992); Davidson Douglas, *Reading, Writing, and Race: The Desegregation of the Charlotte Schools* (Chapel Hill: University of North Carolina, 1995).
27. *Manning, et al v. The Board of Public Instruction of Hillsborough County Florida*, Opinion and Order (July 2, 1971), 6.

28. *Manning, et al v. The Board of Public Instruction of Hillsborough County Florida*, Opinion and Order (July 2, 1971), 7.
29. Altamese Hamilton, interview with the author (August 13, 2001).
30. Ward Sinclair, Desegregation's Quiet Success, *Washington Post* (June 17, 1978), 1A.
31. George S. Middleton high school was scheduled to open in 2002.
32. Gary Orfield, *Dismantling Desegregation*.
33. Douglas Massey and Nancy Denton, *American Apartheid: Segregation and the Making of the Underclass* (Cambridge, MA: Harvard University Press, 1993).

Chapter 6

Imagined Communities and Special Education

Sherman Dorn

As other chapters in this book describe, schools have often been at the symbolic and real center of communities, a notion that is both powerful and problematic. Other chapters have discussed the ways that imagined communities of schools have interacted with race and ethnicity as well as the position of teachers as employees and community members. In other contexts as well, community building through schools have raised issues of both exclusivity and the cognitive awareness of common interests and experiences. The two are intimately linked, as Lois Weis has argued in her analysis of working-class identities in upstate New York. In hard economic times, Weis claimed, working-class white youth defined themselves in reference to a collective (racial and social-class) identity.[1] But social class and race are not the only areas where an awareness of commonality is important to the definition of community. In special education, advocates maintain the notion that parents and students with a wide variety of conditions share common interests, even if what students face in their everyday lives is very different. From World War II through the passage of federal legislation in the 1970s, a growing if shaky disability-rights movement built a political coalition out of just such disparate elements.

Until the 1970s, schools and states treated population groups differently, including them in schools and excluding them from schools in myriad ways. Between 1970 and 1975, advocates for the education of children with disabilities successfully labeled their concerns as a matter of educational rights, the right to a formal education at public expense regardless of the nature and degree of disability. Disability-rights advocates convinced courts and legislatures that schools had discriminated against individuals with disability, a group who needed protection as a class. The disability-rights movement defined two communities—the community of the school and the community of the disabled. Before World War II, admission rules of schools excluded hundreds of thousands of students with disabilities from the notion of a school community. By defining a school community to include children with disabilities, advocates relied on the post–World War II civil rights movement that had attacked racial segregation in schools. Advocates of gender equality, equalized school funding, and disciplinary due process also relied on the philosophical arguments of *Brown v. Board* and advocates of integration, but *Brown* had a particular connection with disability-rights advocates. In defending segregation before the Supreme Court, South Carolina Democrat John W. Davis argued that *Brown* would be a noxious precedent for inclusion. If every school had to admit African American students, Davis said, they would be unable to "segregate its pupils . . . on the ground of mental capacity."[2]

Davis's prediction was correct, and advocates have occasionally used his comment to link the fate of disability rights to social justice in general: Discrimination against the disabled parallels discrimination against African Americans. But for all his prejudices, John W. Davis was not speaking against the education of all children with disabilities in schools with nondisabled peers, only the education of children with retardation (a common mid-century term used to describe a broad range of skills and problems among children). Davis's comment symbolized official discrimination not only because schools across the country did exclude or underserve students broadly but also because advocates consciously created a broad coalition, a political community of disability that stretched far beyond retardation. In part, this political coalition fed on new rhetoric about disability that emerged in the middle of the twentieth century. Franklin Delano Roosevelt was president for 12 years while using a wheelchair. During and after World War II, thousands of veterans returned home as amputees—and heroes. Author Pearl S. Buck wrote a book about her child with retardation, and the Kennedy family acknowledged the institutionalization of Rosemary Kennedy. By the 1960s, at least in public images, disability neither shamed families nor respected privilege.

This new public face of disability did not create a disability-rights coalition by itself. That coalition required the conscious efforts of parents, educators, lawyers, and also individuals with disabilities who all had their own parochial interests but worked together. In schools, they worked together because they perceived a common adversary, school routines that excluded and marginalized students with disabilities. Parents and students faced the most obvious facts of common discriminatory practices. Before the 1970s, schools commonly excluded individuals with moderate or severe retardation because many educators and school board members saw them as uneducable. Where states created central residential schools for students who were blind or deaf, local public schools could justify the exclusion of children with sensory impairments as a diversion to more appropriate facilities.[3] When they were allowed in schools, children who used wheelchairs or had other restrictions on mobility were shut out of gyms and other parts of the school with stairs or relied on classmates or school staff to carry them.[4] But this coalition included special educators, who consistently felt themselves marginalized and in a common effort to build programs serving students with disabilities.

In the 1970s, members of this coalition successfully sued school systems and lobbied for new state and federal laws to guarantee a right to public education. To a remarkable degree, the court cases and laws dramatically expanded the right to a public education. More than three decades after the first federal disability-rights law, public schools educate millions of children with a broad range of disabilities, most of them with individualized, annual programs.[5] This expansion of educational rights was a significant and real accomplishment of the disability-rights coalition. But the real accomplishments did not create a permanent redefinition of schools as communities or disability as a community. As organizations, local school districts most readily include students with sensory and mobility impairments in all parts of school programs. Students with severe behavior problems are some of the students most likely to be taught separately from nondisabled peers, and the most contentious special-education policies since the 1970s have consistently been disciplinary issues. Many educators and parents have continued to define school communities in ways that exclude students with severe behavior problems, including students with disabilities that affect behavior. Within schools, the expansion of special education has been a significant and still partial victory.[6]

Within disability circles, the definition of students with disabilities as a community of interest has also been partially successful. In a few cases, that community had factions at cross-purposes shortly after the expansion of educational rights, as advocates forced schools to reprioritize resources. In Tennessee, for example, alumni of the state school for the blind fought the shift in admissions priorities to students with multiple disabilities because that shift in purpose threatened their image of the school as an academically intensive program for bright students with visual impairments. In the last 30 years, more broadly, the interests of children with disabilities and their families have diverged. In some cases, this division is by degree and category of disability; the interests of students with hearing impairments are substantially different from the needs of students with mobility limitations. But even within any category of disability, children and their families have developed individual perspectives on needs. Some parents of children with moderate and severe cognitive disabilities have pushed for the inclusion of their children within general education classes throughout the school day; others have pushed for the isolation of their children within special-education schools that they hope can shelter the students; and hundreds of thousands of parents are somewhere between the ends of this spectrum. The community of special education historically and currently makes the most sense as a political coalition that has created and defended common procedural and substantive rights. In addressing local school practices, those interests have often been less coherent than the imagined community of disability rights.

To understand both the redefinition of these communities and also the incomplete victories of disability-rights advocates, one must look at both national developments and at some local dynamics. Nationally, the expansion of educational rights for children with disabilities piggybacked on the broader expansion of the "school community" in the postwar civil-rights era, after advocates developed a broad network and lobbying skills. But the broad definition of special-education rights also conflicted with many educators' and parents' desires to limit the community of schools to well-behaved students. And the tentative community of disability-rights activists has fragmented when the topic is appropriate placement of children (and how much of a day a student should spend with nondisabled peers). In Nashville, Tennessee, the local special-education community absorbed parents who felt isolated with a disabled child, tied parents to teachers and national researchers, and successfully pressured the state government at several points in the postwar era. But the victory of special-education advocates also created fragmentation, as the new state law and trends undermined the perceived interests of some parents and former students as well as teachers.

This chapter ties the history of special education in one community (Nashville) to the national history of special education after World War II.[7] The sources for Nashville included both archival sources and oral history interviews conducted between 1995 and 1999. There are two reasons for combining the local and national perspectives. First, the combination provides both detailed texture of local communities (where families have typically first perceived a community centered on disability) and the larger context of national events (where the redefinition of school community has been cemented through political alliances and law). But, in addition, this multilevel history challenges the local orientation of James Coleman's social capital and James Comer's definition of community. Special-education advocates at the local level drew strength from crossing a number of barriers, and one of them was geographic. By building strength within both local and national networks, parents, students, and advocates went beyond the geographically limited networks created by face-to-face and frequent contacts. In both its successes and limitations, the consciously-created disability community operated at multiple geographic levels after World War II.

Special Education and the (Re)Definition of Community

Since the mid-1970s, special education has appeared to comprise a coherent part of public school systems, protected by federal law. There are similar expectations about assessments, eligibility decisions, annual program meetings, and due-process protections, regardless of where a student lives in the country or the skills and conditions she or he has. An umbrella of federal policy has expanded and protected special education, significantly changing historical school practices in several ways. As discussed earlier in this chapter, this umbrella was a concrete achievement of a political coalition that expanded the educational rights of millions of children in the United States. Federal law and regulations have protected and maintained these rights. Moreover, federal policy responded to and has helped support a rhetorical umbrella over all the pieces of what we now call special education. Even the term "special education" implies something coherent, tying together children, parents, and teachers who may have very different substantive needs and skills. In 1920, there was no such commonly-used term, even though many schools and states had established programs for children with sensory or mobility impairments, residential institutions for children and adults labeled mentally retarded, and "ungraded classes" for students thought to be slow or retarded.[8]

Thus, advocates for disability rights in education won a dual victory in the establishment of the federal umbrella over special education. The most obvious victory was the expansion of schools to include all children, regardless of skills or disabilities. With this victory, the umbrella of educational rights extended to children with disabilities. The second victory—and the victory that made the expansion of rights possible—was the creation of a community of interests through the concept of disabilities (or "handicap" as was the more common term in the 1960s and 1970s). This second victory relied on the common experiences of thousands of students, families, and educators who slowly claimed the terms "special education" and "handicapped" as useful umbrella terms in the creation of educational programs and educational rights. This section explores the political victory of the disability-rights coalition through the mid-1970s and then the lesser-known, crucial establishment of a community of special education that made the political victory possible.

Expanding the Imagined Community of Schooling

The establishment of legal educational rights for children with disabilities was the last of five areas of school law where courts and legislatures expanded student rights after World War II. *Brown v. Board* thus represented a watershed for more than just the prohibition of racial segregation in schools. It was a rhetorical and legal wellspring for the establishment of other educational rights. In the 1960s and 1970s, legal and political advocates pushed for the expansion of student rights in other areas: the protection of individual student due-process rights, the equalization of school funding for students who lived in poor communities, the prohibition of sex discrimination in schools, and the creation of specific educational rights for children with disabilities. Advocates were more successful in some areas than in others. After decades of school intransigence in the 1950s and 1960s and then legal retreats in succeeding decades, the concrete legacy of *Brown v. Board of Education* for racial equality is still unclear more than 50 years after the original decision. Advocates for funding equity have been more successful since the late 1980s, after a switch in tactics. In the mid-1970s, the Supreme Court ruled that the federal constitution did not require equal school funding, so funding equalization efforts have relied on state constitutions and arguments that funding was inadequate as well as unequal. Although courts expanded the due-process rights of students in the 1960s and 1970s, federal courts have reasserted the authority of educators since. Only in the areas of gender and disability rights have the advocates maintained clear policy victories won in the 1970s. In the case of disability rights, advocates have been bolstered by a reliance on fundamental and politically powerful arguments about access to education.[9]

Of those five areas, the expansion of legally-enforceable educational rights for children with disabilities was perhaps the most unexpected. In the middle of the political fight for disability rights, one author called people with disabilities the "hidden minority," only faintly discernible on the political radar screen.[10] The successful political coalition did not exist immediately after World War II. In the 1950s, there was only a faint argument in local circles and parent organizations that all children were educable and should be assumed to be able to benefit from formal schooling. Even many special educators argued that children with moderate and severe cognitive disabilities had only a faint hope of having a useful education.[11] From the early nineteenth century through the 1950s, one could only find inconsistent development of programs for students who did not easily fit into schools (in educators' eyes). Program existence was inconsistent both by geography (with programs existing in some school districts and not in others) and also by the degree and nature of disability (with children having access to programs only if they had some conditions and skills and not others). Immediately after World War II, the most consistent experiences of children with disabilities and their families was uncertainty about their education and their future.[12]

Because of this uncertainty in the 1940s and 1950s, parents of children with disabilities developed dual approaches toward educational program development. In one approach, small groups of parents in different locations began pushing school systems to create programs for their children. This public advocacy at the local level had begun earlier, but it expanded as a growing postwar middle class expected more from governments and as parents of children with disabilities wanted their lives to be "normal," like those of parents without disabled children who sent their children to school at age five.[13] In addition to the public approach, groups of parents also pooled their resources to create private programs, most vividly private day schools for children with mild and moderate mental retardation. These two approaches were not inconsistent. Parents who created private programs often anticipated turning over control of private schools to public systems when local public school boards were willing to fund and oversee the programs.[14]

With the early postwar experience in public lobbying and private program development, networks of parents and their supporters had learned how to be effective advocates by the late 1960s and early 1970s. Often connected with volunteer associations that had different levels of organization at national, state, and local levels (such as the National Association for Retarded Children, the Kiwanis Club, the March of Dimes, etc.), a critical mass of parents and other advocates acquired experience working with and lobbying local school officials, negotiating the logistical matter of setting up private day schools and treatments for their own children, and lobbying federal officials for research tied to disabilities. They found funding and emotional support from local service organizations, newspapers willing to publicize events, a growing cadre of service and research professionals, and the knowledge that powerful politicians like the Kennedy family were sympathetic.[15]

So, when lawyers began having significant successes in educational civil rights in the 1960s, they found willing partners and plaintiffs in a growing disability advocacy network. One important case that was about both race and disability was *Hobson v. Hansen* (1967), where lawyers convinced federal judge Skelly Wright that the District of Columbia's tracking system concentrated African-American students in "educably mentally retarded" classes that carried a stigma and low expectations without significant educational opportunities. In 1972, two federal cases focused specifically on schools that excluded children with disabilities. In the District of Columbia, a federal judge ruled that the District's schools had unconstitutionally violated the rights of children through exclusions based on disability. Pennsylvania's state school system settled its case in a consent decree that opened up educational access.[16]

Within a few years of the D.C. and Pennsylvania cases, more than three dozen right-to-education cases were filed in federal court. The 1972 right-to-education cases came on the heels of several court cases and laws that expanded student rights: the 1968 *Green v. New Kent County* decision putting the onus on schools to desegregate, the 1968 *Tinker v. Des Moines* case that gave students considerable free-speech rights in schools, the 1971 *Swann v. Charlotte-Mecklenberg* Supreme Court case that gave federal judges the authority to order busing for desegregation purposes, the 1971 *Serrano v. Priest* decision in California that used a state constitution to equalize school financing, and Title IX of the 1972 Education Amendments, guaranteeing equal treatment by sex for programs receiving federal funding. Special-education advocates used their successful cases and the context of other successful educational rights fights to pressure the states to open up access to special education. In 1972 and 1974, respectively, Tennessee and Massachusetts wrote special-education rights laws, and in floor debate Tennessee legislators explicitly talked about the legal threats they knew were hanging over the head of the state if they didn't pass the law. In the floor debate in the Tennessee House, legislators explicitly mentioned the legal threats if they failed to pass the bill, and sponsor Rep. Curt Weldon said that courts would "ram it down our throats" without legislation. Rep. Darnell noted that advocates had "held in abeyance" a potential lawsuit until the legislature acted (or failed to). Several members wondered about the fiscal costs—Weldon admitted it might be "astronomical"—but the Tennessee legislature passed the bill anyway.[17] The U.S. Congress added a disability nondiscriminatory provision to the Rehabilitation Act in 1973. And in 1975, Congress passed Public Law 94–142, the Education for All Handicapped Americans Act, which President Ford signed even with significant misgivings about both its cost and the authority it would give the federal government. With some modifications, the basic structure of this law remains today as the Individuals with Disabilities Education Act (also known as IDEA).[18]

Special-education advocates created a political and legal steamroller in the early 1970s that was successful even as the Supreme Court was beginning a retreat from its earlier expansion of educational rights. In 1973, the Supreme Court ruled that the federal constitution did not require equal funding for education. In 1974, the Court ruled that the constitution did not require busing plans that crossed district boundaries, even if that would result in more effective desegregation. These defeats for advocates in other areas did not hurt the disability-rights movement significantly at the time. Despite these rulings, advocates for disability rights in education were successful, for two reasons. First, earlier successes created significant legal uncertainties for states that faced unknown costs for special education if they lost a case. Given this uncertainty, states preferred a predictable mandate to the potential for much greater costs. The 1975 law was thus a compromise, establishing federal educational rights for children with disabilities in return for predictability and the promise that the federal government would eventually fund 40 percent of the extra cost for special education.[19]

Second, the argument in favor of educational rights for individuals with disabilities rested on a politically secure foundation. Advocates for children with disabilities used the postwar expansion of educational rights in other areas to make the case that all children had a right to education if a state already provided schooling to most children. Even when the Supreme Court ruled against advocates for equal school funding and metropolitan busing, the broader argument still applied for children with disabilities. Experienced parents and advocates—including members of Congress with disabled relatives—helped persuade a majority of Congress that the proper community of schools included children with disabilities.

Using a Special-Education Community

The network of disability-rights advocates achieved substantial successes in part because they defined a community of interest through the concept of disability. This definition of a community turned an historical basis for stigma into a civil-rights model. Yet that broad statement is misleading. To say that disabilities in general were historically stigmatized is simplistic, because definitions of disability and deviance have changed over the decades and centuries. An obvious example of that shifting is how people have used different words to describe disabilities. The words used to label cognitive disabilities in the last hundred and fifty years have included idiot, imbecile, moron, retarded, backward, borderline, delayed, learning disabled, dyslexic, developmentally disabled, and more. But the shifting language is about hard-to-define concepts as well. For example, blindness is not restricted to individuals with no eyesight. The vast majority of individuals who are legally blind have some residual vision. And state schools for the blind after World War II typically were the primary care facilities for children with multiple sensory impairments. Sometimes, shifting labels reflect changing norms about stigma. Individuals having academic difficulties—or whom educators thought were having extreme academic difficulties—may have been labeled educably mentally retarded in the 1950s and 1960s. But individuals with similar difficulties in the 1980s and 1990s were more likely to be labeled with learning disabilities than retardation, at least in the United States, in part because parents did not want their children labeled as retarded.[20]

Finally, these terms were not just clinical descriptions. The concept of retardation early in the twentieth century was fraught with moral repudiation, despite some attempts to put deviant behavior in a medical context. Retardation was associated with sin as well as with cognitive problems. Henry Herbert Goddard successfully portrayed this association in his fraudulent 1912 study of the Kallikak family, where he claimed that the children of a retarded woman and Martin Kallikak (a pseudonym) were more likely to commit crimes and be social dependents than the children he had with his (normal-intelligence) wife. Goddard manufactured and distorted evidence, including retouching photographs. But he was able to carry off this fraud because of the preexisting prejudices about retardation at the time. The Kallikak fraud fed the prejudice, which itself fed into the early-twentieth-century eugenics movement in the United States. Until the 1930s rise of the Nazis in Germany stigmatized eugenics, American eugenicists promoted both voluntary birth control and involuntary sterilization as a way to improve the American population. When the 1927 Supreme Court ruled in favor of involuntary sterilization of those labeled retarded, Justice Oliver Wendell Holmes used common eugenics assumptions of morality and disability when he pronounced, "Three generations of imbeciles is enough."[21]

If this moral stigma attached with disabilities had risen especially high in the early twentieth century, especially in connection to retardation, the stigma receded after World War II. Public images began to portray individuals with disabilities and their families as either heroic or pitiable. Individuals with disabilities affecting their senses, limbs, and mobility were most often portrayed as heroic—Helen Keller, President

Franklin Roosevelt, and World War II veterans. Images of cognitive disabilities after World War II emphasized pity for the families. Author Pearl S. Buck's 1950 book *The Child Who Never Grew* was a watershed in that shift, as Buck described her agonizing decision to move her daughter Carol to a residential institution for the retarded. Local parent organizations and fraternal orders traded on that pity beginning in the 1950s, soliciting donations in annual drives, as often as they could with local celebrities and the images of a specific poster child.[22]

A half-century later, the twin stereotypes of the heroic/pitiable person with a disability now jar against modern sensibilities and ethics. Starting in the late 1980s, disability-rights groups have protested against the Jerry Lewis Labor Day telethon, concerned that the telethon maintained the stereotype of the people with disabilities as helpless, dependent, and not worthy of autonomy. But in the immediate postwar era, pity was an improvement over moral approbation. The origins of the postwar disability-rights network was in this environment, having to fight against remaining stereotypes of children with disabilities as morally corrupt and attempting to use whatever sympathies existed.[23]

Postwar disability-rights networking was the result of tactics after World War II. The disability-rights movement that began to be visible in the 1970s was not the first effort of individuals with disabilities and their families to convert social stigma to a practical use.[24] There are examples of earlier explicit discussions of disability from the perspectives of individuals with disabilities—for example, pacifist Randolph Bourne's 1911 essay, "The Handicapped."[25] In the mid-twentieth century, however, there were three conditions that nurtured a broader community of interest that could fight for the educational rights of children with disabilities. The first condition was the growing trend of public images sympathetic to individuals with disabilities and their families, discussed in the preceding section. The second condition was a growing acceptance of and support for the American welfare state, in both its private forms (of retirement and private-employer medical insurance) and in its public forms (with Social Security and food stamps as direct supports of families and tax incentives indirectly supporting private home ownership). In the postwar era, American families relied on and expected more from this welfare state than had been possible before the Great Depression.[26]

One part of the American welfare state since the mid-nineteenth century has been public schooling. Parents of children with disabilities saw their neighbors sending children to school at age 5 or 6, but that tax-supported institution was not always available to their families. The discrimination they and their children faced in school jarred against the growing opportunities in the United States after

World War II. In addition, expectations of schools were becoming more common after World War II, as parents' experiences from their own schooling and their children's established a common foundation for discussion. In the first half of the century, schools had become more standardized, more bureaucratic, more uniform in the experiences of children. This standardization came with the decline of community-level variation in many aspects of schooling, especially in rural areas. Yet one consequence of this standardization was a common set of experiences that made a national debate about schooling easier, as a critical mass of adults acquired the same sense of what a "real school" is. With the shift from real community-level control to a national educational debate, parents in the postwar era could build upon a foundation of common experience in defining a national community of interest in disability rights.[27]

That national standardization of education and national debate had real consequences for the building of local networks. As key players participated in journeys involving school—as students, parents, and faculty moved to and from school and other social-service agencies, as students and faculty moved from room to room within postwar schools—they helped build an imagined community of special education in important ways. The literature on parents of children with disabilities is rife with the apparent loneliness of parents in the first half of the twentieth century when told by doctors of their children's conditions.[28] At mid-century and later, pediatric specialists in Nashville, as elsewhere, were pessimistic about the possible lives of children with disabilities. In an oral-history interview, Nashville parent Alvin Tidwell explained about his child's pediatrician,

> But at the time, not only was the educational system short, but the medical profession, too. They didn't know what to do with someone like this. That's why the doctor recommended to my wife, "Send him to Clover Bottom, let him become a ward of the state, and you all get on with your life."[29]

(The Tidwells refused to.) That literature of isolation was no longer entirely accurate in the postwar era, as parents started to create a community. Some Nashville parents did feel isolated after hearing a diagnosis of mental retardation, as parent Pat Butler explained:

> We didn't realize that so many people had children that had mental retardation. When you have a child with mental retardation, you think you're probably the only one that's having this particular thing happen. Of course as you get into the field, you realize that there's an awful lot of people.[30]

Butler's phrase "as you get into the field" indicates that the isolation for her family existed immediately after her son Matt Butler's diagnosis. But the isolation could easily be broken. Tidwell felt bombarded by his fellow parents of children with disabilities:

> We had people calling us to visit with us to try to counsel with us that had handicapped people. And we got insulted because it always happened to someone else. It wouldn't happen to us. We just didn't want to cooperate in any way until finally one day, we finally came to our senses and said "Hey, we've checked all the bones in our closets, and you're not to blame and I'm not to blame. This is God's will. We've got to pick up and go on and do what the best we can for our son."[31]

The parent who felt isolated, Pat Butler, eventually became active in the local advocacy association for individuals with developmental disabilities, now known as the Arc of Davidson County. In Nashville, isolation was broken in at least two ways. One was individual effort, the path Butler took:

> We didn't get a whole lot of help from anybody, I can tell you that right now. We did a lot of adapting things for ourselves because there was not a lot out there. And even in going to school, we felt that they were lacking in a lot of things also. I mean, the fact that I did the words, the pictures and [our son's] vocabulary, and the little cards that I got, and showed him pictures of things, because [he]—[his first teachers] didn't feel that he was capable of doing a lot of this.[32]

Through a determined effort, Matt Butler's family searched for and found fellow advocates at the local level. The other path to community was recruiting from the existing community, as Tidwell experienced. In either case, to become a self-identified member of the special-education parenting community required asserting links to other families that were not automatic aspects of raising children with disabilities. They were part of creating a community.

These parents were interviewees nominated by others as aware and part of the existing disability community in Nashville.[33] Both schools and parent organizations (such as the Davidson County Council for Retarded Children, now the Arc of Davison County) served to alert these parents of their commonality with other parents. These common interests, discussed primarily in reference to social-service organizations (including schools and the state residential institutions for individuals with retardation at mid-century), called into being an imagined community in two ways. First, tangible social contacts demonstrated a commonality of interest among parents as well as providing a set of resources among themselves. The Davidson County Council included parents and teachers, as well as researchers at Peabody College for Teachers.[34] Second, the implicit comparison between themselves and parents of nondisabled children (or between themselves before and with disabled children) showed them the way that public schools at the time excluded the interests of their children and themselves.[35]

By circulating among themselves and among different schools, these parents, their children, and some teachers created a sense of commonality that spread by recruitment to others. One parent who was a member of the local Arc in the 1950s and 1960s was an artist and drew the pictures that Lloyd Dunn used when he created the Peabody Picture Vocabulary Test.[36] Faculty members in special education at Peabody College typically knew the special education administrators and many teachers at local public schools. One might say that a special education community existed in Nashville. Yet that community did not share much time or continuity. Parents passed through the school system or became more interested in adult service issues as their children aged. Faculty members left Peabody or administrators left the public schools (with four special education directors between 1950 and 1967 in Nashville's schools). In addition, everyday life interfered with intentions to create a special community. Parents had to take care of family finances as well as day-to-day care of children (both those with disabilities and siblings). Teachers had to respond to supervisory directives and prepare for work daily. Faculty members at colleges and universities had teaching and research obligations that competed with potential activism. Each of those issues was a potential barrier for the creation of a continuous culture of special education.

These mundane requirements of daily limits had two consequences for a local community of special education in Nashville. On the one hand, without easy mechanisms for transmitting cultural values (to the extent they may have existed) and ways of enculturating new "inductees" into special education, new parents, teachers, and researchers reinvented the social wheel constantly. New members of special education have felt that they were at the frontier of special education not only because of changing circumstances but because, without anyone passing along a history (or even mythology) of the field to them, they have only seen the immediate events around them and not the larger context of their lives. Many in special education (especially teachers and family members) may have had limited contact with others in special education and thus have been outside the building self-conscious disability community. In these ways, the practical limits of created communities contributed to the sense that special education was a frontier. Sam Ashcroft, former Peabody College faculty member, explained the origins of the visual education and training program in Nashville as a type of folk (and certainly humorous) myth:

> [The American Foundation for the Blind] decided to search for a site for the southern region. So they sent [Iowa School for the Blind principal] Georgie Lee Abel and a man who was vice president at the time of San Francisco State College, Leo Cain. So Cain and Abel did a tour of the sixteen southern states to find a site for a regional program in cooperation with the Southern Regional Education Board, and they selected Peabody College. And there was another leader in the field named Francis Lord, so the Lord sent Cain and Abel to the southeastern region.[37]

The insiders' joke, "The Lord sent Cain and Abel," revealed the self-consciousness of researchers trying to institutionalize a new field in special education.

Daily routines may have limited consciousness in one way, but the routines also may have formed opportunities for ordinary journeys that shaped consciousness and social networks. Parents around the world at the beginning of the twenty-first century arise, get themselves and their children dressed and fed, out the door of a home, and toward school (in those places with formal schooling). Children come home from school or some child-care facility, and parents try to find out what happened as they urge the child to complete a routine at the end of the day. Those activities seem intensively private, even (or maybe especially) where there are publicly-funded, mass schools. However, even in those privatized moments are opportunities for reflection, comparison, and social networking. Parents can compare their concerns and even their everyday routines with those of other parents (real or imagined). They can talk with other parents, in person or on the telephone, about events they have witnessed or heard about and what reasonable expectations are. They can send notes to and from school. When more formal opportunities for comparisons and networking exist—weekly meetings of religious congregations or the monthly or quarterly meetings of special-interest organizations—parents and families can plan for some further action. The community organizations to which Nashville parent Alvin Tidwell belonged or contributed comprise a case in point: West End High Lunch Bunch, American Legion, VFW, Boy Scouts, Elks Club Lodge, Fleet Reserve Association, South End United Methodist Church, Phylis Holt Sunday School, and the Rochelle Center Parents Association (centered on a facility operated by the Arc of Davidson County).[38] Out of this network of church, veterans, and service organizations came a set of connections that provided frequent opportunities for passing information and generating ideas. The opportunities for action can thus spring out of daily experience. The accomplishments of special-education activists in the 1970s depended on a network of very busy, often tired people. As in other civil-rights movements after World War II, parents in Nashville and elsewhere made time to change the treatment of their children, in part despite their daily routines but perhaps also because of their daily routines.[39]

The Fracturing of Communities in Special Education

Advocates of educational rights for children with disabilities won court and legislative victories in the 1975 by enlarging the national definition of a "community of schools" to include children with disabilities and by coopting the concept of disabilities to advance civil rights, creating (or recreating) a community of interest around special education. Implementation of the newly-won rights faced several obstacles. As with desegregation, local school districts in many places resisted the new obligations to educate all children and to follow the procedural requirements of the federal law. When courts restricted schools' ability to discipline students with disabilities with arbitrarily-long suspensions, school officials complained. The long-term debate established in the wake of federal educational rights for students with disabilities redefined the community of schools once more, with a common acceptance of the rights of individuals with sensory, mobility, and mild or moderate cognitive disabilities and some acceptance of the rights of individuals with more severe cognitive disabilities. However, with the continuing debate over how schools enforce rules when children with severe behavior problems violate them, and what discretion educators should have, the debate has kept children with behavior problems from being accepted as full members of schools.

The definition of communities has also been debated within the coalition that won the expansion of rights in the 1970s. Nationally, the question of the proper placement of students with disabilities—how much time they should spend in general classrooms or other settings with nondisabled students, how much time in more specialized environments—split educators, parents, and advocates, as the debate over inclusion and advocacy of full inclusion heated up in the 1990s. The debate over the Harris-Hillman School in Nashville is one local example of that larger tension within special-education and disability-rights advocates. The potential tension became evident long before the debate over inclusion, however, beginning almost immediately after the expansion of rights in Tennessee. The tactical use of disabilities as a concept and common interest pitted the interests of some children with disabilities against the image of a particular special-education school community that others had crafted in Tennessee.

The Limits of Educational Rights

By the mid-1990s, the legal and political debate over special education had established some topics as key disagreements while acknowledging the expansion of educational rights up to a point, and for most children with disabilities. Although there are still fights over how schools may discipline students with disabilities and where schools can place students with disabilities, much of the structure of special education law is an established fact of educational politics with robust constituencies. The tacit agreement is as important as the continuing conflict for delineating who "belong" to schools for most Americans and who are still excluded from that understanding of a school community. The tacit agreement was made possible through the implementation process for federal special-education law, through a regulatory and judicial process that set boundaries for acceptable disagreements.[40]

Nationally, the implementation of federal special-education guarantees required regulatory, legal, and political battles to make sure that schools followed the law. The federal government did not release implementing regulations until 1977, two years after President Gerald Ford signed Public Law 94–142. Parents and their lawyers then were able to contest school decisions through two mechanisms: quasi-judicial hearings that could be appealed to courts and complaints to the federal Office of Civil Rights. These mechanisms were sufficient for the clearer mandates of the law, including opening up access to schools, making eligibility decisions within the law's deadlines, and planning individual educational programs every year. But the most substantive conflicts still required interpretation. In 1982, the Supreme Court established the standard for what type of education schools had to provide. The court ruled that schools had to provide a program reasonably calculated to provide some educational benefits, but that federal law did not require that schools maximize learning. In 1988, the court ruled that schools could not suspend students with disabilities for more than 10 days, if the violation of school rules was related to the child's disability (or disabilities) and if the parents had not agreed to a longer suspension.[41] In the same years that the Supreme Court was considering these key special-education cases, special-education advocates were also defending the legal rights of students with disabilities in Congress, as the Reagan Administration floated trial balloons to relax special-education. When President Reagan appointed Madeleine Will to supervise special-education programs in 1983, advocates had won that battle.[42]

The overall result of the legislative and legal battles was a political and legal compromise. The general rights of children with disabilities were established legally. These included the enforcement of the clearest, "bright-line" standards in the law guaranteeing access to public schools, due process protections, individual assessment, and annual education planning meetings. The 1982 Supreme Court decision limited the substantive educational obligations of school districts to providing programs that were likely to provide some benefits to children.[43] And educators discovered that the majority of students with disabilities either had sensory or mobility impairments, relatively mild speech and language problems (concentrated among younger students in elementary schools), or students with some real academic difficulties but no severe cognitive problems (typically labeled as learning-disabled). Because many local public schools districts received some minimum subsidies from the federal government in exchange for providing these services, within a few years educators in many districts welcomed most of these children as members of school communities.[44]

But some children remained the focus of battles over special education, and so they were not commonly recognized as valuable (or even legitimate) members of schools. The students most often excluded for easy acceptance in school communities were children with severe behavior problems. After the Supreme Court limited suspensions for students with disabilities, educators battled parents bureaucratically in the 1980s and 1990s and also successfully fought for a modification of those rules in Congress in the 1990s. First, in response to several court decisions schools established a bureaucratic process for deciding if a student's behavior was a consequence of her or his acknowledged disabilities. These "manifestation-determination" hearings were splitting hairs—it was often difficult in practice to say clearly whether a student's misbehavior was indirectly related to academic difficulties and classroom frustrations. But by insisting on the hearings, school officials raised procedural obstacles against parents who have fought to keep their children in school past the ten-day annual suspension limit. In addition to the manifestation-determination hearings, schools discovered that they could legally bar children from transportation if inappropriate behavior were documented on buses. In practice, "bus suspensions" have become a largely undocumented way of suspending students repeatedly, past the ten-day limit.[45]

Finally, school officials convinced Congress to modify the limits on disciplining students with disabilities. One myth that spread in the late

1980s and early 1990s was that schools could not legally discipline students with disabilities, both because of the Supreme Court's interpretation of federal law and also because of the threats that parents would sue the local schools. This myth was incorrect—federal law left schools with several options apart from suspension, and schools had several ways to separate students with disabilities from school, as described in the prior paragraph—but it provided fodder for educators, parents, and eventually lawmakers who thought that federal special education law established double standards for behavior. In the early 1990s, Congress explicitly included students with disabilities when it gave local schools the authority (and mandate) to suspend and move children who brought guns and other weapons to school. In 1997, the reauthorization of federal special education law further modified the discipline rules, giving school officials a 45-day grace period during which they could provide alternative placement for children who had behaved in ways dangerous to other students, teachers, or staff. The 1997 rules were a compromise—an early proposal would have given educators the 45-day alternative placement option on mere suspicions rather than documented behavior. In addition, under pressure from disability-rights advocates, Congress added a requirement that students' annual programs have support for positive behavior where appropriate. Even with a compromise, the battle over discipline in the 1990s clearly marked the boundaries of "easily-accommodated" students—those who had behavior problems were not necessarily welcome in public schools. By the 1990s, educators and communities acknowledged that the "borders" of the school community included the majority of children with disabilities. But they still patrolled those borders against students who deviated from school rules.[46]

The Limits of a Community of Interest

The other major 1990s conflict over special education was not just a conflict between some educators and advocates for children with disabilities. The debate over inclusion and full inclusion also split the special education community, demonstrating the limits of the disability-rights community of interest. That split began after the 1970s victories. When signed in 1975, Public Law 94–142 provided an ambiguous mandate: Students must be in the "least restrictive environment," with as much contact with nondisabled peers as was consistent with an appropriate education. There was some controversy about the appropriate extent of mainstreaming students (the term used at the time), but little among advocates for special-education rights. In the early

1970s, the primary concerns were basic: access to school for those who had been excluded before, fair assessment, the inclusion of parents in individualized educational planning, and due-process protections. Although the statistics from the 1960s and early 1970s are sketchy, parents and advocates observed that hundreds of thousands of students with sensory impairments and mild cognitive disabilities were unnecessarily separated from nondisabled peers in self-contained classes and that tens of thousands of students with more involved cognitive disabilities were in separate schools with no possibility of contact with nondisabled peers. While there was resistance from some educators, most advocates were firmly convinced that the vast majority of students with disabilities needed and had a right to more contact with nondisabled peers.[47]

By the early 1990s, the majority of students receiving special-education services did have meaningful, frequent contact with nondisabled peers in school. Public Law 94–142 had significantly changed where students spent their time in school as well as opening up access and requiring annual planning of individualized education. Public Law 94–142 created several options in its continuum of placement options, from full-time placement in a general-education classroom without any help to residential institutionalization, and within 15 years the vast majority of students were concentrated closer to the nonrestrictive end than in 1975. By the 1990s, students with disabilities were far more likely to spend part of the day with nondisabled peers than in separate settings; for all students aged 6–17 receiving special-education services in 1990–1991, 69 percent spent at least 40 percent of their time in the general-education setting, with nondisabled peers. That fact did not mean that most students with disabilities spent all of their time with nondisabled peers or that they were succeeding academically in a general classroom setting. A plurality received services in "resource rooms" and other part-time settings where special-education teachers have juggled responsibilities for groups of students who shuttle in and out for "pull-out" academic instruction during the day. Other students had very limited social contact with nondisabled peers, outside academic instruction—a more common routine for interaction between nondisabled peers and students with more severe cognitive disabilities. (Among all 6–21 year olds labeled mentally retarded in 1990–1991, 58 percent spent 60 percent or more of their time in a separate classroom, and another 12 percent were outside regular schools entirely.) Yet other students with disabilities spent academic instructional time in general-education classrooms with little support.[48]

This dramatic change in the placement pattern of special education helped ignite additional debate about moving students more systematically into general-education settings—what educators and parents began to call inclusion in the 1980s. Having some success in changing where schools placed students, some advocates pushed for more inclusion. They had an ally in Reagan appointee Madeleine Will, who launched what she called the Regular Education Initiative in 1984, including focusing millions of federal grant dollars on research to improve the support of students with disabilities in general classroom settings. Beginning in the late 1980s, some parents, researchers, students, educators, and advocates for children with the most severe cognitive disabilities argued that any separation from a general education classroom was inappropriate, and they began to argue for the full inclusion of all students with disabilities in classrooms with nondisabled peers.[49]

Very quickly, other parents, researchers, students, educators, and advocates within special education argued against full inclusion and against some other inclusion proposals. Some called themselves preservationists (to maintain the continuum of placement options). The details of the arguments over inclusion and full inclusion are less important for this chapter than the nature of the split within special education over inclusion and full inclusion. Much of the split came between different areas of special education. The most visible advocates of full inclusion were tied to the education of individuals with severe cognitive disabilities, an area that was still on the margins of many schools more than a decade after Public Law 94–142. For these students, their appropriate curriculum stressed learning the social and survival skills necessary to live as adults with cognitive disabilities. On the other hand, many of the most visible opponents of full inclusion were tied to the education of individuals with relatively mild cognitive disabilities, whose most urgent concerns were effective academic instruction, not social contact with nondisabled peers. Parents, students, researchers, educators, and advocates closely tied to other areas of special education had their own particular concerns that they used to judge inclusion proposals, whether concerns that most general classroom teachers did not have the skills or time to reward good behavior for students with severe behavior problems or concerns that full inclusion (or something close to it) might endanger the ties between students with hearing impairments and the Deaf community that many adults with hearing impairments identified with.[50]

Legally and politically in the 1990s, full-inclusion advocates faced an uphill struggle. Legally, the ambiguous wording of the least-restrictive-environment mandate did not clearly require full inclusion. Despite claims to the contrary, full-inclusion advocates were unable to convince judges that the law required full inclusion. Where a school system followed due-process guidelines and provided documentation of decision-making, courts have generally accepted the professional judgment of educators about a variety of discretionary matters in special education, including the appropriate placement for students with disabilities.[51] Politically, full-inclusion advocates have faced the opposition of many educators and some parents of students with disabilities. Part of the opposition of administrators has been concern with the practical problems of full inclusion—most especially, the potential for students whose proper curriculum was not academic in focus to distract from the academic education of other students. Part may well be a residual exclusion of students with severe cognitive disabilities from educators' notion of a school community.[52]

But in addition to facing the opposition of educators, full-inclusion advocates also have faced the opposition of many within special education. And this opposition includes some parents of children with severe cognitive disabilities. In many local school districts throughout the United States, administrators dismantled separate special-education schools, moving those students into schools where most pupils are nondisabled. However, in places where some educators and parents have fought the dismantling of separate schools, they have survived as legacies of an older system and as evidence of a fragmented community within special education. In Nashville, the survival of the Harris-Hillman special education school through the 1990s showed the ability of a talented administrator to rally parents in support of a separate special-education school. In the 1960s, several patrons of special education in Nashville pushed for the creation of a specially-designed school for individuals with moderate-to-severe disabilities. When completed in the mid-1970s, the Harris-Hillman School served individuals with sensory impairments, orthopedic problems, and severe intellectual disabilities. Over the next twenty years, however, as the Nashville public schools began to accommodate the education of individuals with sensory and motor impairments, Harris-Hillman slowly became the enclave of families of children with severe health or cognitive disabilities who were unwilling to place their children in other, local public schools. When activists pushed the Nashville schools to close five of its seven separate special education schools in the 1990s, Terry Kopansky, the principal of Harris-Hillman, rallied parents and staff to keep the school alive as a special place where the students were safe. He explained to some parents that, with the school across the street from the Vanderbilt University Medical Center, he could literally carry a child to emergency medical care if necessary. Through the cultivation of a unique identity for the school, Kopansky saved the school's existence as a separate facility for children with disabilities.[53]

Kopansky's battle to save Harris-Hillman was itself the echo of a struggle in the 1970s over the identity of the Tennessee School for the Blind. In the mid-1970s, alumni of the school became active in defending their notion of an imagined community against a law that would have placed all academically-achieving children with visual impairments with local school districts. For several decades, the state school for the blind served a small number of children with visual impairments with a college-preparatory curriculum. The classes were very small (typically under ten students per teacher). Many of these students came from rural backgrounds, and experienced quite literal sponsored mobility. As former school superintendent Ralph Brewer explained,

> [We lived then] about 55 miles southwest of Nashville in a little town [called] Hickman, or Centerville, Tennessee, which is in Hickman County. We were a very poor family. My father cut cord wood or pulp wood for a living. Back in that time, they didn't have chain saws, so he did it with crosscut saws and chopping axes and, occasionally, he would become a tenant farmer and live on somebody's farm and work the farm, [a] dairy farm or just general farm. My father had about a fifth grade education. I would imagine it was very sporadic. As far as I can determine, my mother did not have any education at all. She was illiterate: She could not read or write.[54]

According to Brewer, one of his teachers contacted the state welfare department and in effect nominated him for admission to the state school. When he graduated, he (along with many other alumni) became a professional and a member in the alumni association. To many former students of the school, it had served to provide a very concrete opportunity for them.

Ironically, what threatened their imagined community was the 1972 state law guaranteeing special education for all students with disabilities. Following in the steps of two federal lawsuits in Pennsylvania and Washington, D.C., activists in Tennessee threatened the state with a right-to-education lawsuit unless the legislature passed a bill guaranteeing access to education for all children. In the first year after passage, the state refused to comply with the law. An interdepartmental committee in the fall of 1972 decided that the state would not actively seek out children with disabilities who had not previously been identified but would instead compile a list of any known children with disabilities. According to Barry Vickrey, a member of the governor's staff, the primary reason not to find more children was the fear that schools would have to serve more children: "All the committee members considered it unwise to establish a vigorous program of identifying handicapped children when it is unlikely that sufficient money will be available to provide services to all those children." Vickrey also advised that the state pay little attention to the requirement for an implementation plan, writing in October 1972 that "the plan has not been prepared. Although it is probably a waste of time and effort, the department should develop a plan, but at the least possible expense."[55]

In filing *Val Rainey et al. v. Tennessee Department of Education* in November 1973, Memphis attorney Donald Hollingsworth asked for court intervention "on behalf of all handicapped children" in Tennessee against the Department of Education "for their failure to implement certain provisions of Tennessee's Mandatory Education Law."[56] These provisions included the failure to write a state plan, initiate a comprehensive child census in the state, provide in-service teacher and staff training, and monitor local implementation. Some state officials saw the lawsuit as designed, in part, to embarrass the incumbent governor. Assistant Attorney General Henry Haile warned general counsel Lee Smith in January 1974 to be careful in preparing answers to written questions in the *Val Rainey* case: "In my personal opinion these interrogatories can be and are intended to be used for political advantage in the legislature and elsewhere by those who are seeking to increase the amount of the Special Education (Ch. 839) appropriation. Some caution should be used in formulating answers; the plaintiffs' attorneys are agressive [sic] and vindictive."[57] After several embarrassing depositions of department of education officials, the state capitulated and signed a consent decree to follow the law.[58]

One of the provisions in the consent decree, though, directly threatened the college-preparatory identity of the state School for the Blind. To provide services first to children whom schools had never served, the state had to accept children with multiple disabilities into the state schools as a priority. In February 1975, Hal Hardin filed a motion objecting to the consent agreement in the *Val Rainey* case on behalf of eighteen parents of children with visual impairments. The motion argue that the consent decree violated the state's law insofar as it extended deadlines beyond the original schedule in Chapter 839 and focused on children entirely excluded from school and those deprived of all special education services. One provision of Chapter 839 had suggested that students in the state schools could choose whether to remain in that placement or enroll in a local public school. In addition, plaintiffs argued, the threat of withholding funds could put "the student in the middle of a funding struggle, and could cause delay an uncertainty in the educational process of the visually handicapped child."

The specific claims of parents showed the identification of students and their families with the college-preparatory nature of the school. Virginia Cole, a grandparent of two children and who lived in Nashville, explained her concerns bluntly:

> In my opinion it would be disastrous to blind pre schoolers through or to high school age if require to attend public schools. With the fine state school already equipped, staffed with qualified teachers, the cost alone would be unthinkable plus the time and individual attention needed per student to insure that child an adequate education.

Janice Whitley, the mother of a 13-year-old student at the school, wrote:

> I cannot see any circumstances that would prove to be a benefit for Tim to be put in a public school. T.S.B. (Tennessee School for the Blind) offers him so many things he cannot get in a public school. He has teachers who are trained for working with the visually handicapped, who are there every day to help him, whereas if he was in a public school, he would be competing with normal children with a teacher who is not trained for his handicap. He cannot possibly get what he would need from a teacher who would come in a few hours a week to help him.

She concluded, "I recommend that T.S.B. remain open as it is today, without it serving anyone but the visually handicapped. I feel like mixing handicaps would be bad for each handicap person who is blind." To Whitley and the others represented in the petition, the imagined community of the school explicitly excluded connections to local schools and other children with disabilities. Ralph Brewer acknowledged that members of the alumni association had provided funds for the legal petition. He explained the perspective of the alumni:

> At that time, I was president of the Alumni Association of the school, and there was a tremendous, tremendous resistance by the Alumni, who graduated from the school, to these acts because these people knew the quality of education they had gotten at the TSB. And they saw the children not being able to access—there was not a resistance to children of multiple disabilities accessing the school, but it was the philosophy that says that now a residential school is the worst possible thing that can happen to children.[59]

The push to deinstitutionalize individuals with disabilities was offensive to those who not only had benefited from the state school but also saw themselves as part of an imagined community.

The school had, by the end of 1975, become a target of the *Val Rainey* plaintiffs' criticisms. On December 4, 1975, Donald Hollingsworth filed a petition that, among other claims, stated, "There is ample evidence of waste, duplication and inequities which bear both to the defendants' ability to comply and their willingness to assure equal educational opportunities." The 3 : 1 staff ratio at the Tennessee School for the Blind was one of the examples of alleged waste. Later that month, Hollingsworth argued in a letter he co-wrote to the Memphis-area legislative delegation that the students over 21 at the school were inappropriate when some children still had no access to public schooling.[60] The Tennessee School for the Blind continued to refuse to admit students with multiple disabilities, and in October 1977, the *Val Rainey* plaintiffs filed a contempt-of-court petition. The specific case at hand was of the refusal to admit John Wayne Mitchell, a child with multiple disabilities (including blindness). Mitchell's parents had, while he was enrolled at the Royer Greaves School for the Blind (in Pennsylvania), requested placement at the Tennessee School for the Blind (as had Memphis City Schools officials). The Tennessee School for the Blind had refused the request, and the state had not provided an administrative (or due process) hearing for the parents. The plaintiffs asked that the court require the state to provide due process hearing procedures and officers for state-run schools. In addition, the plaintiffs also asked to prevent parents of blind children who were "normal" in other respects from choosing the state school when appropriate placements were available locally (as that discriminated against children with multiple disabilities). The court sided with the plaintiffs and ruled, in August 1978, that Tennessee had to serve academically-able blind students in local school systems and open up the state school to children with multiple disabilities.

The battle over the admissions to the Tennessee School for the Blind, however, was largely symbolic by the late 1970s. For most of a decade, the school's population had been changing. In 1969, the school opened the year with 223 students, few of whom had multiple disabilities. A wave of children who had suffered through rubella in the early 1960s was just about to hit the school, and many of those had multiple disabilities, including developmental disabilities that affected cognition. The school hired its first teacher of the deaf-blind in 1973, and by the court petition, was clearly facing a shift in its population. Former Superintendent Brewer described the shifting mission as a way of serving blind students in different ways. By 1984, one-third of students had multiple disabilities, the result of easily foreseeable changes.[61] The battle over whether a few blind children could continue to attend the state school for a college preparatory program was over the identification of the school with those special opportunities and a community of academically focused students. Even after the changes began to push the School for the Blind toward serving more children with multiple disabilities, key people connected with the school continued to emphasize the history of its college-preparatory achievements. In 1979, a local newspaper article featuring principal Gary Coker emphasized his discussion of the professional alumni: "We have graduates who are successful businessmen. One of the top lawyers in Knoxville is one of our graduates."[62] The Alumni Association of the Tennessee School for the Blind provided assistance in the 1990s for a laudatory history of the school subtitled "the first 150 years" (emphasis added), which included lists of every single teacher and graduate (from the high school program) known to the author.[63]

The limitations of special education before the 1970s established the conditions for the awkward definition of the School for the Blind's imagined community. The origins of this conflict over the identity of the Tennessee School for the Blind was in the restricted access to services and the real sense of its students (and thus alumni, in the 1970s) that they were members of a lucky few. In the deinstitutionalization of special education and the placement of children with disabilities in communities and local schools, the changed norms threatened the self-identification of parents and alumni with that individual school. In both of these cases in Tennessee, the development of an imagined community linked with a school outlasted the specific conditions that supported that imagined community. As the expectations shifted for what special education should be—and in which imagined community children with disabilities belonged—defenders of those schools as ideals summoned up both the literal and figurative reasons for believing in them as communities. In each of these cases, the defenders of the schools had to negotiate the swaying ground underneath them, avoiding direct criticism of the newer values while asserting the right of parents and students to attend a specific school. Implied in those arguments, however, were clear statements of who did belong at separate schools. Blind students with high academic aims could benefit greatly from a separate experience, alumni of the Tennessee School for the Blind asserted. Fragile children with multiple disabilities could often grow best in a sheltered environment, Harris-Hillman Principal Terry Kopansky assured parents and his superiors. Each of these cases made for separate schools relied on important elements of an imagined community—the routine journeys of teachers, parents, and students to circulate ideas and personal connections; the implicit comparison of the community and its members with Others; and the use of a community to exchange ideas about itself and life—thus illustrating that formal schools, one of the institutions contemporary societies rely heavily on for exchanging ideas about life, have both the potential for creation and problematic change in the definition of imagined communities.

Conclusion

The expansion of educational rights for children with disabilities is one of the signal achievements of the post–World War II civil-rights era. This new set of civil rights redefined school communities across the country to include all children. There are disagreements at the margins of the new definition—the removal of students for disciplinary reasons and the extent to which children already in the school system should spend more time with nondisabled peers—but the scope of the redefinition is still breathtaking. It came with the combination of two forces. First, the federal government overruled local politics in the expansion of civil rights after World War II. In addition to the federal government, we must also credit the local, state, and national organizations that pushed for the expansion of educational rights to children with disabilities.

After World War II, the notion of a "community" tied to school has become increasingly entangled with a common national language about education. A continuous national debate over education became easier after World War II as adults shared a common experience of schooling and as a unique American welfare state evolved during and after the Great Depression. This welfare state combines both public and private institutions and both public and private interests. At the same time, American citizens are uncomfortable with the notion of a welfare state and the idea of even partial dependence on large organizations. Schooling is perhaps the best emblem of this welfare state because most schooling is publicly financed, because people associate it with citizenship rights, because people see it as a means to adult independence, because it structures dependence for a significant part of the lifespan, and because most people do not think of schooling as part of the welfare state. Yet the postwar welfare state has changed the debate over education in the United States, including notions of what a school community is.[64]

That change shaped postwar special-education history in two ways. One change came with the national debate over education and educational rights. The politics of the American welfare state has seen significant successes for those who claim a universal right of citizenship, seeking access to a welfare institution for independence and productivity. In those cases, the politics of the welfare state has trumped local political decision-making. The 1954 *Brown* decision and the roiling conflict over its implementation both changed a specific legal doctrine (racial segregation) and also sparked additional fights over who belongs in school (and which schools). Although many school districts did have special-education programs in the 1940s, they did not include all children with disabilities, and many communities had no educational services for children with disabilities (whether they were allowed in schools or not). By the late 1970s, the courts and Congress rejected local choice on the education of children with disabilities. More than 25 years after the passage of Public Law 94–142, the federal government maintains national standards that control local schools. The federal government has helped define what a school (and school community) can be.[65]

In addition to a federalist legal structure that partially defines a school community, voluntary civic activity has operated on multiple levels in special education. Individuals with disabilities, parents, educators, and other advocates can belong to independent local organizations, to local groups that are part of a larger national entity, and also to national entities themselves. In an era when some social critics bemoan the disintegration of civic organizations and the tendency to "bowl alone," this multilevel structure remains in education and special education. These organizations provide both support services to programs, families, and individuals and also help organize advocacy activities like lobbying and lawsuits. They send newsletters and other publications (and now e-mail) to educate and retain members. Where there are local chapters, the local meetings help define communities of interest and later action. Many special-education teachers joined both the national Council for Exceptional Children and also state chapters. Many parents and individuals with developmental disabilities have belonged to local chapters of the Arc (which began as the National Association for Retarded Children). There are also unaffiliated local groups, and there are also national organizations (like the American Foundation for the Blind) that have not developed state or local subunits. These organizations at both local and higher levels helped craft the legal and lobbying strategies that resulted in state and national victories for educational rights. The national organizations also have fragmented in later debates over inclusion and full inclusion. Within special education, the communities have been defined at multiple levels, in part because of how organizations have evolved. In the 1940s, 1950s, and 1960s, that multilevel organization allowed considerable flexibility in defining a community of special education. Even with the occasional disagreements that remain, it is an example of continuing efforts to maintain a community and communities of interest around disabilities.[66]

This redefinition and creation of community at multiple levels has real consequences for schools. To whom are they most accountable? Before federal guarantees of civil rights, the "local community" of a school often meant the local political elites that could and did exclude many parents and children from active participation, including children with disabilities. But a central government may not be the best authority to make decisions on what a good school is, even if that is the import of more than 20 years of school reform that has emphasized test-driven accountability. This multilevel story also should make us question the way we talk about social capital. The contemporary discussion of community social capital typically assumes a local community and set of social networks. But does one gain from social capital only from one's geographic neighbors? Many advocates of desegregation hoped that social networking across race barriers would significantly change the outcomes of students as they aged into adulthood. The history of special-education rights after World War II shows the ability of local activists to learn from and influence national players. The history of postwar special education has to be told at both the local and national levels, and in doing so, we confront an additional problem in thinking about schools as communities.

Notes

1. Lois Weis, *Working Class without Work: High School Students in a De-industrializing Economy* (New York: Routledge, 1990). Weis explored the issues of identity, which are intimately tied up with collective definitions of community.
2. Both Title IX of the Educational Amendments of 1972 and Section 504 of the Rehabilitation Act of 1973 echoed Title VI of the Civil Rights Act of 1964, tying federal funding to nondiscrimination clauses. The investigation of complaints in all areas came under the Office of Civil Rights in the Office of Education (before 1980) and the Department of Education (after its creation in 1980). Davis opened his presentation in the 1952 oral arguments in *Brown* by pointing out that the argument of the NAACP lawyers went beyond race: "I think if the appellants' construction of the Fourteenth Amendment should prevail here, there is no doubt in my mind that it would catch the Indian within its grasp just as much as the Negro. If it should prevail, I am unable to see why a state would have any further right to segregate its pupils on the grounds of sex or on the ground of age or on the ground of mental capacity." Oral argument December 9, 1952, retrieved July 1, 2004, from

<http://www.yale.edu/lawweb/avalon/curiae/html/347-483/old/13.htm>.
3. When faced with a request to allow blind children into city programs for visually-impaired students, the Nashville Board of Education initially refused; minutes, July 5, 1956. Over the next year, the city schools slowly agreed to a pilot program that became permanent; minutes, January 8, 1957; March 14, 1957; April 16, 1957; May 21, 1957.
4. Seymour Bernard Sarason and John Doris, *Educational Handicap, Public Policy, and Social History: A Broadened Perspective on Mental Retardation* (New York: Free Press, 1979), 460.
5. U.S. Office of Special Education and Rehabilitative Services, *Twenty-Fourth Annual Report to Congress on the Implementation of the Individuals with Disabilities Act* (Washington, D.C.: Department of Education, 2002).
6. Mitchell L. Yell, "*Honig v. Doe*: The Suspension and Expulsion of Handicapped Students," *Exceptional Children* 56 (1989): 60–69; Yell, "Reclarifying Honig versus Doe," *Exceptional Children* 57 (1991): 364–368; Antonis Katsiyannis, Mitchell L. Yell, and Renee Bradley, "Reflections on the 25th Anniversary of the Individuals with Disabilities Education Act," *Remedial and Special Education* 22, 6 (2001): 324–335; Sherman Dorn and Douglas Fuchs, "Trends in Placement Issues," Audrey McCray Sorrells, Herbert J. Rieth and Paul T. Sindelar eds., *Critical Issues in Special Education: Access, Diversity, and Accountability* (Boston: Pearson, 2004), 57–72.
7. This chapter reports on research supported by the U.S. Department of Education's Office of Special Education Programs Awards H023N50013 and H023N60001. Views expressed here do not represent those of the granting agency.
8. Philip L. Safford and Elizabeth J. Safford, *A History of Childhood and Disability* (New York: Teachers Coll. Press, 1996), 342.
9. Eric Blumenson and Eva S. Nilsen, "One Strike and You're Out? Constitutional Constraints on Zero Tolerance in Public Education," *Washington University Law Quarterly* 81 (2003): 65–117; Trudy Saunders Bredthauer, "Twenty-Five Years under Title IX: Have We Made Progress?" *Creighton Law Review* 31 (1998): 1107–1129; Avidan Y. Cover, "Is 'Adequacy' a More "Political Question" Than "Equality?" The Effect of Standards-Based Education on Judicial Standards for Education Finance," *Cornell Journal of Law and Public Policy* 11, 2 (2002): 403(37); Gregory T. Gledhill, "Up a Creek . . . but not without a Paddle: Public School Corporal Punishment in the Fifth Circuit," *George Mason University Civil Rights Law Journal* 13, 1 (2003): 121–149; Shari Golub, "Tinker to Fraser to Hazelwood—Supreme Court's Double Play Combination Defeats High School Students' Rally for First Amendment Rights," *DePaul Law Review* 38, 2 (1989): 487–515; Gary Orfield, Susan E. Eaton, and Harvard Project on School Desegregation, *Dismantling Desegregation: The*

Quiet Reversal of Brown v. Board of Education (New York: New Press, 1996), 424; David C. Thompson and Faith E. Crampton, "The Impact of School Finance Litigation, A Long View," *Journal of Education Finance* 28, 1 (2002): 133–172.
10. Sonny Kleinfield, *The Hidden Minority: A Profile of Handicapped Americans* (Boston: Little, Brown, 1979), 213.
11. See, e.g., the debate between I. Ignacy Goldberg and William M. Cruickshank, "The Trainable but Uneducable: Whose Responsibility?" *NEA Journal* 47 (December 1958): 622–623.
12. Sarason and Doris, *Educational Handicap, Public Policy, and Social History*, 460; Safford and Safford, *A History of Childhood and Disability*, 342.
13. Gunnar Myrdal, former executive director of the National Association for Retarded Children (now the ARC) made this point to me in a personal conversation in Nashville in December 1995.
14. Sherman Dorn, "Public-Private Symbiosis in Nashville Special Education," *History of Education Quarterly* 42, 3 (2002): 368–394.
15. See, e.g., discussions of voluntary-organization participation in activities of the Davidson County Association for Retarded Citizens (now the Arc of Davidson County) in its scrapbooks: "Aid to Retarded Cited at Rotary," Nashville *Tennessean*, n.d. (probably 1953 or 1954); "Rotary to Sponsor Retarded Child Aid," other publication information not provided (probably late 1954); in 1952–1955 clipbook in offices of the Arc of Davidson County. The local Rotary Club sponsored the creation of the private Edgehill School; see Nashville City Board of Education minutes, August 11, 1955; October 6, 1955; November 15, 1955; December 15, 1955; May 21, 1957; September 12, 1957; July 22, 1958; August 14, 1958; September 11, 1958; Davidson County Board of Education minutes, August 15, 1957; Nashville *Banner*, September 1, 1953; May 7, 1954; October 6, 1953; October 6, 1955.
16. *Hobsen v. Hansen*, 269 F.Supp. 401 (D.C., 1967); *Mills v. D. C. Board of Education*, 348 F.Supp. 866 (D.C., 1972); *Pennsylvania Association for Retarded Children v. Commonwealth of Pennsylvania*, 348 F.Supp. 279 (1972).
17. Remarks made in the Tennessee House, April 4, 1972, at Tennessee State Library and Archives, 87th General Assembly, 33rd House day, vinyl audio disks H-188, H-189.
18. Katsiyannis, Yell, and Bradley, "Reflections on the 25th Anniversary of the Individuals with Disabilities Education Act;" Congressional Record, May 20, 1974, p. 15270; *Green v. County School Board of New Kent County* (1968); *Swann v. Charlotte-Mecklenburg Board of Education* (1971); *Serrano v. Priest* (1971); Public Law 92–318, Title IX (1972); Tennessee Public Acts of 1972, Chapter 839; Massachusetts Public Acts of 1974, Chapter 766; Public Law 93–112, Section 504 (1973); Public Law 94–142 (1975).

19. *San Antonio Independent School District v. Rodriguez (1973); Milliken v. Bradley I (1974)*.
20. Safford and Safford, *A History of Childhood and Disability*, 342; Michael J. Tobin, "Assessing Visually Handicapped People: An Introduction to Test Procedures,"; Scott B. Sigmon, *Radical Analysis of Special Education: Focus on Historical Development and Learning Disabilities*, Anonymous (London: Falmer, 1987), 124.
21. Safford and Safford, *A History of Childhood and Disability*, 342. Stephen Jay Gould, *The Mismeasure of Man* (New York: W. W. Norton, 1981): 168–174; *Buck v. Bell*, 274 U.S. 200 (1927).
22. Dorothy Herrman, *Helen Keller: A Life* (Chicago: University of Chicago Press, 1989); Helen Keller, *Midstream: My Later Life* (Garden City, N.Y.: Doubleday); Pearl S. Buck, *The Child Who Never Grew* (New York: John Day, 1950); James W. Trent, *Inventing the Feeble Mind: A History of Mental Retardation in the United States* (1994: University of California Press, 1994).
23. Lynda Richardson, "In Wheelchairs and on Crutches, some Disabled Protest a Telethon," *New York Times*, September 7, 1993, p. B2.
24. For an example see David Pfeiffer's criticism of Shapiro's disability-rights history: David Pfeiffer, "Hip Crip 101," *Mainstream: Magazine of the Able-Disabled*; Joseph P. Shapiro, *No Pity: People with Disabilities Forging a New Civil Rights Movement* (New York: Times Books, 1993), 372.
25. Randolph Bourne, "The Handicapped—By One of Them," *Atlantic Monthly*, September 1911: 320–329; also see Paul K. Longmore, "The Life of Randolph Bourne and the Need for a History of Disabled People," Longmore, *Why I Burned My Book and Other Essays on Disability* (Philadelphia: Temple University Press, 2003).
26. Stephanie Coontz, *The Way We Never Were: American Families and the Nostalgia Trap* (New York: Basic Books, 1992), 391; Michael B. Katz, *The Price of Citizenship: Redefining America's Welfare State* (New York: Metropolitan Books, 2001), 469; Emilie Stoltzfus, *Citizen, Mother, Worker: Debating Public Responsibility for Child Care after the Second World War* (Chapel Hill: University of North Carolina Press, 2003), 328.
27. Mary Haywood Metz, "Real School: A Universal Drama amid Disparate Experience," D. Mitchell and M. E. Goertz, eds., *Education Politics for the New Century: The Twentieth Anniversary Yearbook of the Politics of Education Association* (Philadelphia: The Falmer Press, 1990), 75–91.
28. James W. Trent, Jr., *Inventing the Feeble Mind: A History of Mental Retardation in the United States* (Berkeley: University of California Press, 1994), 230–237, discusses the parent "confessional" literature in the 1950s as a reflection and stimulation of parent responses to developmental disabilities. *The Child Who Never Grew* is the paradigmatic example.

29. Interview with Alvin Tidwell (December 4, 1995).
30. Interview with Pat Butler (March 22, 1996).
31. Interview with Tidwell.
32. Interview with Butler.
33. I sent direct invitations to researchers I knew of from discussing the history of special education in Nashville with Peabody faculty in the mid-1990s; I recruited parent, teacher, and student interviewees through the school district and several community organizations.
34. Tidwell interview; also, interview with Franelle Wood (July 4, 1996).
35. Gunnar Dybwad, in a personal conversation in December 1995, described one of these interests as the child-care role that schools served at midcentury.
36. Interview with Lloyd Dunn (February 9, 1996).
37. Interview with Samuel C. Ashcroft (September 28, 1995).
38. Nashville *Tennessean* obituary, June 10, 2002, available online at <http://tennessean.com/obits>.
39. Benedict R. Anderson, *Imagined Communities: Reflections on the Origin and Spread of Nationalism*, 2nd ed. (New York: Verso, 1991).
40. For a similar analysis of how bureaucratic politics set limits to conflict, see Ira Katznelson, *City Trenches: Urban Politics and the Patterning of Class in the United States* (New York: Pantheon Books, 1981), 267.
41. *Federal Register* 42, 153 (August 23, 1977); *Board of Education v. Rowley*, 458 U.S. 176 (1982); *Honig v. Doe* (1988); Dena Kleiman, "Handicapped in Classroom: The Case before the Court," *New York Times*, March 23, 1982, C1, 6.
42. E.g., Susan Heller Anderson, "Goals on Handicapped Meet Wide Resistance," *New York Times*, November 14, 1982, FSE45-46; James G. McCullagh, "Challenging the Proposed Deregulation of P.L. 94–142: A Case Study of Citizen Advocacy," *Journal of Sociology and Social Welfare* 15, 3 (1988): 65–81.
43. For a discussion of how school officials negotiated the maximum-education requirement of Massachusetts' special-education law, see Richard Weatherley and Michael Lipsky, *Street-Level Bureaucrats and Institutional Innovation: Implementing Special Education Reform in Massachusetts* (Cambridge: Joint Center for Urban Studies of the Massachusetts Institute of Technology and Harvard University, 1977), 90; Richard Weatherley, *Reforming Special Education: Policy Implementation from State Level to Street Level* (Cambridge, MA: MIT Press, 1979), 187.
44. For discussions of the mixed attitudes of teachers toward special education in the decade after passage of Public Law 94–142, see Benjamin L. Brooks and Rochelle B. Simms, "Are Handicapped Children Welcome in Catholic Schools?" *Momentum* 15, 1 (1984): 44–46; Ronald E. Childs, "Perceptions of Mainstreaming by Regular Classroom Teachers Who Teach Mainstreamed Educable Mentally Retarded Students in the Public Schools," *Education and Training of the Mentally Retarded* 16, 3 (1981): 225–227; Margaret C. Coleman

and James E. Gilliam, "Disturbing Behaviors in the Classroom: A Survey of Teacher Attitudes," *Journal of Special Education* 17, 2 (1983): 121–129; David Feldman and and others, "The Effects of Differential Labeling on Professional Concepts and Attitudes toward the Emotionally Disturbed/Behaviorally Disordered," *Behavioral Disorders* 8, 3 (1983): 191–198; Mary Elizabeth Hannah and Susan Pliner, "Teacher Attitudes toward Handicapped Children: A Review and Synthesis," *School Psychology Review* 12, 1 (1983): 12–25; Barbara Larrivee, "Factors Underlying Regular Classroom Teachers' Attitude toward Mainstreaming," *Psychology in the Schools* 19, 3 (1982): 374–379; Daniel P. Morgan and Ginger Rhode, "Teachers' Attitudes toward IEP's: A Two-Year Follow-Up," *Exceptional Children* 50, 1 (1983): 64–67; Anita Nader, "Teacher Attitude toward the Elementary Exceptional Child," *International Journal of Rehabilitation Research* 7, 1 (1984): 37–46; Bill J. Reynolds et al., "Elementary Teachers' Attitudes toward Mainstreaming Educable Mentally Retarded Students," *Education and Training of the Mentally Retarded* 17, 3 (1982): 171–176; Thomas M. Stephens and Benjamin L. Braun, "Measures of Regular Classroom Teachers' Attitudes toward Handicapped Children," *Exceptional Children* 46, 4 (1980): 292–294.

45. For a critical look at manifestation-determination hearings, see Antonis Katsiyannis and John W. Maag, "Manifestation Determination as a Golden Fleece," *Exceptional Children* 68, 1 (2001): 85–96. For the U.S. Department of Education's interpretation of how bus suspensions fit into IDEA, see the *Federal Register* 64 (March 12, 1999): 12619.

46. Yell, "*Honig v. Doe*," 60–69; Yell, "Reclarifying *Honig versus Doe*," 364–368; Mitchell L. Yell, Michael E. Rozalski, and Erik Drasgow, "Disciplining Students with Disabilities," *Focus on Exceptional Children* 33, 9 (2001): 1–20, for a taste of the debate over the 1997 reauthorization, see Bruce Alpert, "Schools Request Right To Remove Discipline Cases," *Cleveland Plain Dealer*, May 25, 1996, retrieved from Lexis-Nexis Academic Universe. The discussion here is about the broader arguments over school community membership, not the practical issues involved in classroom order or teaching students with disabilities.

47. 20 U.S. Code §1412(5)(B); Sarason and Doris, *Educational Handicap, Public Policy, and Social History*, 460; Scott B. Sigmon, "The History and Future of Educational Segregation," *Journal for Special Educators* 19, 4 (1983): 1–15.

48. U.S. Office of Special Education and Rehabilitative Services, *Twenty-Fourth Annual Report*, Tables AB7-AB8, retrieved July 2, 2004, from <http://www.ed.gov/about/reports/annual/osep/2002/index.html>. In the 1990s, students in special education on average spent more time with nondisabled peers. By 1999–2000, 76 percent of all 6–17 year old students in special education spent at least 40 percent of their time in general-classroom settings.

49. Madeleine C. Will, "Educating Children with Learning Problems: A Shared Responsibility," *Exceptional Children* 52, 5 (1986): 411–415; D. K. Lipsky and A. Gartner, "Inclusion, School Restructuring, and the Remaking of American Society," *Harvard Educational Review* 66, 4 (1996): 762–796; Maynard C. Reynolds, "An Historical Perspective: The Delivery of Special Education to Mildly Disabled and At-Risk Students," *Remedial and Special Education (RASE)* 10, 6 (1989): 7–11; Susan Stainback and William Stainback, *Inclusion: A Guide for Educators* (Baltimore: Paul Brookes Publishing Company, 1996), 416; Margaret C. Wang and Maynard C. Reynolds, "Progressive Inclusion: Meeting New Challenges in Special Education," *Theory into Practice* 35, 1 (1996): 20–25; Susan Stainback and William Stainback, *Curriculum Considerations in Inclusive Classrooms: Facilitating Learning for All Students* (Baltimore: Paul Brookes Publishing Company, 1992), 275.
50. Douglas Fuchs and Lynn S. Fuchs, "Inclusive Schools Movement and the Radicalization of Special-Education Reform," *Exceptional Children* 60, 4 (1994): 294–309; Naomi Zigmond et al. "When Students Fail to Achieve Satisfactorily—Reply," *Phi Delta Kappan* 77, 4 (1995): 303–306; Douglas Fuchs and Lynn S. Fuchs, "Counterpoint: Special Education—Ineffective? Immoral?" *Exceptional children* 61, 3 (1995): 303–305; Douglas Fuchs and Lynn S. Fuchs, "Sometimes Separate is Better," *Educational Leadership* 52, 4 (1995): 22–26; Douglas Fuchs and Lynn S. Fuchs, "Competing Visions for Educating Students with Disabilities: Inclusion Versus Full Inclusion," *Childhood Education* 74, 5 (1998): 309–316; Daniel J. Gallagher, "Neutrality as a Moral Standpoint, Conceptual Confusion and the Full Inclusion Debate," *Disability & Society* 16, 5 (2001): 637–654; James M. Kauffman et al. "The Regular Education Initiative and Patent Medicine—A Rejoinder," *Exceptional Children* 56, 6 (1990): 558–560; James M. Kauffman, "How we might Achieve the Radical Reform of Special-Education," *Exceptional Children* 60, 1 (1993): 6–16; D. L. MacMillan, F. M. Gresham, and S. R. Forness, "Full Inclusion: An Empirical Perspective," *Behavioral Disorders* 21, 2 (1996): 145–159; Naomi Zigmond et al. "When Students Fail to Achieve Satisfactorily—Reply ," 303–306; Naomi Zigmond, "Where Should Students with Disabilities Receive Special Education Services? Is One Place Better than Another?" *Journal of Special Education* 37, 3 (2003): 193–199.
51. Mitchell L. Yell, "Least Restrictive Environment, Inclusion, and Students with Disabilities: A Legal Analysis," *Journal of Special Education* 28, 4 (1995): 389–404; Mitchell L. Yell and Erik Drasgow, "A Legal Analysis of Inclusion," *Preventing School Failure* 43, 3 (1999): 118–123.
52. E.g., Albert Shanker, "Full Inclusion Is Neither Free nor Appropriate," *Educational Leadership* 52 (December 1994–January 1995): 18–21.

53. Frederick Lawrence Patrick, "An Ethnographic Study of a Special Education School: The Harris-Hillman Story" (Ph.D. diss., Vanderbilt University, 1996).
54. Interview with former Tennessee School for the Blind student and then-superintendent Ralph Brewer (April 18, 1997). In this case, I am shifting the meaning of "sponsored mobility" to include sponsored *upward* mobility as well as maintenance of socioeconomic position, unlike Ralph H. Turner, "Sponsored and Contest Mobility and the School System," *American Sociological Review* 25 (1960): 855–867.
55. Vickrey to Leonard K. Bradley, October 11, 1972, in Tennessee State Library and Archives, Winfield Dunn Papers (Record Group 49), box 124.
56. *Val Rainey et al. v. Tennessee Department of Education*, Davidson County Chancery Court Docket No. A-3100, filed November 6, 1973; the earlier case was *Val Rainey* et al. *v. Juanita Watkins* et al. Shelby County Chancery Court Docket No. 77620–2, filed April 6, 1973. All of the petitions and decrees discussed here have copies in the *Val Rainey* docket boxes in Davidson County, Tennessee (Nashville).
57. Henry Haile to M. Lee Smith, January 18, 1974, in Tennessee State Library and Archives, Winfield Dunn Papers (Record Group 49), box 124. Considering my earlier statements about political narratives, I note that I do not know what personal connections Hollingsworth had to disability activists. Many of the parents active since the early 1950s in the state's developmental–disability organization (now the Tennessee Arc) had been professionals and were likely to know quite well how to contact and employ lawyers.
58. Consent decree entered July 29, 1974, M.B. 90, page 419, Davidson Chancery Court.
59. Interview with Brewer (April 18, 1997).
60. Donald M. Hollingsworth and J. Richard Rossie to "Members of the Shelby County delegation," December 18, 1975, in folder 2, box 2, Halbert Harvill Papers, Record Group 75, Tennessee State Library and Archives.
61. John H. Waddey, *Tennessee School for the Blind: The First One Hundred Fifty Years* (Nashville, Tenn.: Tennessee School for the Blind, 1995), 259, 271, 307; interview with Brewer (April 18, 1997).
62. Max York, "School for the Blind Teaches Skills," Nashville *Tennessean* (April 22, 1979), F-1, F-2.
63. John H. Waddey, *Tennessee School for the Blind, 1844–1944: The First 150 Years* (Nashville: Tennessee School for the Blind, 1995).
64. For discussions of the politics of schooling and the democratic state, see Martin Carnoy and Henry M. Levin, *Schooling and Work in the Democratic State* (Stanford, CA: Stanford University Press, 1985), 307; W. Norton Grubb and Marvin Lazerson, *Broken Promises: How Americans Fail their Children* (New York: Basic Books, 1982), 358; Katz, *The Price of Citizenship*, 469; Ira Katznelson and Margaret Weir,

Schooling for All: Class, Race, and the Decline of the Democratic Ideal (New York: Basic Books, 1985), 258; David Tyack and Larry Cuban, *Tinkering toward Utopia: A Century of Public School Reform* (Boston: Harvard University Press, 1995), 190.

65. Technically, both the Individuals with Disabilities Education Act and Section 504 of the Rehabilitation Act of 1973 rely on monetary incentives rather than directly ordering local schools to take certain actions. A state is legally free to reject federal funding, and New Mexico refused federal special-education funding for several years to avoid having to comply with its requirements.

66. See, e.g., Robert Putnam, *Bowling Alone: The Collapse and Revival of American Community* (New York: Simon & Schuster, 2000).

Chapter 7

The Glover School Historic Site: Rekindling the Spirit of an African American School Community

Elgin Klugh

Several groups of African Americans seeking to preserve and advance the educational history of their communities, and also seeking facilities to offer various kinds of educational and community programming, have focused their efforts on the buildings that once served as segregated schoolhouses. These schools, generally known as Rosenwald Schools, symbolize an important part of African American cultural history.[1]

Pre-desegregation-era Black schools were a part of the larger institution of American education in which acceptable standards for curriculum, teaching-styles, student behavior, and most school-related activity, was defined by the dominant class of society. However, African American school communities were overwhelmingly reliant on community initiative and collective action. Thus, these schools developed as community institutions wherein community members could focus their collective energies toward a common goal—where they could "invest in each other" and actively create "palpable resources" to improve their lives.[2] And because these were community institutions that everyone had a vested interest in, they reinforced the educational and communal values that allowed their construction.

Several authors have explored what constitutes the shared values/ motivations/inspirations that drew people together to create viable, self-help community institutions—in the form of schools. Using terms and phrases such as "core values" or "sense of group consciousness and collective identity"[3] or "cultural ethos" or "cultural capital and African American agency,"[4] these authors describe how people with almost no economic power, and possessing very little inside of the dominant paradigm for acceptable cultural/social capital, were able to capitalize on the resources that they did have—a shared cultural background, shared goals, and collective ability. Thus, the ability to marshal productive, collective action proved to be a potent form of cultural capital within itself.[5]

Social capital, unlike cultural capital, does not primarily concern values that are "lodged" within individuals, but refers to the functioning of relations within social networks and institutions.[6] As schoolhouses, and the inherent social structure within them, took shape, a community's bonds were strengthened through the productive interaction of its members. And, as schools became the central point of community activity, the potential for productive social capital development grew. In many cases, tight social networks existed among parents, administrators, and school employees. These networks were only strengthened by interaction in other segments of small community life—the church, family, benevolent organizations, and the like.

The end result of the process of schooling is increased human capital. According to James Coleman's 1988 article, "human capital is created by changes in persons that bring about skills and capabilities that make them able to act in new ways."[7] Even in the grip of a Jim Crow society that offered few opportunities for advancement to educated African Americans, the educated individuals and communities fared much better. Thus, the progression concerning segregation-era African American schoolhouses appears that cultural capital, which led to social capital development, resulted in the development of human capital that improved community life.

In spite of their contextual existence in an oppressive, Jim Crow society, these schools left lasting impressions on those who were educated in them. Though not advocating a return to the past, many of these former students are actively trying to bring the values they were taught there into the present. Through preserving these buildings and the inherent symbolism within them, it is hoped that an important part of their heritage will not be forgotten, but will be passed down to future generations.

In Bealsville, Florida, residents formed a nonprofit community organization, Bealsville, Incorporated, for the purpose of taking control of their segregation-era schoolhouse that was closed by the county in 1980.[8] In the years since, residents have embarked on a project aimed at renovating the school for noneducational use, and reviving the complex as a center for community activity. At the Glover School Historic Site in Bealsville, Henry Davis and William Thomas, Sr.—both over 50 and still working full-time—spend several hours each week pulling weeds, planting flowers, cutting tree limbs, and making minor repairs around the six-building complex. Meanwhile, Herman Hargrett, a retired schoolteacher, drives his tractor over the ten acres of land to cut the grass without any kind of financial reimbursements.[9] These jobs are on top of their existing voluntary responsibilities as president, vice president and co-treasurer of the organization handling the Glover School renovation project.

Though the actions Bealsville residents are independent, their preservation efforts are reflective of similar community-based efforts in communities throughout the southeast. The work of preserving schools is a painstaking process with few tangible rewards. Money must be raised, grounds must be kept, community support must be encouraged, local political support must be won, and contract work must be managed. In most cases these and other tasks are completed by individuals who are not paid to do them. Instead, they believe they have duties to preserve and pass on the educational legacy that was handed down to them. To fully understand the significance of this legacy and why it would inspire individuals to invest so much of their time and energy in preserving it, we must first understand how education was a crucial component of African American "ethnogenesis."[10]

African Americans and Education: The First Crusade

African American attitudes toward education developed within the context of slavery. In an effort to keep slaves more submissive, southern states enacted laws making it progressively more difficult to teach Blacks to read or write, especially after Nat Turner's rebellion in 1831. Punishments were often severe for slaves found to be literate, and also for those caught teaching slaves to read and write. Those who chose education, or to educate, in spite of the prevailing laws, risked bodily mutilations and even death.

Still, many risked everything for the sake of education. Whether its was in the form of secret group meetings, under the guise of bible study, or the result of defiant mistresses or masters simply tutoring their favorite slaves (who sometimes happened to be their children), a theme of educational agency exists throughout the history of slavery. Anderson proffers a reason for this when he explains that, "Black adaptation to slavery imbued them with the ideas of literacy as a contradiction to oppression [. . .]."[11] Thus, the quest for literacy offered a direct form of resistance to slave society—a less direct and immediate method than running away or open revolt, but dangerous just the same.

At slavery's end, it was the literate contingent of African Americans (those free during slavery, and those recently freed who had become literate during slavery) that assumed many of the leadership roles within flowering African American communities. They, along with almost all African Americans, carried with them a view of education as the means to safeguard against exploitation, to express freedom and distance themselves from slavery, and to secure appropriate knowledge for informed political participation.[12] In efforts to secure their freedom through education, Reconstruction Era Black politicians led the fight for universal, state-financed, public education.[13] And by 1870, "every southern state had specific provisions in its constitution to assure a public school system financed by a state fund."[14]

On the local level, the African American fervor for education did not wait for a state-financed school system to be instituted. Though taxes were paid, educational benefits stemming from tax money were slow in coming to African American communities. Thus, people used their personal resources to create schools that should have been provided. Many undocumented schools sprang up all over the South. Some of these were schools sponsored by well-intentioned northern philanthropists. However, many of these schools were set up by community members who pooled their collective resources to procure books, supplies, facilities (if possible), and teachers. And in many cases, outside help from northern philanthropists and missionaries was shunned so that Blacks could maintain direct control over their schools.

It is not clear exactly how many African American schools were started in the years immediately after slavery. Surely, some of them were started before slavery's end and simply came out of hiding, and others were erected by recognized organizations that kept records of attendance and expenditures. But vast numbers of small, uncounted community initiated educational efforts also existed. Popular manifestations of these were in the form of "Sabbath Schools"—schools that had their beginnings in the church.[15]

For many communities religion and education were intimately connected. Both pursuits provided a sustaining sense of protection against the mental and physical realities of oppression. Thus, it made symbolic and practical sense for fledgling communities to locate religious and educational activities in the same place. As resources and population permitted, permanent, independent structures were built for the purpose of education. And as communities grew to have more than one church, the school provided a central, neutral, meeting place. Also, because members of the community all had a personal stake in these schools they took on a central importance and became beacons of community pride and togetherness.

Rosenwald Schools and Community

The Rosenwald school-building program arose when industrial education was being advocated in African American communities. African Americans desired education to live as free and efficacious citizens. Conversely, most southern Whites desired that Blacks remain uneducated, intimidated, and exploitable.[16] And northern philanthropists wanted an industrially trained, politically passive class of laborers. Falsely presented as a compromise, Industrial Education "was the logical extension of an ideology that rejected Black political power while recognizing that the South's agricultural economy rested on the backs of Black agricultural workers."[17]

The proponents of this industrial education desired a "cultural hegemony" that "mitigated the necessity for the State to use its coercive apparatus to control" African American ideology, protest, and labor.[18] Instead of control by force, ideological control appeared much more economically sound. However, the paradigm of industrial education was not blindly accepted in African American communities.[19] This opposition is most clearly stated in the arguments put forward by W.E.B. DuBois.

In his 1903 essay on Booker T. Washington, Dr. Dubois, though acknowledging contributions that Mr. Washington had made to the Black community, condemned Washington's prescription that African American people give up "political power," "insistence on civil rights," and the "higher education of Negro Youth" in exchange for focused concentration on labor, and the accumulation of wealth and property.[20] Pointing out the deteriorating political and social conditions of African Americans since Reconstruction, Dr. Dubois asks a pivotal question:

> The question then comes: Is it possible, and probable, that nine millions of men can make effective progress in economic lines if they are deprived of political rights, made a servile caste, and allowed only the most meager chance for developing their exceptional men? If history and reason give any distinct answer to these questions, it is an emphatic No.[21]

In concert with wealthy philanthropists, Washington waged a fierce ideological campaign in support of Industrial Education, but the sentiments of the masses sided with Dubois. Still, the ideological sensibilities of Dubois's arguments were limited when it came to combating wealthy philanthropists who desired Industrial Education for Blacks, and the philanthropists had seemingly endless resources to finance their plans.[22]

The Julius Rosenwald Foundation arose during the Industrial Education movement. With the aid of Booker T. Washington, Julius Rosenwald, a Sears Company executive, instituted a program to help finance small schools for African Americans across the south. Though the foundation was an outgrowth of an ideology with serious flaws, the benefits of its programs had a significantly positive impact on the development of Black America. Henry Allen Bullock writes:

> The work of the Rosenwald Fund, however, permeated the educational experiences of the Negro more deeply than that of any other fund. It inspired the construction of Negro schools where none had ever been before, facilitated the development of more specialized industrial high schools for Negroes, sponsored libraries and provided reading materials where books had been rare objects, and financed the development not only of Negro teachers but of doctors and other professionals as well. The corresponding assistance to Negro schools that it stimulated from other sources ranked the Rosenwald Fund as the most influential philanthropic force that came to the aid of Negroes at that time.[23]

When Rosenwald died in 1932, he had contributed $4.4 million[24] to help build "5,357 public schools, shops, and teachers' homes" in "883 counties of fifteen Southern states" between 1913 and 1932.[25]

Fisk University graduate Clinton L. Calloway inspired the idea for the Rosenwald school-building program. Calloway, who had experience in organizing communities to build schools, saw a collective educational determination within southern Black communities that, with some outside help, could potentially be used to launch a large-scale school-building program.[26] He suggested to Booker T. Washington that Washington propose this idea to his friend, and literary fan,[27] Mr. Julius Rosenwald. Mr. Washington put forth the proposal and the rest is history.

The school-building program organized under the auspices of the Rosenwald Fund constituted the "second crusade for Black common schools in the rural south."[28] These schools symbolized a movement— not an authoritarian directed reception of educational goods—because of the required financial, material, and physical contributions of communities receiving the schools.

For those investigating the character of this second crusade, it is imperative to understand that Rosenwald funds did not provide all of the money to build schools. In fact, the Rosenwald fund "never gave even one-half the cost of a schoolhouse, and it generally contributed an average of about one-sixth of the total monetary cost of the building, grounds, and equipment."[29] Anderson explains some conditions under which Rosenwald funds could be received:

> ... black residents of the selected school district were required to raise enough money to match or exceed the amount requested from the Rosenwald Fund, which initially was a maximum of $350; the approval and cooperation of the state, county, or township school officers were required; all property, including the land, money, and other voluntary contributions by blacks, was to be deeded to the local public school authorities; the school building to be erected had to be approved by Tuskegee's Extension Department; and the efforts in each state were to be coordinated by the state agents of Negro education and the Jeanes Fund supervisors.[30]

In spite of these rather stringent and demanding requirements, Black communities showed an incredible capacity to mobilize their collective resources and take advantage of the opportunity presented by Rosenwald.

Community Initiative

There are rather fascinating stories of community, and individual, mobilization and agency in organizing, building, and maintaining schools.[31] Gill tells of how a poor, rural, Black community in Texas "voted a $1.00 school tax to fund a $3,000 bond issue" ($1.00 being a lot of money in 1925, and more than any other community in the state, White or Black, chose to levy on themselves). This same community also "held picnics, staged plays, and took up church offerings to raise additional money."[32]

Anderson provides several examples of communities, and individuals who stretched themselves to painful extents to finance educational initiatives. In one Alabama community where the "combined annual incomes of about seven black male adults" was $700, and "not a house had a screen or a glass window," people pooled their collective labor and built a two-teacher school. In another community of "boll-weevil stricken sharecroppers," a Rosenwald school agent reported that community members, inspired by a former slave's tear-filled donation of his life's earnings, raised $1,365 when he had initially expected to raise only $10.[33]

While other schools (schools for Whites) were able to grow, many African American schools remained small, one-room/one-teacher schools that had to perform many functions with a minimum of resources.[34] Beyond initial fundraising campaigns to procure school facilities, communities had to keep raising funds to provide maintenance and support for the buildings. To this end, "In the late 1920s, each of fourteen southern states established 'Rosenwald School Day,' an annual event that punctuated the year-long campaigns to raise money and contribute labor for school improvement activities."[35] These activities even persisted during the years of the Great Depression. Walker tells of how right up until desegregation, Black parents and community members regularly contributed various necessities to schools, such as, "stage curtains, band uniforms, pianos,"[36] money to raise funds for a bus, and whatever else was needed. Though people may have been poor, Vanessa Siddle Walker correctly ascertains that there was "No Poverty of Spirit" when it came to education within these communities.[37]

Peggy B. Gill writes, "The need to raise additional funds within the community stands in stark contrast to the reality for white school districts."[38] Anderson reflects on the fact that Blacks had to raise money to attain public education while paying taxes that, in an equal society, would have covered the costs. He writes:

> On one hand, the process of double taxation and collective social action enabled them to improve tremendously the material conditions of their educational system; on the other, this same process was unjust and oppressive, and their accommodation to double taxation helped extend over them the power of their oppressors.[39]

This "double taxation" was exceedingly punishing due to the fact that many White employers simply channeled the taxes that they paid into lower wages for their Black employees.[40]

Though the willingness of African Americans to fund their own educational efforts may have helped to make some White educational administrators feel justified in using public tax funds primarily, and in some cases exclusively, for the education of White children. The reality was that large segments of southern society were against paying any money that could end up helping to finance education for Black children. Thus, Black communities could either wishfully wait for society to change, or strive to change society by taking the initiative to make their corner of the world a better place for their children.

It was within the act of taking initiative for education that cultural capital was reinforced within communities. The theoretical perspective of cultural capital derives from the writings of Pierre Bourdieu.[41] Yelvington writes:

> For Bourdieu, there are four forms of capital: economic capital, or productive property (money and material objects that can be used to produce goods and services); social capital, or positions and relations in groups or social networks; cultural capital, or lifestyle, taste, skills,

educational qualifications, and linguistic styles; and symbolic capital, or the use of symbols to legitimate the possession of varying levels and configurations of economic, social, and cultural capital.[42]

When referring to cultural capital, Bourdieu places emphasis on upper and elite classes of society that control which "lifestyle[s], taste[s], skills, educational qualifications, and linguistic styles"[43] are deemed of worth and therefore exchangeable for those things associated with a respectable status in society—such as, positions in powerful social networks and high-paying jobs.

Explaining this emphasis on elite classes as a limitation of Bourdieu's theory, Greenbaum writes:

> Class relations are reproduced by monopolizing access to cultural goods, in much the same way that more tangible goods are controlled. The poor have less of both kinds of capital, and the lack of one prevents obtaining the other. This perspective has been criticized for its "static reproductionism," leaving too little room for agency or change (Yelvington 1995:5; Jenkins 1992:80–84). Nor can his ideas adequately explain the persistence of cultural differences in spite of economic success...[44]

Challenging this "static" view of cultural capital, Greenbaum focuses on the ability of the "less powerful to marshal the effectiveness of collective action" by creating institutions that allow them to "invest in each other [therefore,] creating palpable resources they can use to change their lives."[45] Referring to Bourdieu's lack of investigation into "institutional underpinnings of group identity," Greenbaum writes, "Bourdieu neglected the role of institution building, focusing on individual habits rather than collectivized structures."[46]

The segregated, self-help schooling that African Americans had developed existed in an oppressive context. However, whole communities dedicated toward the education of their children were able to create strong, nurturing environments that instilled a lasting moral fiber within individuals. And, cohesion within communities was strengthened by the constant communication, interaction, control, and sense of mission directed at the collective goal of education.[47]

Desegregation

In writing about the development of segregated schools in the south, Barbara Shircliffe states,

> On the one hand, segregated schools emerged as part of a system designed to uphold the economic exploitation and political disenfranchisement of African Americans. On the other hand, segregated

schools grew out of the efforts of African Americans to utilize local resources and knowledge to provide African American children an education.[48]

It is this latter statement that this essay seeks to focus on as the dominant cause for the significance of these schools. However, it is important to note that though the history of these schools reveals an important story of self-determination and overcoming odds, it also reveals a past of attempted political indignation and disenfranchisement.

It is ironic that the community cohesiveness that inspired collective actions to create and maintain these institutions was eventually responsible for their demise.[49] It was these schools that imbued students with the moral fiber necessary to protest and demand equality. Graduates of these schools provided a base for the leadership and manpower of the civil rights movement, and the first wave of qualified applicants to newly desegregated jobs and institutions of higher learning.

However, once desegregation was won, immediate change did not take place. Often, years of "litigation, noncompliance, and bureaucratic maneuvering" postponed actual desegregation.[50] When desegregation finally did occur, some African Americans considered the way it was implemented as a punishment rather than as the justice they were seeking. Many White parents simply refused to send their children to formerly Black schools. Thus, when change did occur it resulted in Black students being shipped around counties to integrate White schools while many of their schools were used for less significant purposes (such as a bus depot or storage facility), or closed all together.[51]

Sacrifice

The saga of desegregation entails many stories of immense sacrifice and struggle.[52] David S. Cecelski writes, "Black communities repeatedly had to sacrifice their leadership traditions, school culture, and educational heritage for the other benefits of desegregation."[53] Certainly there were conscious sacrifices made collectively by African Americans. But it appears that more was taken than people were willing to give.

Certainly, the average person expected some school closings and racial problems. However, African Americans were correctly estimating the extent to which their schools would be closed and their teachers and administrators demoted and/or fired, or the persistence of racism within integrated schooling—such as "racial bias in student disciplining, segregated busing routes, unfair tracking into remedial and other lower-level classes, low academic expectations, and estrangement from extracurricular activities."[54] It is not likely that anyone could have calculated the disillusionment concerning education reflected in generations of Black students separated from their community's educational heritage, and exposed to the adverse educational environments that led educational theorists such as John Ogbu to expound on concepts like "secondary cultural discontinuities."[55]

"Cultural ignorance" may have played a factor in the minds of both Whites and Blacks that felt "African Americans would benefit from merely associating with the dominant culture."[56] But it is a disservice to all who struggled to describe the damaging effects of desegregation as resulting from cultural ignorance without also pointing to the fact that several individuals consciously worked to thwart the goals of desegregation, and to make it exceedingly punitive on the Black community.[57]

Cecelski attributes the "mass closing of black schools" as "part of a broader pattern of racism that marred school desegregation throughout the South." He writes:

> As desegregation swept through the region in the 1960s and 1970s, white southern school leaders routinely shut down these black institutions, no matter how new or well located, and transferred their students to former white schools. [. . .] Instead of reconciling black and white schools on equal terms, white leaders made school desegregation a one-way street.[58]

To provide examples of patterns of routine discrimination that existed, Cecelski discusses the impact of desegregation on Black teachers and school administrators.

When it came to Black teachers, the first years of desegregation were not a time of advancement and opportunity. Initially referring to the firing of Black teachers in North Carolina, Cecelski writes:

> These patterns were similar to those in other states, where an estimated 3,150 black teachers were displaced by 1970. In a five-state survey, the U.S. Department of Health, Education, and Welfare (HEW) confirmed that between 1968 and 1971 alone, at least 1,000 black educators lost jobs while 5,000 white teachers were hired. Teachers unions, a U.S. congressional committee, and several scholars documented widespread displacement of black educators across the South. Holding less than 2 percent of local school board positions in the region, black citizens did not have the political power to stem this tide. The phenomenon was so widespread that in 1966, when New York City faced a severe teacher shortage, it developed Operation Reclaim specifically to recruit black teachers who had been fired below the Mason-Dixon line.[59]

The fact that experienced Black teachers were fired while White teachers were actively recruited is indicative of discriminatory practice.

When it came to Black principals, Cecelski writes:

> In North Carolina, typical of the southern states in this regard, school closings and mergers eliminated an entire generation of black principals. From 1963 to 1970, the number of black principals in the state's elementary schools plunged from 620 to only 170. Even more striking, 209 black principals headed secondary schools in 1963, but less than 10 still held that crucial job in 1970. By 1973, only three had survived this wholesale displacement.[60]

Surely, more than 10 out of 209 Black principals were qualified to head integrated secondary schools. Several other authors, such as Everett Franklin and V. P. Abney, also reported on this trend.[61]

Capital Loss

The closing of buildings, dismissal and demotion of revered educational leaders, and transfer of education outside of the community under the control of the dominant culture, had significant impacts on the educational value system that had been consciously, and unconsciously, building in Black communities throughout the South. These impacts would have been lessened if desegregation had occurred as a sharing and mixing of staff, facilities, and resources, instead of as a White dominated project done through a paradigmatic lens of Black inadequacy. Cecelski writes:

> When black schools closed, their names, mascots, mottos, holidays, and traditions were sacrificed with them, while the students were transferred to historically white schools that retained those markers of cultural and racial identity. When former black high schools did not shut down, they were invariably converted into integrated junior high or elementary schools. White officials would frequently change the names given the school buildings by the black community and would remove plaques or monuments that honored black cultural, political, or educational leaders. They hid from public view trophy cases featuring black sports teams and academic honorees and replaced the names of black sports teams with those used by the white schools.[62]

These kinds of actions had alienating impacts on both parents and students.[63]

The fact that several Black communities did not passively accept the closure of their schools attests to the ideas that several of the school closings that occurred during desegregation were not anticipated and that many African Americans felt that they had an educational heritage, and educational resources, of high exchange value for the purposes of desegregation—one that they were willing to share in an integrated setting but not sacrifice for the sake of integration. Cecelski's *Along Freedom Road* is the story of the struggle to prevent two Black schools from closing. Cecelski writes, "Between 1968 and 1973, school boycotts, student walkouts, lawsuits, and other black protests challenging desegregation plans grew common at the southern grass roots."[64]

Cecelski describes the story of protest in Hyde County, North Carolina, where "For an entire year, Hyde County's black students refused to attend school," "marched twice on the state capital," "held non-violent demonstrations almost daily for five months," "organized alternative schools in their churches," and even had to drive the KKK "out of the county in a massive gunfight" to protest a desegregation plan that required closing two historically black schools in this poor, rural community."[65] Other, less documented, less extreme, and less successful fights to stop school closures certainly occurred throughout the South.

To be sure, many of the historically Black schoolhouses across the South were not adequate to serve as schools in the larger, integrated setting. And these smaller, inadequate one and two-room schools were not the scenes of large protests to halt closures. However, just as with large schools that should not have been closed, an intangible aspect of community was lost when they were closed.

Walker writes:

> Although black schools were indeed commonly lacking in facilities and funding, some evidence suggests that the environment of the segregated school had some affective traits, institutional policies, and community support that helped black children learn in spite of the neglect their schools received from white school boards.[66]

To some, the closing of schools felt like death had come to the community. Others felt as if the community had lost its center.[67]

In their discussion on schooling and community, Van Dempsey and George Noblit elaborate on the importance that continuity of place, purpose, and people have for a community's "sense of itself."[68] These, and the cultural and social capital that they allowed to develop, were all thoroughly disrupted by the way desegregation was allowed to take place. For the purposes of his discussion, Julian Savage analyzes the concept of cultural capital in terms of "resource development, community leadership, and extraordinary service." He defines these in the following way:

> Recourse Development: Because of the limited funding of their schools (whether private or public), southern African Americans taxed themselves to provide the resources—monetary or material—that ensured the success of their schools.
> Community leadership: Community members, as individuals or as part of a group, created a public will within their community to establish and maintain their schools in spite of the opposition from the larger white community.
> Extraordinary Service: Although teaching was their profession, principals and teachers provided extraordinary service to their students. Principals maneuvered district policies and provided resources to equip their schools and introduced new curricula and activities to enrich their students.[69]

As shown from examples cited in this essay, these three components of cultural capital were severely, and negatively, impacted by the way that desegregation occurred.

Reclamation

The purpose of my discussion is not to advocate the reinstitution of segregated schools. The schooling that exists today, though having some problems, is arguably the most organized, efficient, and equal schooling that has existed in the history of the United States and in much of the world. However, an accurate historical perspective is necessary in order to properly engage current issues concerning education in the African American community. Watkins writes:

> Among the most disturbing phenomena in today's debates on the quality of African American schooling is that we seem to have lost sight of our history. Reforms such as multicultural education and the Afrocentric curriculum are presented and discussed as if they only recently fell from the sky. Our collective amnesia has decontextualized and separated much of the current dialogue from any historical antecedents. We have all but ignored the rich intellectual tradition of theory and practice in the protracted battle to provide, reform, and improve the schooling and education of African Americans.[70]

The history of African American education displays the potential that can be realized when whole communities get involved in the educational process. This legacy should not be lost as its remembrance may well have current benefits. Franklin writes:

> With the Supreme Court's *Brown* decision and the federal government's efforts in the 1950s and 1960s to insure African American children's access to all publicly supported schools, many African Americans came to believe that they would no longer have to use their collective resources to provide excellent, or even adequate, public or private schooling for their children. Now, at the beginning of the twenty-first century, we know (or should know) that this is not the case.[71]

Many currently failing schools could potentially thrive if the kind of community involvement that existed in past school communities was revived.

Many of those who were involved in past African American school communities are not willing to let their educational legacies fade. Instead, the have focused their attention and collective efforts upon the actual structures that once served as educational centers within their communities. Writing about these schools, Cecelski explains:

> Like chimneys standing in the cold ashes of a tragic fire, the old buildings endure in towns and rural communities across the southeastern United States. A few have been reincarnated as textbook warehouses, old-age homes, or cut-and-sew factories. More commonly, though, they sit vacant and deteriorating in older black neighborhoods.[72]

These schools, generally the last remaining of the Rosenwald Schools explained earlier in this essay, are valued by former teachers, alumni, and community members for the legacy of cooperation and collective action that they represent. They are also more practically valued as facilities to offer supplemental educational programming (such as tutoring and educational museums), and/or space for other community activities.

Noting the historical importance, public interest, and decreasing number of old Rosenwald schools, the National Trust for Historic Preservation (NTHP) placed them on their 2002 list of the "11 Most Endangered Historical Sites." The NTHP has also started a "Rosenwald Initiative" with goals of:

> developing and publishing public education materials; developing and launching a web site on Rosenwald schools; developing a network of individuals and organizations working toward documentation and preservation of Rosenwald schools and continued fundraising to meet the goals of the initiative.[73]

The first Rosenwald School conference to be sponsored by this initiative occurred in May of 2004 at Fisk University in Nashville Tennessee. This conference was attended by 160 participants from 15 states—many representing school renovation projects in various stages of completion.[74] For the purposes of this essay I discuss the renovation of the Glover School in Bealsville, Florida—a community in which I have conducted ethnographic research over the past three years.

Bealsville and the Glover School Historic Site

Bealsville (not to be confused with the more popular Eatonville)[75] is a small, semirural community about 40 miles east of the city of Tampa. It does not have its own post office, and the mailing address for its 1,200 residents reveals that they officially reside in Plant City, Florida. For those driving on the main thoroughfare, Highway 60, there is nothing to distinguish the community except for small signs on the East and West borders, Ruby William's fruit and folk art stand, and a small brown sign marking the turn for the Glover School Historic Site. However, like many small places, there is a history there that, once uncovered, reveals an insightful story about the American past.

Former slaves homesteaded Bealsville (first naming it Alafia) in the 1860s. Today, though some land has been sold to neighboring phosphate mines, strawberry farms, and families migrating to the area, the majority of the land in Bealsville is still owned by descendants of its first settlers. However, due to the recent encroachment of urban sprawl from suburban Brandon and the farm town of Plant City, Bealsville's rural character is undergoing a slow, but definite, change.

As land prices increase and drive up taxes, more residents are deciding to sell land that was once strictly kept in the family. In many cases, the resultant newcomers—often representing a diversity of ethnicities—lack a shared sense of historical connection to the community, and tend to prioritize their commitments to surrounding urban areas. In fact, many long-time Bealsville families also have a greater involvement in affairs located outside of Bealsville. Thus, for the first time in the history of this small community, residents are experiencing the more urban and suburban associated sense of estrangement from their neighbors. This fraying of social capital within the community is compounded by the fact that there are now seven churches in this small community that used to have one central church for all to fellowship.

Like many communities, another force that destabilized continuity was the fact that in order to find opportunity, many young people had to leave. However, many individuals are now feeling a "call to home,"[76] and choosing to retire in Bealsville. Thus, there is an eclectic mix of large, spacious homes with pools and two-car garages, and early-twentieth-century houses in need of care. But as these individuals return, and as demographic shifts make it possible for younger generations to find opportunity without leaving the community, Bealsville is able to draw on organizational talents and energy.

The history of Bealsville mirrors broader historical trends in rural African American communities in many ways. When former slaves settled the area, they quickly became part of the first crusade for African American education. In the years immediately following slavery's end, their first communal project was the building of the Antioch Baptist Church—which also functioned as school. This church is still operating in the heart of the Bealsville Community. Their next project was the construction of a separate school building. This school was named the Jameson School and was opened in or around 1870.

Teachers for the Jameson School were sought out and funded by members of the community. Though many were not able, those who had the opportunity to go to high school had to migrate to nearby Bartow, Lakeland, or Tampa until a Black high school was built in Plant City. And those who went to college had to completely leave the area—going east to Daytona, Florida (Bethune-Cookman College) or north to Tallahassee and the Florida Agricultural and Mechanical University. Unfortunately for these earlier scholars, job opportunities were generally limited to teaching.[77]

In the early 1930s, Bealsville was able to improve its educational facilities. Though personal recollections and archival documentation from the Rosenwald Fund do not show that Bealsville was officially included in the Rosenwald school-building program, the model of the program appears to have been closely imitated.[78] Families went "around the world"[79] collecting money, and in-kind items, from all who resided in the community. In this manner, and through fundraising in the form of BBQ's and Fish Fries, the community was able to put $1,100 and ten acres of land toward the construction of a new school building.

Residents of the community decided to name the new school after an elder in the community named William Glover. To lessen confusion between them and another nearby community that was also named Alafia, they also chose to change the name of the community to Bealsville after Alfred Beal, a member of one of the original families who helped to keep the community together by buying foreclosed land and returning it to its former owners.[80]

According to Rosenwald protocol, the $1,100 and the ten acres of land were turned over to the Hillsborough County School Board. In 1933 the first building of the Glover School was constructed. In the

1940s additional classrooms were added.[81] This new school quickly became a central point of activity in this small community.

Classrooms at the Glover School consisted of about 20–25 students.[82] Though students also came from surrounding communities, Bealsville students were often in classes with, and taught by, cousins, neighbors, and fellow church members. Local people also staffed the lunchroom and made up most of the custodial staff. Close relationships were formed among students, teachers, administrators, and parents in this environment. This was the ideal community school that reigns positively in popular nostalgia about the past.

One former student, whose mother was a teacher, remembers the principal playing basketball with students. This same person was later hired as a high school teacher by that principal.[83] As I looked through a Glover School reunion booklet with another former teacher, she pointed out former custodians, cafeteria workers, and other teachers, who were all born and raised in Bealsville.[84] Still, another former teacher mentioned that she saw most of her class in church on Sundays where she was also their Sunday School teacher.[85] Though some students may not have appreciated the abundance of guidance and supervision at the time, in hindsight they realize that this kind of social capital had had positive impacts in their academic, professional, and personal successes.[86]

Change came in 1971 when a court ordered plan was enacted to desegregate Hillsborough County schools. To adhere to the Federal Judge's recommendation of a "black-white ratio of 20 to 80" in each school, Black students were bused to formerly all-White schools for nearly all of their schooling, and former all-Black schools were turned into sixth or seventh grade centers.[87] This plan, though constructed in a manner that was more appeasing to resistant Whites, worked well in relation to plans enacted by other school districts where boycotts and other hostilities broke out.[88] Due to these changes, the Glover school was converted to a sixth grade center. For their sixth-grade year White students were bused to the Glover School from surrounding areas, and several Glover teachers were moved around the county to help desegregate other schools. The school operated in this manner for ten years before the county decided to close it altogether due to low enrollment and budgetary concerns.[89]

Bealsville, Inc.

The residents of Bealsville were not passive observers when it came to issues relating to their school. The community accepted desegregation and the changes that it brought to education within their community.

In order to attain the positive benefits of integration, this community was willing to send its children outside of its borders for their formative years of education—the first time that had occurred. Residents were also willing to accept a diminished function and new student population for their own school that used to serve students from the early grades until they went to high school. These changes disrupted established patterns of interaction and involvement within the Bealsville community—such as the Glover School PTA, and community-school activities like the annual May Day celebration. However, residents were willing to sacrifice comfort and familiarity for progress.[90]

Though integration had occurred rather smoothly in the Bealsville community,[91] problems arose when residents started hearing whispers that the school board had plans to close the school. Concerned residents went to school board hearings and argued that their school be kept open. Eventually, the community started a lawsuit against the school board's decision to close the school. However, their suit was unsuccessful.

Having lost their fight to keep the Glover School open, residents shifted their demands to having the buildings and property deeded back to the community. In order to have a legal body to which the Hillsborough County School Board's could deed the recently closed Glover School, in 1981 residents formed the nonprofit group, Bealsville Incorporated. From that time, the members of Bealsville, Inc. have been responsible for maintaining the grounds of the school, and for directing all activities that occur there.[92]

Though the community now had the school, it lacked a formal plan about what to do with it. Also lacking was the money to make necessary repairs and renovations, and energetic volunteers with knowledge of how to raise funds, and get a large renovation project started. The board of Bealsville Incorporated, determined not to let their school fall into total disrepair, made sure that the ten acres of grass was mowed, and that necessary repairs were done. However, due to lack of funds, and inconsistent usage, the Glover School complex was slowly deteriorating.

In the mid-1990s, though the community was doing well overall, residents started noticing the some of the younger individuals were starting to get involved with drugs. And there were signs that some were using the empty Glover School complex as a place to use drugs. Upon learning that this type of activity was beginning in their own community, in 1995 the members of Bealsville Incorporated quickly moved to start the Glover School renovation project, and in 1998, Bealsville, Inc. received 501(c)(3) status, which made it eligible for various sources of funding to help in the renovations. The goal of the project is to completely renovate the old school buildings and to make them available to house various kinds of social programming directed at the old and the young alike, a historical museum/archive, and community events.

One particular returnee who had a positive impact on the Glover School renovation was Mrs. Carrie Johnston. Mrs. Johnston, retired from a career as a psychiatric nurse outside of the state, moved back into the area just as interest in getting the renovation project was gaining momentum. A former student of the school, she joined the board of Bealsville, Inc. and made the renovation of the school her new, voluntary, full-time job—becoming the first Renovation Project Manager.

Throughout the years residents had invested a lot of time and money in the School—holding annual fundraising banquets and even a Glover School homecoming. But through Mrs. Johnston's fundraising and organizational talents, Bealsville Inc. was able to start a daily lunch program for seniors in the community, upgrade the rooms in the facility to house community meetings and tutoring for youth, put a tin roof on the entire facility, raise over $300,000 in funding, and make many other improvements such as getting the school on the National Register of Historic Places. Regretfully, while the building was still under renovation and with much work to do, Mrs. Johnston passed away in 2003.[93]

This project could have easily come to a halt after the passing of such an energetic and pivotal person. However, two months later a new Renovation Project Manager was named and the Board of Directors was getting back on track with the project. Others in the community are making efforts to prepare a book on the accomplishments of individuals who attended the Glover School. In this way they make certain that alumni outside of the area will stay integrated in the Glover School and Bealsville family.

To residents, the Glover School is the "heart of the community," and the closure of the school had a "devastating impact" on community togetherness.[94] However, because of the shared sense of attachment to the school, and the benefits that a fully functioning community center may offer this small, semirural enclave, the residents of Bealsville have found themselves still held together by the centripetal force of the Glover School.

Conclusions

By working with individuals in the Bealsville community, I set out to understand the motivations and values underlying efforts of those involved in the renovations. In order to grasp the various aspects in which the Glover School renovation benefits the community, I have identified six functional categories in which the Glover School represents various levels of meaning ranging from the practical to symbolic. These categories are: (1) Utilitarian; (2) Community Building; (3) Community Reunification and Identification; (4) Community Preservation; (5) Value Transmittal; and (6) Heritage Landmark.

(1) Utilitarian

In its most practical form, the Glover School serves as public meeting facility. Community groups of any kind may request to utilize meeting space within the buildings. This, in turn, can provide a source of income to cover monthly maintenance charges. This aspect of the building will help to publicize its existence. Permitting other groups to utilize space in the buildings will also help in the effort to maintain "good neighbor" relations with nearby communities and organizations.

(2) Community Building

This function pertains to the impact that the Glover School will have on the community. By providing a central space in which to focus community activities and programs, Bealsville, Inc. has increased the community's capacity to engage in bonding and improvement activities.

In Bealsville the School is at the literal center of the community, and will be the only facility in the community directed at providing services for everyone. With a comfortable space, more people will hopefully be encouraged to participate in Bealsville, Inc. and other programs at the school. Also, though specific programs, beyond the senior lunch program and drug relapse prevention programs, have not all yet been decided, the Glover School has space for almost anything that residents can dream up. Some have entertained thoughts of opening a charter school, a post office, or dry cleaners. These kinds of things would be very useful to individuals in the community, and would increase the value and use of the school building for everyone. These kinds of activities would also increase the contact that residents have with each other and help to rekindle neighborly relations.

(3) Community Reunification and Identification

Pulling fragmented community activity into one central location should have the effect of revitalizing and unifying community spirit. The Glover School will also serve the function of a community "home" for those who now live in other parts of the country.

With the museum and archives individuals connected to the community will have a common source in which to share and store their personal and collective histories and artifacts. Tying together history and sentiment in one place help to define the identity of the community. This reunification aspect of the Glover School will be operationalized in terms of school and community reunions occurring at the sites.

(4) Community Preservation

By creating space to unite the community and store community history the Glover School will serve to preserve the legacies of the people who created, attended, and contributed to it. In Bealsville, the preservation activities at the Glover School will also assure that past community achievements are not forgotten. Though the Bealsville community is very much existent, the activities of individuals and families are not as community-centered as they once were. On top of this fragmentation, individuals in the community are starting to sell land to "outsiders" who are not familiar with the history of Bealsville. Setting aside a space to preserving community history will assure that memories do not become fragmented and lost. It will encourage people to record their experiences, and will make the history more accessible to all. This function becomes all the more important as elders in the community pass on, some unfortunately taking their memories with them.

(5) Value Transmittal

As younger generations come to learn about the history of the Bealsville community, it is hoped that the values underlying the community will be passed on. Whether through occasional museum visitations, specific programs run by Bealsville, Inc., or perhaps as a part of a social studies curriculum, young people will learn of how the early residents of the Bealsville community valued education, and were able to accomplish so much with so little—hopefully inspiring young people to take full advantage of their present opportunities.

(6) Heritage Landmark

Beyond specific applications and uses for the local community, the preservation of the Glover School makes a valuable contribution to broader efforts to preserve African American heritage. The example of the Glover School, and other similar projects, will help to counterbalance the loss of thousands of similar school sites, and countless other historical sites of significance for African American history. Thus, the Glover School complex has national importance.

The Glover School has already been the site of family reunions, various community meetings, a health fair, tutoring, a daily senior lunch program, and a drug relapse prevention center—not to mention the fact that a Hispanic church used to rent out the cafeteria. It is a site where community leadership is practiced and expressed—where community members literally come together and decide on local political candidates to vote for based on the candidate's relationship with the community.[95]

The work to revive the Glover School as a center for the convergence and reinforcement for educational values and communal interaction has drawn positive attention to the Bealsville community. Hillsborough County television studios have completed two documentaries on the history of Bealsville.[96] Numerous newspaper articles have also been written about goings-on in the community.[97]

The motivations and values that inspire the work are not isolated in time, but are a part of a pattern that has existed for over a hundred years. Anderson explains this pattern:

> The common patterns of behavior among black men and women of diverse social environments evidence the educational and communal values blacks transmitted from generation to generation. Thus the behavior of blacks in the second crusade for universal schooling [the Rosenwald school-building program] was strikingly similar to the behavior of former slaves in their campaign for universal public education during the Reconstruction era.[98]

The values evidenced by these patterns of behavior are what have moved many to participate in school renovation projects, and are perhaps the most important aspect of what they are trying to preserve and pass on.

Those who attended schools such as Glover were the beneficiaries of some of the best guidance that the African American community had to give at that time. Though not everyone had the same experience, in the best cases students were shown a love inside the school that was repeated throughout their community. Though schools now have much more in the way of resources, some educational environments are lacking in their abilities to imbue students with educational and communal values. That is a gap that these *supplemental* community efforts seek to fill. These school communities were first created because groups of individuals with similar goals and a shared history found themselves excluded from the rights and benefits of mainstream American life. The school became a beacon of light in these communities—only surpassed in significance by the church. Individuals collectively poured their resources into these schools in the hopes of securing social advancement for their children, and for future generations.

As communities became larger and those associated with the schools more dispersed, the significance of the school as a social/symbolic landmark increased. And when these schools were closed, many literally felt as if "death had come to the community,"[99] or as if the heart had been taken out of the community.[100] The schoolhouse had become an important locale for community life that many, at least in Bealsville, did not want to give up—even if an actual school was not in operation within the building.

Schools such as Glover are reference points for community—whether real or imagined. Members who consider themselves a part of these communities may live hundreds of miles away. And many schools now sit in busy areas where most of the local population does not identify with school at all. But for those that do identify with schools such as Glover, the schoolhouse represents the center of their community.

Notes

1. National Trust for Historic Preservation <http//:www.rosenwald-schools.com>.
2. Greenbaum, *More Than Black* (Gainesville, FL: University of Florida Press, 2002), 19.
3. V. P. Franklin, "Introduction: Cultural Capital and African American Education," *Journal of African American History* 87, Spring (2002): 176–177.
4. Carter Julian Savage, "Cultural Capital and African American Agency: The Economic Struggle for Effective Education for African Americans in Franklin, Tennessee, 1890-1967," *Journal of African American History* 87, Spring (2002): 207, 218.
5. Greenbaum, *More Than Black*, 19.
6. James S. Coleman, "Social Capital in the Creation of Human Capital," *American Journal of Sociology* 94 (1988): 98.
7. Coleman, "Social Capital," 100.
8. Griggs, France, "Bealsville Residents Seek Voice in Fate of Glover School," East Hillsborough Tribune, Monday, September 29, 1980.
9. Henry Davis, interview with the author (August 28, 2003).
10. Defined as the "unfolding process of group identification." See Greenbaum, *More Than Black*, 8.
11. James D. Anderson, *Education of Blacks in the South, 1860–1935* (Chapel Hill, NC: The University of North Carolina Press, 1988), 17–18.

12. Ibid., 18; Christopher M. Span, "I Must Learn Now or Not at All: Social and Cultural Capital in the Educational Initiatives of Formerly Enslaved African Americans in Mississippi, 1862–1869." *Journal of African American History* 87, Spring (2002): 196–197.
13. Cantor Brown, Jr., *Florida's Black Public Officials, 1867–1924* (Tuscaloosa, AL: University of Alabama Press, 1998), 27.
14. Anderson, *Education of blacks in the south*, 19.
15. Ibid., 6, 11–13.
16. Ibid., 27–28.
17. Ibid., 44.
18. Robert F. Arnove, *Philanthropy and Cultural Imperialism: The Foundations at Home and Abroad* (Boston, MA: G. K. Hall, 1980), 2–3.
19. Savage, "Cultural Capital," 218.
20. W. E. B. DuBois, "Souls of Black Folk," *In Three Negro Classics*, 207–389 (New York Avon Books, 1965), 246.
21. Ibid., 247.
22. Anderson *Education of Blacks in the South*, 106–109.
23. Henry Allen Bullock, *A History of Negro Education in the South: From 1619 to the Present* (Cambridge, MA: Harvard University Press, 1967), 138.
24. Morris R. Werner, *Julius Rosenwald: The Life of a Practical Humanitarian* (New York: Harper & Brothers Publishers, 1939), 133.
25. Bullock, *History of Negro Education in the South*, 139.
26. Anderson, *Education of Blacks in the South*, 157–158.
27. Werner, *Julius Rosenwald*, 139,
28. Anderson, *Education of Blacks in the South*, 152.
29. Ibid., 154.
30. Ibid., 158.
31. See Ibid., 155–185; David S. Cecelski, *Along Freedom Road* (Chapel Hill, NC: University of North Carolina Press, 1994); Peggy B. Gill, "Community, Commitment, and African American Education: The Jackson School of South County, Texas, 1925–1954," *Journal of African American History* 87, Spring (2002): 256–268; Adah Ward Randolph, "Building Upon Cultural Capital: Thomas Jefferson Ferguson and the Albany Enterprise Academy in Southeast Ohio, 1863–1886," *Journal of African American History* 87, Spring (2002): 182–195; Carter Julian Savage, "Cultural Capital and African American Agency: The Economic Struggle for Effective Education for African Americans in Franklin, Tennessee, 1890–1967," *Journal of African American History* 87 (Spring 2002): 206–235; Vanessa Siddle Walker, *Their Highest Potential: An African American School Community in the Segregated South* (Chapel Hill, NC: The University of North Carolina Press, 1996).
32. Gill, "Community, Commitment," 259.
33. Anderson, *Education of Blacks in the South*, 164–165.

34. Michael Fultz, "African American Teachers in the South, 1890–1940: Powerlessness and the Ironies of Expectation Protest," *History of Education Quarterly* 35, 4 (1995): 408.
35. Anderson, *Education of Blacks in the South*, 173.
36. Walker, *Their Highest Potential*, 200.
37. Ibid., 199–219.
38. Gill, "Community, Commitment," 259.
39. Anderson, *Education of Blacks in the South*, 179.
40. Ibid., 182–183.
41. See Pierre Bourdieu, *Distinction: A Social Critique of the Judgment of Taste* (Cambridge, MA: Harvard University Press, 1984); Pierre Bourdieu, *Outline of a Theory of Practice* (London: Cambridge University Press, 1977); Pierre Bourdieu and Jean-Claude Passeron, *Reproduction in Education, Society and Culture* (London: Sage, 1977).
42. Kevin Yelvington, *Producing Power: Ethnicity, Class, and Gender in a Caribbean Workplace* (Philadelphia, PA: Temple University Press, 1995), 31.
43. Ibid., 31.
44. Susan D. Greenbaum, *More Than Black: Afro-Cubans in Tampa* (Gainesville, FL: University of Florida Press, 2002), 18; Yelvington, *ProducingPower*, 5; Richard Jenkins, *Pierre Bourdieu* (London, Routledge, 1992), 80–84.
45. Greenbaum, *More Than Black*, 18–19.
46. Ibid., 7.
47. See Van Dempsey and George Noblit, "Cultural Ignorance and School Desegregation: A Community Narrative," Mwalimu J. Shujaa ed., *Beyond Desegregation: The Politics of Quality in African American Schooling* (Thousand Oaks, CA: Corwin Press, INC, 1996), 115–137; Van Dempsey and George Noblit, "The Demise of Caring in an African American Community: One Consequence of School Desegregation," *The Urban Review* 25 (1993): 47–61; Russell W. Irvine and Jacqueline Jordan Irvine, "The Impact of the Desegregation Process on the Education of Black Students: Key Variables," *Journal of Negro Education* 52, 4 (1983): 410–422; Maike Philipsen, *Values-Spoken and Values-Lived: Race and the Cultural Consequences of a School Closing* (Cresskill, NJ: Hampton Press, 1999); Barbara Shircliffe, "We Got the Best of that World: A Case Study for Nostalgia in the Oral History of School Segregation," *Oral History Review* 28, 2 (2001): 59–84; Vanessa Siddle Walker, "Interpersonal Caring in the Good Segregated Schooling of African American Children: Evidence from the Case of Caswell County Training School," *The Urban Review* 25, 1 (1993): 63–77.
48. Barbara Shircliffe, "Middleton and Blake High Schools: The Politics of Race and History in the Closing, and Restoration of High Schools in Tampa, Florida," *International Journal of Educational Policy, Research and Practice* 1, 4 (2000): 473.
49. Ibid., 473.

50. Ibid., 480.
51. Ibid., 480–481.
52. See David S. Cecelski, *Along Freedom Road* (Chapel Hill, NC: University of North Carolina Press, 1994); Van Dempsey and George Noblit, "Cultural Ignorance and School Desegregation: A Community Narrative," Mwalimu J. Shujaa ed., *Beyond Desegregation: The Politics of Quality in African American Schooling* (Thousand Oaks, CA: Corwin Press, INC, 1996), 115–137; Van Dempsey and George Noblit, "The Demise of Caring in an African American Community: One Consequence of School Desegregation," *The Urban Review* 25 (1993): 47–61; Barbara Shircliffe, "Middleton and Blake High Schools: The Politics of Race and History in the Closing, and Restoration of High Schools in Tampa, Florida," *International Journal of Educational Policy, Research and Practice* 1, 4 (2000): 471–491; Vanessa Siddle Walker, *Their Highest Potential: An African American School Community in the Segregated South* (Chapel Hill, NC: The University of North Carolina Press, 1996).; Anna Victoria Wilson and William E. Segall, *Oh, Do I Remember!: Experiences of Teachers During the Desegregation of Austin's Schools, 1964–1971* (New York: State University of New York Press, 2001).
53. Cecelski, *Along Freedom Road*, 8–9.
54. Ibid., 9.
55. See John Ogbu, "Frameworks—Variability in Minority School Performance: A Problem in Search of an Explanation," Evelyn Jacob and Cathie Jordan eds., *Minority Education: Anthropological Perspectives* (Norwood, NJ: Ablex Publishing, 1993), 83–111; John Ogbu, "Cultural Discontinuities and Schooling," *Anthropology and Education Quarterly* 13, 4 (1982): 290–307.
56. Dempsey and Noblit, "Cultural Ignorance and School Desegregation," 115–116.
57. See Hall, Leon. "The Implementer's Revenge." *Southern Exposure* 7 (1979):122–124.
58. Cecelski, *Along Freedom Road*, 7.
59. Ibid., 8–9.
60. Ibid., 8.
61. Everett Abney, "Status of Florida's Black School Principals," *Journal of Negro Education* 43 (Winter 1974): 3–8; V. P. Franklin, "They Rose and Fell together: African American Educators and Community Leadership," *Journal of Education* 172 (November 1990): 39–64.
62. Cecelski, *Along Freedom Road*, 9.
63. See James Bolner and Arnold Vedlitz, "The Affinity of Negro Pupils for Segregated Schools: Obstacles to Desegregation," *Journal of Negro Education* 40, 4 (1971): 313–321; Patricia A. Edwards, "Before and After School Desegregation: African American Parents' Involvement in Schools," Mwalimu J. Shujaa ed., *Beyond Desegregation: The Politics of Quality in African American Schooling* (Thousand Oaks, CA: Corwin Press, INC, 1996), 138–161.

64. Cecelski, *Along Freedom Road*, 10.
65. Ibid., 7–12.
66. Walker, *Their Highest Potential*, 3.
67. See Shircliffe, "We Got the Best of that World," 74; Dempsey and Noblit, "The Demise of Caring in an African American Community," 59.
68. Dempsey and Noblit, "The Demise of Caring in an African American Community," 50.
69. Savage, "Cultural Capital," 207.
70. William H. Watkins, "Reclaiming Historical Visions of Quality Schooling: The Legacy of early 20th Century Black Intellectuals," Mwalimu J. Shujaa ed., *Beyond Desegregation: The Politics of Quality in African American Schooling* (Thousand Oaks, CA: Corwin Press, INC., 1996), 5.
71. Franklin, "Introduction," 180.
72. Cecelski, *Along Freedom Road*, 7.
73. National Trust for Historic Preservation, "America's 11 Most Endangered Historic Places," *Preservation* 54, 4 (2002): 13; Also see "Rosenwald Initiative Moves Forward," *Southern Preservation News* 1, 1 (December 2002), 1, available at <http://www.nationaltrust.org/about_the_trust/newsletters/sro/sro-1202.pdf>.
74. <www.rosenwaldschools.com>.
75. Eatonville is noted to be the first black municipality in the country. Due to its association with the anthropologist and writer Zora Neal Hurston it has been the focus of several preservation efforts.
76. See Carol Stack, *Call to Home: African Americans Reclaim the Rural South* (New York HarperCollins Publishers, Inc., 1996).
77. Leola McDonald, interview with the author (September 3, 2003).
78. The Rosenwald Fund papers, housed at the Fisk University Library Special Collections, are known to be incomplete.
79. G. S. Cunningham, interview with author (September 6, 2003).
80. Quintilla Geer Bruton and David E. Bailey, *Plant City: Its Origin and History* (Winton-Salem, NC: Hunter Publishing Company, 1984), 63.
81. Historic Resources Review Board, A Resolution of the Historic Resources Review Board of Hillsborough County, Florida, amending the Landmark Designation for the Glover School Site (Tampa, FL: Hillsborough County Planning & Growth Management, July 14, 2000), 3–4.
82. Leola McDonald, interview with the author (September 3, 2003). Mrs. McDonald attended the Jameson School and taught at the Glover School for 17 years before teaching in integrated schools.
83. Herman Hargrett, interview with the author (September 3, 2003).
84. Ida White, interview with author (September 6, 2003).
85. Leola McDonald, interview with the author (September 3, 2003).
86. Henry Davis, interview with author (August 28, 2003); Herman Hargrett, interview with the author (September 3, 2003).

87. Barbara J. Shircliffe, "Desegregation and the Historically Black High School: The Establishment of Howard W. Blake in Tampa, Florida," *The Urban Review* 34, 2 (2002): 140.
88. C. Sinclair, "Desegregation's Quiet Success," *The Washington Post* June 17, 1978.
89. Marguerite Wingate, interview with author (September 6, 2003).
90. Ida White, interview with author (September 6, 2003).
91. During the time that the Glover School operated as a sixth grade center there were no major incidents, the faculty worked well together, and the environment was peaceful and comforting—this is according to interviews done with Ms. Ida White (a lifetime resident of Bealsville and teacher at the Glover School throughout the years of integration), and Ms. Marguerite Wingate (a White, former secretary at the Glover School who worked there during the time the school was integrated). Ida White, interview with author (September 6, 2003); Marguerite Wingate, interview with author (September 6, 2003).
92. Henry Davis, interview with author (August 28, 2003). Mr. Henry Davis has served as the president of Bealsville Incorporated since the creation of the organization. He was active in initial protests to keep the school open, then in demanding that the county give the property back to the community, and has worked to maintain and improve the property ever since.
93. Carrie Johnston, interview with author (May 16, 2002). Mrs. Johnston made a lot of improvements to the Glover School in a short amount of time. The project goes on but she will be missed. See Janet Zink, "Carrie Johnston," *St. Petersburg Times* May 15, 2003, 7B.
94. Ida White, interview with author (September 6, 2003).
95. Henry Davis, interview with author (August 28, 2003).
96. *Timeline: Bealsville*, produced by Patrick Dowling, 23 min., Hillsborough Television, 2002, videocassette; *Bealsville: Wings of Deliverance*, produced by Thomas H. Mills and Loretta H. Rhoads, 28 min., Florida West Coast Public Broadcasting, Inc., 1988, videocassette.
97. See Deborah Alberto, "Fundraiser is Oct. 16 for Glover School," *Tampa Tribune*. Plant City. October 9, 1999; and Bonnie Dyson, "Common Grounds," *Tampa Tribune* June 10, 2004.
98. Anderson, *Education of Blacks in the South*, 173.
99. Barbara J. Shircliffe, "We Got the Best of that World: A Case Study for the Study of Nostalgia in the Oral History of School Segregation," *The Oral History Review* 28, 2 (Summer/Fall 2001): 74.
100. Ida White, interview with author (September 6, 2003).

Index

Abel, Georgie Lee, 157
The Advocate, 119
Alcott, A. Bronson, 37, 38
Anderson, Benedict, 2, 16, 128
Anderson, James, 183, 203
Anthony, Otis, 125, 128, 135, 139
Antioch Baptist Church (Bealsville), 197
Arc of Davidson County, 155–56, 157
Ashcroft, Sam, 157

Bailey, Walter T., 83
Barber, Marlena, 126
Beal, Alfred, 197
Bealsville (Hillsborough County, Fla.), 25, 182–83, 196–204
Bealsville, Incorporated (Hillsborough County, Fla.), xi, 182, 198–200
Beecher, Thomas, 59, 61–62, 64, 68–69
Bellamy, Edward, 17
Bethel African Methodist Episcopal Church (Champaign, Ill.), 99
Black Alumni and Ex-Student Project (University of Illinois), 81, 89–92
Blake High School (Tampa), 125, 126, 129–38
  closing of, 135–37
  reopening of, 137–38
Blake, Howard W., 129–30
Bourdieu, Pierre, 16, 188–89
Bourne, Randolph, 153

Braddock, Charlotte, 65
Bradley, Tom, 121
Brewer, Ralph, 165, 167, 168–69
Brichford, Maynard, 90–92
Briggs, John, and Briggs Initiative (California), 117–21
Brisbane, Albert, 40
Briscoe, John William, 91
Brognard, Mary, 54
Brook Farm, 21–22, 33–46
Brown v. Board of Education, 10, 129, 143–44, 148–51, 171, 195
  see also discrimination in education; segregation and desegregation
Brown, Lavern Jean Hill, 130–31
Brown, Maudelle Tanner, 83
Bryant, Anita, 24, 116–18
Buck, Pearl S., 144, 153
Bullock, Henry Allen, 186
Bunce, James, 54, 55
Burbank, Katherine, 67
bureaucracy in education, 9–11, 16–17, 64
Bushnell, Horace, 53
Butler, Matt, 154–55
Butler, Pat, 154–55

Cain, Leo, 157
California Federation of Teachers, 113
Calloway, Clinton L., 186
capitalism, *see* industrialization; social class and education

Capron, William, 59, 61, 65, 68
Carpenter, Josie, 68
Cecelski, David S., 190–93, 195
Champaign County Housing Authority, 96
class, *see* social class and education
Clifford, Geraldine, 51–52
Codman, John, 44
coeducation
  elementary and secondary, 8
  University of Illinois, 83
  see also gender and education
Coker, Gary, 169
Cole, Virginia, 167
Coleman, James, 2, 182
Comer, James, 2
common school reform movement, 33–36
communes in the U.S., 7, 38–39
community
  building of, 8–9, 11–12, 16, 35–36, 38–40, 55–57, 58–62, 63–64, 85–86, 105–106, 110–11, 113–16, 125, 126–28, 130–35, 137–38, 144–45, 147–48, 151–58, 171–72, 181–204
  definition of, 2–3, 169
  exclusions from, 1, 3–6, 11, 17–18, 70–72, 95–99, 102, 103–4, 111–12, 113, 116–21, 122, 144–45, 159–64, 188, 191–92; *see also* discrimination in education; segregation and desegregation
  explanations of imagined, 12–16
  images of, 1, 6, 12, 33–34, 67–68, 69, 105–106, 125, 126, 130–35, 139–40, 143, 144, 149, 170–71, 182–83, 194–200, 202–3; *see also* nostalgia
  inclusion within, 8, 15, 16, 18, 52, 54–57, 95–99, 148–51; *see also* segregation and desegregation

politics of, 1–2, 10–11, 13, 14–15, 53, 58, 68–73, 116–21, 136–37
tensions within, 14, 18–20, 33–34, 44–45, 57–58, 61–62, 69–73, 90–91, 95–99, 109–10, 118–19, 120, 137–38, 145–46, 158–59, 161–70
community of interest, and special education, 147–48, 161–70
"community of limited liability," 19
Cooke, George Willis, 39, 43, 44
Cooke, McLauren, 70–71
Coontz, Stephanie, 20, 127
The Crisis, 85–87
Crocker, Anna, 60
cultural capital, 15–16, 181–82, 188–89, 193–94
curriculum, 41, 181
Curtis, Edith, 33
Curtis, James Burrill, 43
Curtis, Thomas, 59, 60–61, 64, 68, 72–73
Cutler, William, 10–11

Daughters of Bilitis, 112
Davidson County Council for Retarded Children (now the Arc of Davidson County), 155–56, 157
Davis, Henry, 182–83
Davis, John W., 144
Day, Olivia, 22–23, 54, 55, 60, 61–62, 63–64, 65, 68
D'Emilio, John, 16, 111
definitions of disability, 151–53
Dempsey, Van, 131, 193
Denton, Nancy, 139
desegregation, *see* segregation and desegregation
Dewey, John, 1, 2
discrimination in education
  disability, 25, 144–45, 148–50, 151–53, 158, 160–61, 162

racial and ethnic, 1, 4–6, 8, 9, 10,
   23, 79, 80–82, 91, 95–99,
   102–6, 127, 129–31, 135–37,
   138–39, 148, 182, 183, 185,
   188, 189–94, 197, 198
religious, 8
sexual orientation, 23–24,
   109–12, 116–22
sexual orientation
   nondiscrimination policies,
   115, 116–17
social-class, 3–6, 18, 19,
   140, 148
*see also Brown v. Board of
   Education*; segregation and
   desegregation
Dodge, Abby, 51, 53, 56, 57,
   60–61, 62–63, 64, 67
Don Thompson Vocational School,
   129, 134
Dougherty, Jack, 11
Draper, Andrew Sloan, 84
DuBois, W.E.B., 85, 87, 185
Dunn, Lloyd, 156
Dwight, John S., 40–42

Eaton, Susan, 20, 127
educational rights, *see Brown v.
   Board of Education*
Ellis, Charles Mayo, 36–37
Emerson, Ralph Waldo, 36, 37
Emile, 36

Fass, Paula, 7
Favor, Ortha, 135
Fifties Black Alumni (University of
   Illinois), 106
Fourier, Charles, 40, 44–45
Fowler, Ellen, 71–72
Franklin, V.P., 195
Freedman, Estelle, 111
Fruitlands, 38
Fuller, Hiram, 38
Fuller, Margaret, 37
Fuller, Richard, 43–44
full inclusion in special education,
   161–65

gender and education
   African American enrollment in
      University of Illinois and,
      92–93, 100, 101
   at Brook Farm, 41, 52, 66–67
   ideology of true womanhood,
      81–82
   see also coeducation
G.I. Bill (Servicemen's
   Readjustment Act of 1944), 79,
   80, 92–93, 101
Gillette, Lilly, 67–68
Gill, Peggy, 187, 188
Gish, John, 113–14
Glover, William, 197
Glover School (Hillsborough
   County, Fla.), 25, 182–83,
   196–204
Goodrich, Marion, 54–55, 60, 65,
   66, 72
Gore, Malvina, 54
Greeley, Horace, 40
Greenbaum, Susan, 189

Haile, Henry, 166
Hamersley, Elizabeth, 56
Hamilton, Altamese, 136–37
Hamilton, Alvin, 132, 133
Hansot, Elisabeth, 51
Hargrett, Herman, 183
Harris-Hillman School (Nashville),
   158, 164–65, 169
Hartford, 22, 51–73
Harvard College, 44
Hawes, Erskine, 54
Hayes, Betty Jo, 131–32, 137
Hearns, Fred, 138
Hirsch, E.D., 16
Hitchcock, Stephen, 70
Hochschild, Jennifer, 2
Hollingsworth, Donald, 166
Holloway, Mark, 44
Hooker, Sarah, 61
Hubbard, Virginia, 61
Human capital, 13, 182
Hunter, Albert, 17
Hyde County, N.C., 193–94

Illinois Industrial University, 82
Inclusion in special education, 161–65
Industrial Education, 185–86
industrialization, 1, 34, 35, 39, 40, 82, 83
  see also social class

Jacobs, Edward, 85
James, Edmund J., 84
Jameson School (Bealsville), 197
Janowitz, Morris, 19
Johnson, Nancy, 60
Johnston, Carrie, 200
Julius Rosenwald Foundation, 25, 186–87, 197–98
  see also Rosenwald Schools

Katznelson, Ira, 17
Kay, James, Jr., 41
Kennedy family, 144, 149
Kenney, Rosemary, 144
Kinsey, Alfred, 111
Kopansky, Terry, 164–65, 169
Krentzman, Ben, 136

Lane, Charles, 38, 43
Leach, Cephas, 71–72
League of Women Voters of Champaign County, 96
Lee, Albert R., 79, 83–87, 92, 98–99, 104
lesbian, gay, bisexual, and transgender (LGBT) educator organizations, 113–15
lesbian, gay, bisexual, and transgender (LGBT) educators, 23–24, 109–22
Lesbian Tide, 120
Lewis, Jerry, 153
Lexington School for the Deaf, 15
liberalism, 103–4
local control, 7, 10

MacDonald, Victoria-Maria, 51
manifestation determination hearings, in special education, 160

marital status and education, 61–62, 100–1
Marshall High School (Hillsborough County, Fla.), 134
Massey, Douglas, 139
Mattachine Society, 112
McCarthy, Eugene, 24
Middleton Alumni Association, 138
Middleton High School (Tampa), 125, 126, 128–38
  closing, 135–37
  reopening, 137–38
Mitchell, John Wayne, 168
morals and education, *see* values and education
Morgan, J. Pierpont, 65
Morrill Act of 1862, 43
Muncie, Indiana, 15

Nashville, 25, 146, 154–58, 164–70
National Association for the Advancement of Colored Peoples (NAACP), 135, 171
National Education Association, 113
Niles, William W., 61, 65
Noblit, George, 131, 193
nostalgia, 6, 20–21, 126–28, 139
  see also community, images of

Ocean Hill-Brownsville (New York City), 11
Ogbu, John, 191
Olmsted, Bertha, 61
Olmsted, Frederick Law, 55
Olmsted, John, 54, 55, 61–62
opportunity hoarding, 14–15
Orfield, Gary, 1, 20, 127, 139

parents and education, 10–11, 15, 131–32
Parker, Theodore, 37
Peabody College for Teachers, 156–57
Peabody, Elizabeth, 37, 38
Perkins, Emily, 56

Perkins, Linda, 81–82
Person, William, 27n10
Pestalozzi, Johann Heinrich, 36
Petalson, Jack W., 91
Pinney, Morgan, 113
post-World War II education
  sexual orientation, 110–12
  special education, 144, 152–54, 170–71
  University of Illinois, 88–90, 92–103
Pratt, Frederick, 44
Preston, Jo Anne, 64
Pride, Richard, 137
property values, 5, 15

reclamation of closed schools
  Blake and Middleton High Schools (Tampa), 137–38
  Glover School (Bealsville), 194–204
  see also segregation and desegregation
Reconstruction Era and education, 183–84, 197
Reed, Billy, 133
Reese, William, 51
Regular Education Initiative, 163
religion and education, 5, 6, 8, 25, 53, 54, 68, 94, 99, 110, 117, 132, 157, 182, 184, 193, 197, 198, 203
  Catholics, 8
  churches, 19, 35, 99, 132, 182, 184, 187, 193, 197, 198, 203
  communes and religion, 34–38, 42
rights, see Brown v. Board of Education
Riley, George W., 83
Ripley, George, 39, 41, 46
Ripley, Sophia, 38, 41, 43
Robinson, Anne, 55–56
Robinson, David, 55–56
Robinson, Sarah, 56, 57

Rogan, Jonathan, 83
Roosevelt, Franklin Delano, 144, 153
Rosenwald Fund, see Julius Rosenwald Foundation
Rosenwald Schools, 181, 185–87, 195–96
  historic landmarks, 195–96, 200, 202–3
  see also Julius Rosenwald Foundation
Rousseau, Jean Jacques, 36
Rubin, Marc, 114
Russell, Eddie, 89–92

Savage, Julian, 193–94
school discipline, and disabilities, 159–61
Scovronick, Nathan, 2
Scruggs, Amus Porter, 83
segregation and desegregation, 8, 9, 10
  desegregation, 1, 189–94
  minority enrollment in Tampa Palms, 5
  minority enrollment in University of Illinois, 87–89, 92–95
  resegregation in Tampa, 138–39
  segregated schools, and community, 126–35, 179–204
  segregation in higher education, 103
  Tampa desegregation, 135
  Tampa school facilities, 129, 135–36
  unequal resources, 183–89
  University of Illinois student housing, 95–99
  see also Brown v. Board of Education; discrimination in education
Servicemen's Readjustment Act of 1944 (G.I. Bill), 79, 80, 92–93, 101

sexual orientation in schools, 16, 109–10
  see also discrimination in education
Shimkin, Dimitri, 90
Shircliffe, Barbara J., 189–90
Siddle-Walker, Vanessa, 1, 188, 193
Sims, Yvette Ballard, 132, 134
Smith, Lee, 166
Smith, William Walter, 83
Snow, Mehitable, 60
social capital, 2, 15–16, 20, 172, 181–82, 193
social class and education, 3–6, 7, 10–11, 18, 19, 34–35, 40–42, 53–57, 61–62, 93–94, 96–97, 105, 126, 130, 132, 139, 140, 143, 148, 150, 151, 153–54, 165, 182, 185, 187–88, 189, 193, 196–97, 199
  see also discrimination in education; industrialization
Socrates, 38
Soul Bowl (Tampa), 133
special education, 14, 143–72
special education laws, national, 150–51
Stephens, Carl, 87
Stevens, Sophia, 22–23, 54, 55, 56, 57, 58, 60, 62, 64–65, 68, 70, 71–72
Stonewall riots (New York City), 24, 110, 112–13
Student Community Interracial Committee (Champaign, Ill.), 79, 104
Student Human Relations Council (Champaign, Ill.), 79
student-teacher relations, 66–68, 69, 70–71, 159–61
Sumner, Arthur, 45
Suttles, Gerald, 17, 18–19

Tallant, Caroline, 60
Tampa, 3–5, 24, 125–40
teacher roles, 11, 51–52

teacher turnover, Hartford, 52, 59
Temple School, 38
Tennessee, 145, 150, 165–70
Tennessee School for the Blind, 165, 166–70
Thomas, William, Sr., 182–83
Thoreau, Henry David, 37
Tidwell, Alvin, 154, 157
Torres, Mary, 54–55, 62
Towles, Ella Madalyne, 86
Transcendentalism, 21–22, 33, 36–39, 45
Trumbull, Eliza, 56
Turner, Nat, 183
Tyack, David, 51

University of Illinois, 23, 79–106
urbanization and education, 7–8, 9, 17

Val Rainey v. Tennessee Department of Education (1973–74), 166–70
values and education, 11, 34–36, 43–45, 69–70, 111–13, 116–21, 132–33, 152–53, 181–82, 189, 200–4
Vermette, James, 92
Vickrey, Barry, 165–66
volunteer organizations and education, 16, 149, 157, 171, 182, 198–200

Washington, Booker T., 185, 186
Watkins, William H., 194
Weiler, Kathleen, 51
Weir, Margaret, 17
Weis, Lois, 143
Weldon, Curt, 150
welfare state and education, 153–54, 170–71
Wheaton, Helen, 54
Whitley, Janice, 167
Will, Madeleine, 163

Willard, Arthur C., 88
William, Ruby, 196
Williams, Carlton, 19, 134–35
Williams, Laura, 132
work and education
    Brook Farm, 39–40, 42
    Hartford, 55, 57, 62–63, 64
    see also Industrial Education; industrialization; social class and education

Wright, Skelly, 150

Yelvington, Kevin, 188–89

Zimmerman, Jonathan, 10

GPSR Compliance

The European Union's (EU) General Product Safety Regulation (GPSR) is a set of rules that requires consumer products to be safe and our obligations to ensure this.

If you have any concerns about our products, you can contact us on

ProductSafety@springernature.com

In case Publisher is established outside the EU, the EU authorized representative is:

Springer Nature Customer Service Center GmbH
Europaplatz 3
69115 Heidelberg, Germany

www.ingramcontent.com/pod-product-compliance
Lightning Source LLC
LaVergne TN
LVHW041956060526
838200LV00002B/42